·汉语 101·

Survival Chinese

生活汉语 101

（第二版）

袁芳远（Yuan Fangyuan） 著

外语教学与研究出版社
FOREIGN LANGUAGE TEACHING AND RESEARCH PRESS

北京 BEIJING

图书在版编目（CIP）数据

　生活汉语101 ／ 袁芳远著. — 2版. — 北京：外语教学与研究出版社，2016.2（2023.11重印）
　（汉语101）
　ISBN 978-7-5135-7139-5

　Ⅰ. ①生… Ⅱ. ①袁… Ⅲ. ①汉语－口语－对外汉语教学－自学参考资料 Ⅳ. ①H195.4

　中国版本图书馆CIP数据核字(2016)第038739号

出 版 人	王　芳
策划编辑	李彩霞
责任编辑	刘虹艳　孟佳文
封面设计	姚　军
版式设计	赵　欣　姚　军
插图设计	姚　军
出版发行	外语教学与研究出版社
社　　址	北京市西三环北路19号（100089）
网　　址	https://www.fltrp.com
印　　刷	北京捷迅佳彩印刷有限公司
开　　本	787×1092 1/32
印　　张	11
版　　次	2016年4月第2版　2023年11月第7次印刷
书　　号	ISBN 978-7-5135-7139-5
定　　价	45.00元（附赠MP3光盘一张）

如有图书采购需求，图书内容或印刷装订等问题，侵权、盗版书籍等线索，请拨打以下电话或关注官方服务号：
客服电话：400 898 7008
官方服务号：微信搜索并关注公众号"外研社官方服务号"
外研社购书网址：https://fltrp.tmall.com

物料号：271390001

记载人类文明
沟通世界文化
www.fltrp.com

前　言

　　"汉语101"是一套为在华留学生、外籍工作人员以及汉语初、中级学习者编写的口语系列手册，内容简单实用、针对性强。本系列手册旨在帮助读者于较短时间内学会基本句子，并在相关语境中模仿、使用，以达到迅速消除语言障碍、提高汉语交际能力、轻松融入中国生活的目的。

　　"汉语101"由《生活汉语101》《商务汉语101》《旅游汉语101》等组成。每一本包含若干主题单元，每个单元下设若干话题，每个话题以一个核心句开头，在其基础上扩展成短小实用的对话。每分册共有101个核心句/话题篇，因此冠名为"汉语101"。

　　各话题篇包含以下要素：

　　主题：即该话题篇所属的主题单元。以本册《生活汉语101》为例，由15个主题单元构成，包括"见面寒暄""到中国去""学校生活""住宿""就餐""购物""娱乐休闲""出行""银行"等，基本涵盖了在中国日常生活、学习和工作中的吃、喝、住、行、玩各个方面。

　　话题：由主题分解细化为更具象的若干情景话题，如："见面寒暄"细分为"询问姓名""问好""交换名片""介绍相识""朋友相遇"等，供读者学习使用。

核心句：每个话题篇有一个核心句，如"询问姓名"的核心句是"请问，您贵姓？"，"交换名片"的核心句是"这是我的名片，以后多联系"等。读者应反复练习核心句，以便在实际交际中熟练应用。

句型与替换：这一部分提供2–4个替换词语、短语或句子，如"请问，您贵姓？"可以由"怎么称呼您？"替换，供读者选择使用。

扩展：这一部分提供3–5个与话题有关的常用句，读者应反复练习，以便在相关语境中选择使用。如"询问姓名"一篇的扩展句为"我姓王"，"免贵姓刘"，"认识您很高兴"等。

对话实例：对话围绕核心句展开，一般为6–8句，目的是帮助读者在相关语境中学习汉语表达方式及中国人的说话习惯和逻辑，以便更好地表达自己、理解对方。读者最好把对话实例背诵下来，以便在交际中熟练使用。

相关词语：这部分列出该单元出现的词汇及与本话题相关的若干其他词汇，旨在为读者的实际应用提供更多可供选择的词语。

文化导航：为了让读者更好地了解中国文化，每个话题篇都选择一个与该话题直接或间接相关的文化现象进行解释，如"询问姓名"一篇中的"中国人的姓与名"，"交换名片"一篇中的"中国的名片文化"等。

为方便读者学习，各册附录都列出了读者在紧急情况下可能用到的一些句子。

本系列附英文翻译，并配有录音，且携带方便，是在华留学生、外籍工作人员不可多得的汉语日常工具书。本系列亦可用作初、中级汉语口语教材和自学教材。

编者在本系列手册编写过程中得到了外语教学与研究出版社汉语分社李彩霞女士的悉心指导和帮助，在此表示衷心的感谢。但书中可能还存在不当之处，希求读者、同行在使用过程中及时指出，以便再版时更正，在此先行致谢。

编者

2013年6月5日

Preface

Chinese 101 is a series of handbooks of conversational Chinese designed for non-native speakers of Chinese who study or work in China as well as primary and intermediate learners of Chinese. The content is reasonably simple with a clear aim. It is developed to enable users to learn, imitate and master useful vocabulary and sentences in a meaningful context so that they can quickly improve Chinese skills and easily adapt to Chinese culture in the short term.

Chinese 101 is composed of *Survival Chinese 101*, *Business Chinese 101* and *Travel Chinese 101*. Each book in the series is divided into thematic units that cover major aspects of living, doing business or traveling in China. Thematic units are subdivided into 101 situational topics or chapters, hence the title of the series. And each unit starts with a key sentence followed by short and practical dialogues.

Each chapter has the following components:

Theme: Title of the theme to which the current chapter belongs. For example, in *Survival Chinese 101*, there are 15 thematic units like "Greeting People", "Dining", "Shopping", "Going to China", "School Life", "Lodging", "Entertainment", "At the Bank" and "Traveling", covering almost all aspects of daily life and work in China.

Topic: Title of the situational topic. For example, under the theme "Greeting People", there are situational topics provided for learners, like "Asking about Names", "Exchanging Name Cards", "Hello", "Introducing Each Other" and "Running across a Friend", etc.

Key Sentence: A sentence that represents the core of the topic. For example, the key sentence in the chapter of "Asking about Names" is "May I know your name?" while in the chapter of "Exchanging Name Cards" is "This is my name card. Keep in touch". Learners should practice as much as possible.

Substitution: Two to four substitutions are provided for readers to learn how to convey similar meanings of the key sentence. For example, "May I know your (last) name?" can be substituted by "How can I address you?"

Extension: Three to five sentences that relate to the topic of the chapter are provided for readers to learn to use. For example, in the chapter of "Asking about Names", sentences like "My last name is Wang", "My last name is Liu" and "Nice to meet you" are listed.

Dialogue: A situational dialogue is presented, through which users can learn how Chinese people express themselves in the context in order to express their opinions and understand Chinese culture. The length of a dialogue is mostly 6-8 sentences. It is suggested that learners recite the dialogue.

Related Words: A list of words closely related to the topic is provided for readers to learn, imitate and use.

Cultural Navigation: A brief explanation is provided about a cultural phenomenon directly or indirectly related to the current topic, in order to enhance the understanding of Chinese culture and the reason behind the phenomenon. For example, "Chinese names" is introduced in "Asking about Names" and "name cards culture in China" is introduced in "Exchanging Name Cards".

For the convenience of the users, each book also provides a list of sentences in the appendix that may be used in emergency contexts in China.

With English translation and CDs, this series of handbooks should be a useful companion and reference book for foreign people living in China. The series can also be used as a textbook for primary and intermediate students' conversational Chinese as well as for self-study.

During the process of material collection, textual preparation, and editorial revision, I received constant guidance, support and assistance from Ms. Li Caixia of the Foreign Language Teaching and Research Press. I am deeply indebted to her. I will appreciate all the suggestions.

Yuan Fangyuan
June 5th, 2013
Tianjin, China

目 录 Contents

住宿
Lodging

就餐
Dining

出行
Traveling

城市交通
Local Transportation

旅馆
At the Hotel

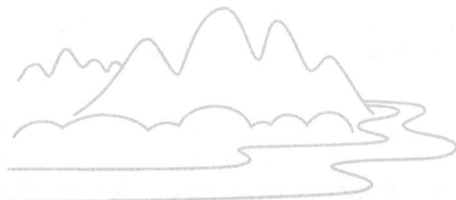

见面寒暄
Greeting People

核心句
Key Sentence

Qǐngwèn, nín guìxìng?
请问，您贵姓？
May I know your last name?

句型与替换
Substitution

Nǐ xìng shénme?
你姓什么？
What is your last name?

Zěnme chēnghu nín?
怎么称呼您？
How can I address you?

✛ 扩 展/Extension

Wǒ xìng Wáng.
1. 我姓王。 My last name is Wang.

Miǎn guì xìng Liú.
2. 免贵姓刘。 My last name is Liu.

Wǒ shì gōng cháng Zhāng, bú shì
3. 我是"弓长"张，不是 My last name is not 立早

lì zǎo Zhāng.
"立早"章。 Zhang, but 弓长 Zhang.

Rènshi nín hěn gāoxìng.
4. 认识您很高兴。 Nice to meet you.

甲: Qǐngwèn, nín guìxìng?
请问，您贵姓？

Hello, may I know your last name?

乙: Wǒ xìng Zhāng.
我姓张。

My last name is Zhang.

甲: Shì yì zhāng zhǐ de zhāng ma?
是一张纸的"张"吗？

Is it "zhāng" as in 一张纸？

乙: Shì. Zěnme chēnghu nín?
是。怎么称呼您？

Yes. May I know your name?

甲: Wǒ xìng Bái, báisè de bái.
我姓白，白色的白。

My last name is Bai. It means color white.

乙: Bái xiānsheng, rènshi nín hěn gāoxìng.
白先生，认识您很高兴。

Mr. Bai, nice to meet you.

甲: Zhāng xiānsheng, rènshi nín wǒ yě hěn gāoxìng.
张先生，认识您我也很高兴。

Mr. Zhang, nice to meet you, too.

相关词语/Related Words

1	guìxìng 贵姓	(honorable) last name	5	chēnghu 称呼	to address
2	xìng 姓	last name	6	rènshi 认识	to know; to meet
3	jiào 叫	to call	7	gāoxìng 高兴	glad; happy
4	míngzi 名字	name; first name			

中国人初次见面时，一般问对方"您贵姓"或"贵姓"，而不是姓和名一起问。"您"是"你"的尊敬说法，"贵"是"尊贵"的意思。"您贵姓"是表示对对方的尊敬。比较传统的回答是"免贵"加上自己的姓，意思是"不尊贵"，以表示谦虚。现在大多数人用"我姓……"来回答。

When Chinese people meet for the first time, they usually ask each other's last name by saying "您贵姓" or simply "贵姓" instead of asking for a full name. Here "您" is the polite form of "你" (you) and "贵姓" is literally translated as "honorable last name" to show respect. The old fashioned reply is "免贵……" whose literal meaning is "not honorable" as a modest response. Nowadays most people simply reply by saying "我姓……".

核心句 / Key Sentence

Nǐ jiào shénme míngzi?
你叫什么名字？
What is your name?

句型与替换 / Substitution

Nǐ yǒu Zhōngwén míngzi ma?
你有中文名字吗？
Do you have a Chinese name?

Nǐ de Zhōngwén míngzi shì shénme?
你的中文名字是什么？
What is your Chinese name?

扩 展 / Extension

Wǒ jiào
1. 我叫……　　　　　　　　My name is…

Wǒ de Zhōngwén míngzi shì
2. 我的中文名字是……　　　My Chinese name is…

Wǒ de míngzi shì　　de yìsi.
3. 我的名字是……的意思。　My name means…

对话实例 / Dialogue

（在迎新会上　At a new students reception）

Nǐ jiào shénme míngzi?
甲：你叫什么名字？
What is your name?

乙： Wǒ xìng
我 姓 William， 叫 Karen。
My last name is William and my first name is Karen.

甲： Karen， nǐ hǎo。 Wǒ jiào
Karen，你好。我 叫 David Lee。
Hello, Karen. My name is David Lee.

乙： Nǐ yǒu Zhōngwén míngzi ma?
你 有 中 文 名字 吗?
Do you have a Chinese name?

甲： Yǒu, Sòng Dàmíng, dàxiǎo de dà, míngtiān de míng.
有，宋 大明， 大小 的 大， 明天 的 明。
Yes. Song Daming. "Dà" as in "big and small" (大小), and "míng" as in "tomorrow" (明天).

乙： Wǒ de Zhōngwén míngzi shì Wáng Xiǎoměi, měi shì piàoliang de yìsi.
我 的 中 文 名字 是 王 小美， 美 是 漂亮 的 意思。
My Chinese name is Wang Xiaomei, and "měi" means pretty.

甲： Nà wǒ yǐhòu jiù jiào nǐ Xiǎoměi, xíng ma?
那 我 以后 就 叫 你 小美， 行 吗?
May I call you Xiaomei?

乙： Xíng. Wǒ yǐhòu jiào nǐ Dàmíng.
行。我 以后 叫 你 大明。
Sure, I will call you Daming.

相关词语／Related Words

1	意思 yìsi	to mean; meaning	3	以后 yǐhòu	thereafter
2	那 nà	then	4	行 吗? Xíng ma?	Is it OK?

文化导航
Cultural Navigation

中国人的姓名由姓和名组成，姓在前，名在后。姓一般随父亲，大部分由一个音节/字组成。中国常见的姓有一百多个，因此很多人的姓是一样的，外国人要记住谁是谁会有一点困难。中国人一般不会只用姓称呼他人。中国人的名一般是一个或两个音节/字，常常带有正面意义，反映了父母对孩子的期望。家族里兄弟姐妹的名字常常有一个字是共用的，比如"志华""志明"。过去中国人很少只用名称呼他人，现在越来越多的人这么做。如果名是一个音节/字，一般就用全称了。如今，中国大城市的很多年轻人都有英文名。

Chinese names are composed of two parts: the last name and the first name with the former proceeding the latter. Last names generally come from father's family and most of them contain one syllable/character. Only about 100 Chinese family names are commonly used and thus you need to make a special effort to tell who is who. It is rare that Chinese people address each other by his/her last name only. Chinese first names usually contain one or two syllables/characters, reflecting parents' hope for their children. Siblings often share a character in their names such as Zhihua and Zhiming. In the past, Chinese people rarely addressed each other by the first name only. But more and more people do it nowadays. However, if the first name has only one syllable/character, the full name is used instead. In large cities, many young people have English names and use them to address each other.

3 问好 | Hello

Nǐ hǎo.
你好。
Hello.

句型
与替换
Substitution

Nín hǎo!
您好!
How are you?/How do you do?

Zǎoshang hǎo!
早上好!
Good morning!

Wǎnshang hǎo!
晚上好!
Good evening!

Wǎn'ān!
晚安!
Good night!

扩 展／Extension

Nín zuìjìn zěnmeyàng?
1. **您最近怎么样?**   How have you been?

Nín shēntǐ hǎo ma?
2. **您身体好吗?**   How about your health?

Nǐ gōngzuò shùnlì ba?
3. **你工作顺利吧?**   Are you doing well in your work?

Dài wǒ xiàng nǐ fùmǔ wènhǎo.
4. **代我向你父母问好。**   Send my regards to your parents.

对话实例/Dialogue

甲: Zhāng lǎoshī, nín hǎo.
张 老师，您好。
Hello, Professor Zhang.

乙: Wáng Tiānxīn, nǐ hǎo.
王 天心，你好。
Hello, Wang Tianxin.

甲: Hǎojiǔ bú jiàn, nín zuìjìn zěnmeyàng?
好久不见，您最近怎么样？
I haven't seen you for a long time. How is everything?

乙: Hái búcuò, jiùshì tǐng máng de.
还不错，就是挺 忙 的。
Pretty good, but still busy.

甲: Nà nín děi zhùyì shēntǐ.
那您得注意身体。
Then you should take care of yourself.

乙: Hǎo. Nǐ xuéxí zěnmeyàng?
好。你学习怎么样？
Yes, I will. How is your study?

甲: Hěn hǎo.
很 好。
Very well.

乙: Nà jiù hǎo. Yǒu shì zhǎo wǒ.
那就好。有事 找 我。
That is good. Come to see me when you need help.

甲: Xièxie nín. Zàijiàn, Zhāng lǎoshī.
谢谢您。再见，张 老师。
Thank you. Goodbye, Professor Zhang.

1	hǎojiǔ 好久	for a long time	5	búcuò 不错	good; not bad
2	zuìjìn 最近	recently	6	tǐng 挺	very
3	zěnmeyàng 怎么样	How is/are…?	7	zhùyì 注意	to pay attention to
4	shēntǐ 身体	health	8	xuéxí 学习	study

文化导航
Cultural Navigation

　　中国人在正式场合常常用职位称呼彼此，比如王经理、李主任、刘教授，在邻居和朋友之间有时也如此。如果一个人是副职，称呼时常常把"副"字去掉。一个人的职位代表了他在社会中的地位，因此用错称呼会被认为是不礼貌的行为。

　　On formal occasions, Chinese people often use official and professional titles plus last name to address each other, such as Manager Wang, Director Li, and Professor Liu, even among neighbors or close friends. If someone is a deputy director, it is better to drop the word "deputy". This, in a way, is a reflection that one's title and rank announce where a person stands in relation to others in society. Those who address others using a wrong title are considered impolite and disrespectful.

4 交换名片 | Exchanging Name Cards

Zhè shì wǒ de míngpiàn, yǐhòu duō liánxì.
这是我的名片，以后多联系。
This is my name card. Keep in touch.

句型
与替换
Substitution

diànhuà
电话
telephone

diànzǐ yóujiàn
电子邮件
email address

zhùzhǐ
住址
address

liánxì fāngshì
联系方式
contact information

扩 展/Extension

Nín yǒu míngpiàn ma?
1. 您有名片吗?

Do you have a name card?

Bù hǎoyìsi, míngpiàn fāguāng le.
2. 不好意思，名片发光了。

I am sorry that I have just sent out all my cards.

Wǒ bǎ liánxì fāngshì xiě xialai.
3. 我把联系方式写下来。

I will write down my contact information for you.

Yǐhòu qǐng nín duō guānzhào.
4. 以后请您多关照。

I will count on your support in the future.

甲： Zhāng jiàoshòu, nín gāngcái jiǎng de tài hǎo le.
张 教授，您刚才 讲得太好了。

Professor Zhang, you have given us a wonderful speech.

乙： Guòjiǎng le. Nín shì
过奖了。您是……?

I am flattered. You are…?

甲： Wǒ xìng Lǐ, zhè shì wǒ de míngpiàn.
我姓李，这是我的名片。

I am Li. This is my name card.

乙： Nín jiù shì Běi Dà de Lǐ jiàoshòu, jiǔyǎng, jiǔyǎng.
您就是北大的李教授，久仰，久仰。

You are Professor Li from Peking University. I have heard about you for a long time.

甲： Nín tài kèqi le.
您太客气了。

It is very nice for you to say so.

乙： Zhè shì wǒ de míngpiàn, yǐhòu duō liánxì.
这是我的名片，以后多联系。

This is my card. Keep in touch.

1	guòjiǎng 过奖	to flatter	4	liánxì 联系	to contact; to be in touch
2	míngpiàn 名片	name card; business card	5	kèqi 客气	polite
3	jiǔyǎng 久仰	to have known your name for a long time			

中国人在职场上交换名片时要用双手，以示尊敬。递名片时，要用大拇指和食指夹住名片的两个角，名片内容对着对方。接到递过来的名片后，不要马上收起来，而是要看一看名片内容，表示对对方的尊重。高级政府官员一般不递名片。很多中国人的名片一面是中文，一面是英文。

For the Chinese, especially in the business setting, a proper way for exchanging name cards is to use both hands to show respect to each other. When giving your card, you should hold the card corners between thumbs and forefingers of both hands with the text facing the receiver. When receiving a card, please don't simply pocket it immediately but take a few moments to study the card for what it says and show some interest in the giver. However, top government officials do not usually present their cards. Chinese name cards are usually printed in both Chinese and English.

5 介绍相识 | Introducing Each Other

Zhè shì wǒ de péngyou.
这是我的朋友。
This is my friend.

句型
与替换
Substitution

tóngxué
同学
classmate, schoolmate

xīn tóngshì
新同事
new colleague

shìyǒu
室友
roommate

lǎobǎn
老板
boss

扩 展／Extension

Lái, nǐmen rènshi yíxià.
1. 来，你们认识一下。   Let me introduce you.

Wǒ lái jièshào yíxià.
2. 我来介绍一下。   Let me introduce you.

Zhè wèi shì
3. 这位是……?   This is…?

Yǒu shíjiān wǒmen zài liáo.
4. 有时间我们再聊。   Let's find a time to have a chat.

对话实例/Dialogue

甲: Gāo Míng, nǐ hǎo. Zhè wèi shì
高明，你好。这位是······?
Hello, Gao Ming. This is…?

乙: Wǒ gěi nǐ jièshào yíxià, zhè shì wǒ de péngyou, Wáng Lì.
我给你介绍一下，这是我的朋友，王丽。
Let me introduce to you. This is my friend Wang Li.

甲: Nǐ hǎo. Wáng Lì, wǒ jiào Gāo Yīshān.
你好。王丽，我叫高一山。
Hello, Wang Li. My name is Gao Yishan.

丙: Gāo Yīshān, nǐ hǎo, nǐ shì liúxuéshēng ma?
高一山，你好，你是留学生吗？
Hello, Gao Yishan. Are you a foreign student here?

甲: Shì, zài Wàiguóyǔ Dàxué xué Hànyǔ. Nǐ ne?
是，在外国语大学学汉语。你呢？
Yes, I am studying Chinese at the Foreign Languages University. And you?

丙: Wǒ zài Běijīng Dàxué jiāo Yīngwén, shì wàijiào.
我在北京大学教英文，是外教。
I am teaching English at Peking University as a foreign professor.

甲: Rènshi nǐ hěn gāoxìng. Yǒu shíjiān wǒmen zài liáo.
认识你很高兴。有时间我们再聊。
Nice to meet you. Let us find a time to have a chat.

相关词语/Related Words

1	jièshào 介绍	to introduce	3	wàiguóyǔ 外国语	foreign language
2	rènshi 认识	to know; to meet	4	Hànyǔ 汉语	the Chinese language

| 5 | liúxuéshēng 留学生 | foreign student | 7 | liáo 聊 | to have a chat |
| 6 | wàijiào 外教 | foreign professor; foreign instructor | | | |

文化导航
Cultural Navigation

　　介绍新朋老友相识时，先介绍谁后介绍谁并不太重要。但在正式场合，例如谈判会议，一定要先介绍职位最高的人。另外介绍时，要用"这位是……"或者"这是……"，而不用"他是……"或"她是……"。同理，在向别人介绍公司、学校、产品时，也只能用"这家公司""这所学校""这个产品"或"这是……"来表达。

　　When introducing a group of people to know each other in a non-formal setting, you don't have to be particular about who you should introduce first. However, in a formal setting such as at negotiation meetings, you should introduce the most senior people in position first. In addition, when you do the introduction, you should use "这位是……" or "这是……", instead of "他/她是……". Likewise, when you introduce a certain company, school or product, you can only use "这家公司" "这所学校" "这个产品" or "这是……".

6 朋友相遇 | Running into a Friend

Wáng Míng, nǐ chīfàn le ma?
王 明，你吃饭了吗？
Wang Ming, have you eaten?

句型
与替换
Substitution

Nǐ qù nǎr?
你去哪儿？
Where are you going?

Nǐ zài gàn shénme?
你在干什么？
What are you doing there?

Mǎi dōngxi ya?
买东西呀？
Are you shopping?

Xiàkè le?
下课了？
Did you just finish class?

扩 展／Extension

Nǐ máng shénme ne?
1. **你忙什么呢？**

Hái méi láidejí chīfàn ne.
2. **还没来得及吃饭呢。**

Nǐ de liǎnsè bú tài hǎo.
3. **你的脸色不太好。**

Yǐhòu zài liáo.
4. **以后再聊。**

What are you busy with?

I am too busy to eat.

You don't look good.

Talk to you later.

对话实例/Dialogue

甲：
Hāi, Wáng Míng, nǐ chīfàn le ma?
嗨，王明，你吃饭了吗？
Hi, Wang Ming, have you eaten?

乙：
Hái méi láidejí ne. Nǐ ne?
还没来得及呢。你呢？
Not yet. How about you?

甲：
Gāng chīguo.
刚吃过。
I just ate.

乙：
Xiànzài qù shàngkè ma?
现在去上课吗？
Are you going to class?

甲：
Shì a, xiàwǔ yǒu liǎng jié kè.
是啊，下午有两节课。
Yes. I have two classes in the afternoon.

乙：
Nà jiù zàijiàn le, yǐhòu zài liáo.
那就再见了，以后再聊。
Goodbye then and talk to you later.

相关词语/Related Words

1	tú shū guǎn 图书馆	library	3	lái bù jí 来不及 did not find time to do something
2	chá zīliào 查资料	to look up something	4	liáo tiān 聊（天） to chat

　　中国人见面时常常问一些日常生活上的事，比如说吃饭的时间碰上会问"吃了吗？"，下课时会问"刚下课呀？"。很多时候，还没等对方回答，问话人已经走远了。其实这些问话并不表示问话人想知道对方是否吃饭或到哪儿去，也无意邀请对方吃饭，只是像"你好"一样在打招呼。回答人一般可以用"吃了"或"还没呢"等回答。

When two Chinese acquaintances come across each other, they may ask each other a casual question about the routine activity that the other party may be engaged in at the moment. For example, one may ask the other "吃了吗？" (Have you eaten?) around the meal time or "刚下课呀？" (Did you just finish class?) at the time when the other party has obviously come back from class. There is a good chance that after such addressing they will simply keep on walking without waiting for any answer. These questions actually don't reflect the addressers' curiosity about these issues. Rather they are just common greeting expressions like "你好". Responses to such greetings might be "吃了" (I have eaten) or "还没呢" (Not yet).

[社会交际
Social Functions]

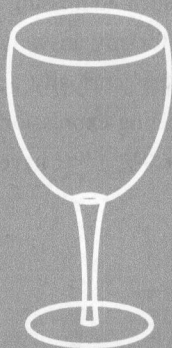

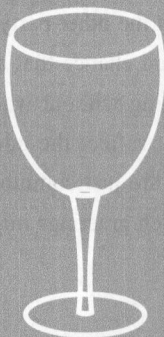

7 称赞 | Complimenting

核心句
Key
Sentence

Nǐ de Zhōngwén zhēn búcuò!

你的中文真不错!

Your Chinese is really good!

句型
与替换
Substitution

qìsè
气色
complexion

fàxíng
发型
hairstyle

nǚpéngyou
女朋友
girlfriend

扩 展/Extension

Nǐ jīntiān chuān de yīfu hǎo piàoliang!
1. 你今天穿的衣服好漂亮!

You look beautiful in the dress today!

Nǐ de Zhōngwén jìnbù zhēn dà!
2. 你的中文进步真大!

You have made an impressive improvement in your Chinese!

Nǎlǐ, nǎlǐ.
3. 哪里，哪里。

I am far from that good.

Chà yuǎn le.
4. 差远了。

I am far from that good.

甲：
Mǎkè, nǐ zài nǎr xué de Zhōngwén? Shuō de zhēn búcuò!
马克，你在哪儿学的中文？说得真不错！
Mark, where did you learn Chinese? You speak Chinese really well!

乙：
Guòjiǎng le. Wǒ zài Měiguó shàng dàxué shí xué de.
过奖了。我在美国上大学时学的。
I am flattered. I started learning Chinese at college in the United States.

甲：
Nǐ kěndìng shì gè hǎo xuésheng.
你肯定是个好学生。
You must be a great student.

乙：
Hái xíng ba. Hěn xìngyùn, wǒ pèngshangle gè hǎo lǎoshī.
还行吧。很幸运，我碰上了个好老师。
I think so. I was lucky to have a good teacher.

甲：
Néng xiě yíxià nǐ de Zhōngwén míngzi ma?
能写一下你的中文名字吗？
Can you write your Chinese name?

乙：
Méi wèntí.
没问题。
Yes, I can.

甲：
Wa, nǐ de zì xiě de zhēn piàoliang!
哇，你的字写得真漂亮！
Wow, your handwriting is beautiful!

乙：
Nǎlǐ, nǎlǐ.
哪里，哪里。
I am far from that good.

1	búcuò 不错	not bad; very good		6	hái xíng ba 还行吧	so so
2	guòjiǎng 过奖	to flatter		7	méi wèntí 没问题	no problem
3	xìngyùn 幸运	lucky		8	Hànzì 汉字	Chinese characters
4	kěndìng 肯定	must be		9	piàoliang 漂亮	beautiful
5	yōuxiù 优秀	outstanding				

文化导航
Cultural Navigation

很多中国人面对别人的赞扬时，常常说"哪里，哪里"，意思是我没那么好。这种回答其实并不是不同意别人的夸奖，而是表示谦虚，否则就会被认为是骄傲。但是现在也有很多人用"谢谢"来回应夸奖。

When faced with other's compliments, many Chinese use "哪里，哪里" as a response. Literally it means "I am far from that good". This does not mean that they don't agree with the compliments; they just want to show their modesty. Otherwise, they will be considered too arrogant. Nowadays, some Chinese use "thank you" to respond to other people's compliments.

核心句 Key Sentence

Wǒmen yùdào *nántí* le.
我们遇到难题了。
We encounter some difficulties.

句型与替换 Substitution

máfan
麻烦
trouble

wèntí
问题
problem

kùnnan
困难
difficulty

扩展/Extension

Wǒ zhèng xiǎng zhǎo nín bāngmáng ne.
1. 我正想找您帮忙呢。 I have meant to ask you for help.

Wǒ yídìng jìnlì'érwéi.
2. 我一定尽力而为。 I will do my best.

Nín yídìng yào bāng wǒ.
3. 您一定要帮我。 You have to help me out.

Nǎ tiān wǒ qǐng nín chīfàn.
4. 哪天我请您吃饭。 Let's find a time to have dinner together.

甲: Xiǎo Zhāng, wǒ zhèng zhǎo nǐ ne.
小张，我正找你呢。
Xiao Zhang, I have been looking for you.

乙: Zěnme la?
怎么啦？
What's up?

甲: Wǒmen yùdào nántí le, nǐ yídìng děi bāng wǒmen.
我们遇到难题了，你一定得帮我们。
We run into some problems and you have to help us out.

乙: Jùtǐ shuōshuo, wǒ yídìng jìnlì'érwéi.
具体说说，我一定尽力而为。
What happened? I will definitely try my best.

甲: Zhǔyào shì ruǎnjiàn chūle wèntí, néng gēn wǒ qù kànkan ma?
主要是软件出了问题，能跟我去看看吗？
There is something wrong with the software. Can you go with me to take a look?

乙: Méi wèntí.
没问题。
No problem.

甲: Tài xièxie le, nǎ tiān wǒ qǐng nǐ chīfàn.
太谢谢了，哪天我请你吃饭。
Thank you very much. Let's find a time to have dinner together.

相关词语/Related Words

1	zhǎo 找	to look for	4	jùtǐ 具体	specifically
2	bāngmáng 帮忙	to help	5	fàngxīn 放心	not to worry
3	pèngshang 碰上	to encounter	6	jìnlì'érwéi 尽力而为	to try one's best

对中国人来说，对别人为自己所做的事情或提供的帮助，表示感激的方式不只是说声"谢谢"或写一个感谢卡，而是要有实在的表示。比如说，得到帮助的人要送给提供帮助的人礼物或请他/她吃饭。这种有来有往的形式有助于建立和维护人际关系。

For Chinese people, the way to show appreciation for what others have done is substantial rather than just saying "thank you" or writing a thank-you card. For example, the one who receives help usually sends a gift or invites the person to dinner. This is a way to establish and maintain relationship/network for long-term benefits.

9 道歉 | Apologizing

Duìbuqǐ, wǒ chídào le.
对不起，我迟到了。
I am sorry for being late.

hěn bàoqiàn
很抱歉
my apologies

qǐng yuánliàng
请原谅
Please excuse me.

zhēn bù hǎoyìsi
真不好意思
I am embarrassed.

扩展/Extension

Shì wǒ de bú duì.
1. 是我的不对。   It is my fault.

Wǒ yǐhòu yídìng gǎi.
2. 我以后一定改。   It will never happen again.

Wǒ zài yuánliàng nǐ yí cì.
3. 我再原谅你一次。   I will give you another chance.

Xià bù wéi lì.
4. 下不为例。   This is your last opportunity.

Méi guānxi, yǐhòu zhùyì jiù xíng le.
5. 没关系，以后注意   It doesn't matter. Be careful next
就行了。   time.

甲：
Xiǎo Wáng, nǐ zěnme yòu chídào le?
小 王，你怎么 又 迟到 了？

Xiao Wang, why are you late again?

乙：
Duìbuqǐ, jīntiān lùshang pèngdào chēhuò le.
对不起，今天 路上 碰到 车祸 了。

I am really sorry. There was an accident on my way here.

甲：
Kěshì Lǎo Lǐ zěnme zhǔnshí dào le ne, nǐmen zhù zài yí gè fāngxiàng.
可是老李怎么 准时 到 了 呢，你们住在一个 方 向。

But Lao Li was here on time. You two come from the same direction.

乙：
Shì wǒ de bú duì, xià cì yídìng zǎodiǎnr chūlai.
是我的不对，下次一定 早点儿 出来。

It is my fault. I will leave home earlier next time.

甲：
Zài yuánliàng nǐ yí cì, xià bù wéi lì.
再 原 谅 你一次，下不为例。

I will give you one more chance.

乙：
Zhēn duìbuqǐ, dānwu de gōngzuò wǒ yídìng bǔshang.
真 对不起，耽误 的 工作 我一定补上。

I am terribly sorry. I will make up for the lost time.

甲：
Bǎ zhè fèn wénjiàn sònggěi Lǐ zǒng, ránhòu zuòchū xià zhōu gōngzuò
把这份文件 送给 李总，然后做出下周 工作
jìhuà.
计划。

Send this document to Manager Li and then draft the work plan for next week.

乙：
Méi wèntí, zhōngwǔ qián wǒ bǎ jìhuà jiāogěi nín.
没问题，中午前我把计划交给您。

Sure. I will finish the plan by noon.

	chídào				dānwu	
1	迟到	to be late		6	耽误	to delay; to hold up
2	chēhuò 车祸	car accident		7	bǔshang 补上	to make up for
3	zhǔnshí 准时	punctual; on time		8	wénjiàn 文件	document
4	fāngxiàng 方向	direction		9	jìhuà 计划	plan
5	yuánliàng 原谅	to excuse				

文化导航
Cultural Navigation

　　在同事、朋友和熟人之间，人们常常用"小"和"老"加上姓来称呼彼此，比如我们对话里的"小王"和"老李"。"小"+姓通常用来称呼年轻人，"老"+姓通常用来称呼比自己年长的人，但不一定真的年老。但是一般很少用"老"+姓称呼女性。

　　Among colleagues, friends and acquaintances, "小" (young) and "老" (old) plus one's last name are often used to address people, e.g. Xiao Wang and Lao Li in our dialogue. "小" plus last name is used to address young people and "老" plus last name is used to address the people relatively elder than the addresser but not necessarily old in age. But "老" plus last name is generally not used to address women.

10 谈天气 | Talking about Weather

Yào xiàxuě le.
要下雪了。
It is about to snow.

句型
与替换
Substitution

xiàyǔ
下雨
rain

guāfēng
刮风
wind blowing

jiàngwēn
降温
drop in temperature

扩 展／Extension

Tiān yòu yīn le.
1. 天又阴了。

It is cloudy again.

Tiānqì yùbào shuō, jīnwǎn yǒu
2. 天气预报说，今晚有
bàofēngxuě.
暴风雪。

The weather forecast has said that there will be a blizzard tonight.

Jīxuě kěnéng yào 4 – 5 límǐ.
3. 积雪可能要4－5厘米。

The accumulation of snow will be about 4-5 cm.

Wēndù kěnéng huì jiàngdào shèshì
4. 温度可能会降到摄氏
língxià 10 dù zuǒyòu.
零下10度左右。

The temperature may drop to 10 degrees below zero Celsius.

甲: Tiān yīn le,　shì bú shì yào xiàxuě le?
天阴了，是不是要下雪了？

It is cloudy. Is it about to snow?

乙: Shì.　Tīng tiānqì yùbào shuō,　jīnwǎn yǒu bàofēngxuě.
是。听天气预报说，今晚有暴风雪。

Yes, it is. The weather forecast has said it is going to have a snowstorm tonight.

甲: Shì ma?　Duō dà?
是吗？多大？

Really? How serious is it?

乙: Jīxuě kěnéng yào dào 10 – 12　límǐ.
积雪可能要到10—12厘米。

The accumulation may be about 10-12 cm.

甲: Wēndù zěnmeyàng?
温度怎么样？

How about the temperature?

乙: Dàyuē yào jiàngdào shèshì língxià 10 dù zuǒyòu.
大约要降到摄氏零下10度左右。

It may drop to about 10 degrees below zero Celsius.

甲: Zhème lěng,　lùshang huì jiébīng de.
这么冷，路上会结冰的。

It should be very cold and there will be ice on the road.

乙: Suǒyǐ zhè liǎng tiān zuìhǎo dāi zài jiā li.　Chūqu lù tài huá.
所以这两天最好呆在家里。出去路太滑。

So just stay home for the next two days. The road must be very slippery.

相关词语/Related Words

1	yīntiān 阴天	cloudy	7	jiébīng 结冰	frozen
2	tiānqì yùbào 天气预报	weather forecast	8	lù huá (路)滑	slippery
3	jīxuě 积雪	snow accumulation	9	nuǎn 暖	warm
4	wēndù 温度	temperature	10	rè 热	hot
5	língxià 零下	below zero	11	mēnrè 闷热	muggy; stuffy
6	lěng 冷	cold			

文化导航
Cultural Navigation

　　中国幅员辽阔，各地气候差别很大。中国跨越多个温度带，最南端属于热带，最北端属于寒温带。比如说，中国最北省份黑龙江的北端几乎没有夏天，而南方的海南岛则常年夏季，没有冬天。黄河流域四季分明，青藏高原整年积雪，云贵高原四季如春，西北内陆地区一天之内温度变化极大。

　　The climate of China is extremely diverse due to its vast size. There are several temperature zones in China. It is tropical in the southernmost place and almost cold temperate in the northernmost place. For example, the northern part of Heilongjiang in Northeast China has almost no summer, while Hainan Island in South China has a long summer with no winter. The Yellow River valley features four distinct seasons; the Qinghai-Tibet Plateau is covered by snow all year round; the Yunnan-Guizhou Plateau is spring-like all the year; and the northwestern inland region sees a great change of temperature in a day.

核心句 Key Sentence

Wǒmen wǎnshang *jiànmiàn*, zěnmeyàng?

我们晚上 见面 ，怎么样？

Shall we meet tonight?

句型与替换 Substitution

chīfàn
吃饭
have dinner

tánhuà
谈话
talk

duànliàn
锻炼
workout

扩 展／Extension

1. Nǐ shénme shíhou yǒu shíjiān?
   你什么时候有时间？
   When do you have time?

2. Xīngqīsì shàngwǔ 9 diǎn zěnmeyàng?
   星期四上午 9 点 怎么样？
   How about nine o'clock on Thursday morning?

3. Jiànmiàn dìdiǎn jiù dìng zài lóuxià kāfēitīng.
   见面地点就定在楼下咖啡厅。
   Let's meet in the café downstairs.

4. Wǒmen míngtiān xiàwǔ jiàn.
   我们 明天 下午 见。
   I will see you tomorrow afternoon.

甲： Wèi, nǐ shì Liú Jìng ma? Wǒ shì Tiānxīn.
喂，你是刘静吗？我是天心。
Hello, is it Liu Jing? This is Tianxin.

乙： Tiānxīn, nǐ hǎo. Yǒu shì ma?
天心，你好。有事吗？
Hi, Tianxin, what's up?

甲： Wǒ xiǎng shēnqǐng dú yánjiūshēng, xiǎng gēn nǐ shāngliang yíxià.
我想申请读研究生，想跟你商量一下。
I plan to apply for the graduate program and need your opinions.

乙： Xíng a. Jīntiān báitiān hěn máng, wǒmen wǎnshang jiànmiàn, zěnmeyàng?
行啊。今天白天很忙，我们晚上见面，怎么样？
No problem. I will be busy today. But shall we meet tonight?

甲： Hǎo a. zài nǎr?
好啊，在哪儿？
It sounds good. Where should we meet?

乙： Jiējiǎo kāfēitīng zěnmeyàng?
街角咖啡厅怎么样？
How about the café in the corner?

甲： Hǎo.
好。
Good.

乙： Nà wǒmen wǎnshang 7 diǎn nàr jiàn.
那我们晚上7点那儿见。
Then I will see you at 7:00 there.

相关词语/Related Words

1	Yǒu shì ma? 有事吗？ What's up?		3	yánjiūshēng 研究生 graduate program
2	shēnqǐng 申请 to apply for		4	shāngliang 商量 to discuss

5	rúhé 如何	How about...?	7	kāfēitīng 咖啡厅	cofé
6	jiējiǎo 街角	street corner			

文化导航
Cultural Navigation

　　中国电话礼仪与西方不同。电话接通时人们不用第三人称单数（it）或指示代词（this、that）介绍自己或称呼对方，而是用"我""你"来直接和对方说话。另一个不同之处是，接电话的人一般不报自己公司的名字或自己的名字，而是问对方"你是哪位？"或"您是哪里？"。但电话中不能用"你是谁？"来询问对方姓名，这种问法不礼貌。用手机通话时，由于有来电显示，可以直接开门见山说事情。

Telephone protocol in Chinese culture is somewhat different from the West. "我" (I) and "你" (you) are used instead of the third person singular (it) or the demonstrative pronoun (this/that). For example, when you call someone, you should start by saying "我是……" (This is...) and "你是……吗？" (Is that...?). Another difference is that people who answer the phone call don't usually give the company's name or his/her name first. They may ask "你是哪位？"（Who is it?）or "您是哪里？" (Who is it?) to know who is calling. Another thing you should be careful about is that people don't use "你是谁？" (Who are you?), since it sounds very impolite. Nowadays when you use cell phones to make a call, since there is a name display on the screen, you usually don't have to ask for the name of the other party.

核心句
Key Sentence

Wǒmen sòng yì hé qiǎokèlì.
我们送一盒巧克力。
We can send a box of chocolate (as a gift).

句型与替换
Substitution

yí shù huā
一束花
a bunch of flowers

yì hé dàngāo
一盒蛋糕
a box of cakes

yì tīng cháyè
一听茶叶
a tin of tea

yì hé kāfēi
一盒咖啡
a can of coffee

yì píng hóngjiǔ
一瓶红酒
a bottle of red wine

扩展/Extension

Wǒmen sòng shénme lǐwù ne?
1. 我们送什么礼物呢？

What gift can we give?

Niánqīngrén xǐhuan bǐjiào xīshì
2. 年轻人喜欢比较西式
de lǐwù.
的礼物。

Young people prefer Western gifts.

Bù kě gěi lǎoniánrén sòng zhōngbiǎo,
3. 不可给老年人送钟表，
tīngzhe bù jílì.
听着不吉利。

Clocks cannot be sent to old people as a gift because it doesn't sound lucky.

4. Lǎoniánrén xǐhuan gèng Zhōngguó de dōngxi.
   老年人喜欢更 "中国" 的 东西。

   Old people like things that are more Chinese.

对话实例/Dialogue

甲: Zhōumò shì Xiǎo Wáng fùqin de shēngrì, tā qǐng wǒmen dào tā jiā chīfàn.
周末是小 王父亲的生日，他请我们到他家吃饭。

This weekend is the birthday of Xiao Wang's father and we are invited to have dinner at their home.

乙: Wǒmen dài shénme lǐwù?
我们带什么礼物？

What gift should we give?

甲: Dài yì hé qiǎokèlì qù ba?
带一盒巧克力去吧？

How about a box of chocolate?

乙: Qiǎokèlì tài tián, lǎoniánrén bù xǐhuan. Tāmen xǐhuan gèng Zhōngguó de dōngxi.
巧克力太甜，老年人不喜欢。他们喜欢更 "中国" 的 东西。

Chocolate is too sweet and old people may not like it. They like things that are more Chinese.

甲: Cóng Měiguó dàilái de nà kuài diànzǐ bàoshízhōng zěnmeyàng?
从 美国带来的那块电子报时钟 怎么样？

How about the electronic alarm clock we brought from America?

乙: Tīngshuō zhōngbiǎo bù kěyǐ sòngrén, tèbié shì gěi lǎoniánrén.
听说 钟表不可以送人，特别是给老年人。

I've heard that clocks cannot be sent as gifts, especially to old people.

甲: Wèi shénme?
为什么？

Why?

乙: Zhōng yǔ zhōng shēngyīn xiāngtóng, tīngzhe xiàng sǐ, bù jílì.
"钟" 与 "终" 声音 相同，听着像 "死"，不吉利。

It sounds like "终" (zhōng) in Chinese whose meaning is death, which is not lucky.

1	礼物 lǐwù	gift	5	吉利 jílì	lucky
2	送礼 sònglǐ	to send something as a gift	6	西式 xīshì	Western
3	听说 tīngshuō	to be told ...	7	喜庆 xǐqìng	joyous
4	喜欢 xǐhuan	to like			

文化导航
Cultural Navigation

　　像很多文化一样，在中国也有一些东西是不能当礼物送的。比如绝对不能送钟表给老年人，因为"送钟"听着像"送终"。鞋也不可以用作礼物，因为"送鞋"听着跟"送邪"一样，是让对方交厄运的意思。绿色的帽子不能送给成年男人，因为在中国文化里，男人戴绿帽子是自己的伴侣跟别人有染的意思。

As in many cultures, there are things that can never be used as a gift in Chinese culture. For example, never give a clock to an old Chinese person as a gift because "送钟" (giving a clock as a gift) sounds like "送终" (attending one's funeral). One should not give a pair of shoes to a Chinese person because "送鞋" (giving a pair of shoes as a gift) sounds similar to "送邪" (giving evil to someone). One must also avoid giving a green hat as a gift to a Chinese man as "wearing a green hat" in Chinese implies that the man is cheated by his wife or girlfriend who has an affair with another man.

核心句
Key Sentence

Nín màn zǒu.
您慢走。
Please take care.

句型与替换
Substitution

Nín zǒu hǎo.
您走好。
Watch your steps, please.

Bù yuǎn sòng le.
不远送了。
Let's say good-bye here.

Yǒukòng zài lái.
有空再来。
Do come again.

扩展/Extension

Nà jiù bù liú nín le.
1. 那就不留您了。   I will not keep you any longer.

Qǐng liúbù.
2. 请留步。   Please stay inside.

Wǒ jiù bù yuǎn sòng le.
3. 我就不远送了。   I will say good-bye here.

Yǐhòu yídìng dēngmén bàifǎng.
4. 以后一定登门拜访。   I will definitely find a time to visit you.

甲：
Tài wǎn le,　　wǒmen děi huíqu le.
太晚了，我们得回去了。

It is getting too late. We should leave now.

乙：
Nà jiù bù liú nín le.　　Tiān hēi le,　　wǒ gěi nín jiào liàng
那就不留您了。天黑了，我给您叫辆
chūzūchē.
出租车。

I will not keep you then. It is dark outside. Let me call a
taxi for you.

甲：
Búyòng,　　wǒ zuò dìtiě huíqu,　　tǐng fāngbiàn de.　　Qǐng liúbù.
不用，我坐地铁回去，挺方便的。请留步。

Please don't bother. I will take the subway. It's very
convenient. Please stay inside.

乙：
Nà jiù bù yuǎn sòng le,　　xièxie nín de bàifǎng.
那就不远送了，谢谢您的拜访。

Then I will say good-bye here. Thank you for coming.

甲：
Hǎo,　　hǎo,　　qǐng huí ba.
好，好，请回吧。

OK. Please go back.

乙：
Nín màn zǒu.　　Zàijiàn.
您慢走。再见。

Please watch your steps. Good-bye.

1	liú 留	to keep	3	chūzūchē 出租车	taxi
2	jiào 叫	to call	4	fāngbiàn 方便	convenient

5	liúbù 留步	to stay inside	7	bàifǎng 拜访	to visit
6	yuǎn sòng 远 送	to see somebody off further	8	màn zǒu 慢 走	to watch one's steps

文化导航
Cultural Navigation

中国有比较特别的送客文化。当客人告别时，主人常常把客人送到门外，直到看不见再回去。主人有时会为客人叫好出租车。主人陪着客人走得越远，就越客气，客人就越会感觉受尊重。如果客人刚离开，主人就关门，会被认为非常不客气，没有礼貌。

Chinese have their own culture for seeing visitors off. When a guest says good-bye, a Chinese host often accompanies the guest to the outside of the apartment or the house and won't go back until the guest is out of sight. Sometimes, the host calls a taxi for the guest. The further the host escorts the guest, the better the guest will feel. It is considered impolite if the host shuts the door immediately after the guest leaves.

核心句
Key Sentence

Wǒ xiǎng shēnqǐng Yīngyǔ fānyì zhíwèi.
我 想 申请 英语翻译职位。
I want to apply for the English translator position.

句型与替换
Substitution

xiàngmù jīnglǐ
项目经理
project manager

chūjí xíngzhèng rényuán
初级行政人员
junior administrator

Yīng-Hàn biānjí
英汉编辑
English-Chinese editor

扩展／Extension

Zhè shì wǒ de jiǎnlì.
1. 这是我的简历。

This is my resume.

Néng jièshào yíxià nǐ zìjǐ ma?
2. 能 介绍一下你自己吗?

Can you tell me something about yourself?

Nǐ yǒu zhèngshū ma?
3. 你有HSK证书吗?

Do you have the HSK certificate?

Nǐ yǒu gōngzuò jīngyàn ma?
4. 你有 工作 经验 吗?

Do you have working experience?

Nǐ dào Rénlì Zīyuán Bù tián
5. 你到人力资源部填
yíxià biǎo.
一下表。

Please go to the HR department and fill out a form.

对话实例/Dialogue

甲: Wǒ jiào Wèi Lì, xiǎng shēnqǐng guì gōngsī de Yīngyǔ fānyì zhíwèi,
我叫魏力，想申请贵公司的英语翻译职位，
zhè shì wǒ de jiǎnlì.
这是我的简历。

My name is Wei Li and I am here to apply for the English translator position of your company. This is my resume.

乙: Néng jièshào yíxià nǐ zìjǐ ma?
能介绍一下你自己吗?

Can you tell me something about yourself?

甲: Wǒ shì Měiguórén, xuéle liù nián Zhōngwén, gāng cóng Běi Dà
我是美国人，学了六年中文，刚从北大
shuòshìbān bìyè.
硕士班毕业。

I am American. I have studied Chinese for 6 years. I have just graduated from Peking University with a Master degree.

乙: Yǒu zhèngshū ma?
有HSK证书吗?

Do you have the HSK certificate?

甲: Gānggāng kǎoguò, zhè shì zhèngshū.
刚刚考过，这是证书。

I have just passed the test. This is my certificate.

乙: Nǐ yǒu gōngzuò jīngyàn ma?
你有工作经验吗?

Do you have working experience?

甲: Yǒu. Wǒ zài Měiguó jiāoguo liǎng nián Yīngyǔ, yě fānyìguo jǐ piān
有。我在美国教过两年英语，也翻译过几篇
wénzhāng.
文章。

Yes. I taught English for two years in America and translated a few articles.

乙： Hǎo, nǐ dào Rénlì Zīyuán Bù tián yíxià biǎo, zài cānjiā yí gè
好，你到人力资源部填一下表，再参加一个

Zhōngwén kǎoshì.
中文考试。

Good! Please fill out a form at the Human Resources Department
and then take a Chinese test.

甲： Shénme shíhou néng zhīdào nín de juédìng?
什么时候能知道您的决定？

When should I be notified of your decision?

乙： Yí gè yuè yǐhòu.
一个月以后。

In about a month.

相关词语 / Related Words

1	shēnqǐng 申请	to apply for	6	zhèngshū 证书	certificate
2	zhíwèi 职位	position	7	gōngzuò jīngyàn 工作经验	working experience
3	jiǎnlì 简历	resume	8	rénlì zīyuán 人力资源	human resources
4	jièshào 介绍	to introduce	9	juédìng 决定	decision
5	bìyè 毕业	to graduate			

文化导航
Cultural Navigation

中国人的个人简历跟美国人的有些不同。在美国，简历上
是不写自己的年龄、性别、婚姻状况的，而把重点放在学历和

工作经验上。但中国人的简历要包括年龄、性别、婚姻状况，甚至健康情况、配偶情况等。有的简历还要求附上求职者的照片。人们这样做的原因是很多招工广告对年龄、性别有具体要求，有的对外表还有要求。

There are several differences between resumes in China and in the United States. In the US, on the resume you don't reveal your age, gender, marital status but focus more on your educational background and professional experience. Resumes in China often include such information as age, gender, marital status, even health and information about one's spouse. Some resumes even have the applicants' photos attached. People do so because some job advertisements have specific requirements in these aspects. Some job advertisements even have specifics about the appearance of the applicants.

核心句
Key Sentence

Zhù nǐ yílùshùnfēng.
祝你一路顺风。
Wish you a good journey.

句型与替换
Substitution

shìyè chénggōng
事业成功
successful career

shēnghuó xìngfú
生活幸福
happy life

hūnyīn měimǎn
婚姻美满
happy marriage

扩 展/Extension

Wǒ lái gēn nín gàobié.
1. 我来跟您告别。 I am here to say good-bye to you.

Huíguó yǒu shénme dǎsuàn ma?
2. 回国有什么打算吗? Do you have any plans back home?

Xièxie nín zhè jǐ gè yuè duì
3. 谢谢您这几个月对 Thank you for your help for the past
wǒ de bāngzhù.
我的帮助。 few months.

Wǒmen bǎochí liánxì.
4. 我们保持联系。 Let's keep in touch.

甲：
Wèi chùzhǎng, wǒ yào huíguó le, gēn nín gào gè bié.
魏处长，我要回国了，跟您告个别。
Director Wei, I will go back to my home country. I am here to say good-bye to you.

乙：
Zhēn de? Shénme shíhou zǒu?
真的？什么时候走？
Really? When do you plan to leave?

甲：
Xià gè xīngqī.
下个星期。
Next week.

乙：
Huíqu yǒu shénme dǎsuàn?
回去有什么打算？
Do you have any plans back home?

甲：
Wǒ dǎsuàn kǎo bóshìshēng, bìyè hòu dào dàxué jiāoshū.
我打算考博士生，毕业后到大学教书。
I plan to apply for the doctoral program and teach at college after graduation.

乙：
Nà wǒmen wò gè shǒu, zhù nǐ yílùshùnfēng.
那我们握个手，祝你一路顺风。
Then let's shake hands and I wish you a safe journey back home.

甲：
Xièxie nín zhè duàn shíjiān duì wǒ de bāngzhù, wǒmen bǎochí liánxì.
谢谢您这段时间对我的帮助，我们保持联系。
Thank you for your help for the past few months. Let's be in touch.

1	gàobié 告别	to say good-bye	4	bāngzhù 帮助	help
2	dǎsuàn 打算	to plan	5	bǎochí 保持	to keep
3	wòshǒu 握手	to shake hands	6	liánxì 联系	contact

文化导航
Cultural Navigation

　　无论久别重逢还是分离告别，中国人通常都是握手。在朋友、熟人、同事、生意伙伴之间，他们初次见面、久别重逢、分离告别或在谈判桌上都会握手。但男女之间一般是女士主动握手，时间不会太长。现在一些人见面或分别时也会拥抱。

　　For Chinese, hand-shaking is more common than hugging when you say good-bye or meet long-time-not-seen friends. It takes place between friends, acquaintances, colleagues and business partners. People shake hands at their first meeting, reunion, farewell and at negotiation table. Generally speaking, hand-shaking between different genders won't last long and it is usually initiated by women. Nowadays some people hug each other when meeting and saying goodbye.

[到中国去]
Going to China

16 申请入学 | Applying for School in China

核心句 / Key Sentence

Wǒ xiǎng shēnqǐng guì xiào de yánjiūshēng.

我想申请贵校的研究生。

I plan to apply for the graduate program of your school.

句型与替换 / Substitution

běnkēshēng
本科生
undergraduate

zàizhí jìnxiūshēng
在职进修生
in-service training student

jiāohuànshēng
交换生
exchange student

扩展 / Extension

Nín nàlǐ shì zhāoshēng bàngōngshì ma?
1. 您那里是招生办公室吗? Is it the admission office?

Nǐ xiǎng shēnqǐng nǎge zhuānyè?
2. 你想申请哪个专业? Which major do you plan to apply for?

Dào xuéxiào wǎngzhàn dú yíxià zhāoshēng jiǎnzhāng.
3. 到学校网站读一下招生简章。 Read the admission brochure on the school website.

4. Shēnqǐngbiǎo kěyǐ cóng xuéxiào wǎngzhàn shang xiàzǎi.

   申请表可以从学校网站上下载。

   The application form can be downloaded from the school website.

对话实例/Dialogue

甲: Wèi, nín nàlǐ shì zhāoshēng bàngōngshì ma?
喂，您那里是招生办公室吗？

Hello, is it the admission office?

乙: Shì. Yǒu shì ma?
是。有事吗？

Yes, it is. What can I do for you?

甲: Wǒ xiǎng shēnqǐng guì xiào míngnián de yánjiūshēng.
我想申请贵校明年的研究生。

I plan to apply for the graduate program of your school next year.

乙: Kàn zhāoshēng jiǎnzhāng le ma?
看招生简章了吗？

Have you read the admission brochure?

甲: Hái méiyǒu.
还没有。

Not yet.

乙: Nǐ kěyǐ dào xuéxiào wǎngzhàn dú yíxià zhāoshēng jiǎnzhāng.
你可以到学校网站读一下招生简章。

You can go to the school website and read the brochure first.

甲: Hǎo. Shēnqǐngbiǎo yě zài wǎngshang ma?
好。申请表也在网上吗？

Yes, I will. Is the application form also on the website?

乙: Duì, shēnqǐngbiǎo yě kěyǐ zài wǎngshang xiàzǎi.
对，申请表也可以在网上下载。

Yes. You can download it there.

1	zhāoshēngbàn 招生办	admission office	5	wǎngzhàn 网站	website
2	bìyè 毕业	to graduate	6	shēnqǐngbiǎo 申请表	application form
3	shēnqǐng 申请	to apply for	7	xiàzǎi 下载	to download
4	zhāoshēng 招生 jiǎnzhāng 简章	admission brochure	8	fǎngwèn 访问 xuézhě 学者	visiting scholar

文化导航
Cultural Navigation

　　如要申请到中国上学，首先需到报考学校网站下载并填写《外国留学生入学申请表》，并同时准备好毕业证书和成绩单（原件或公证件）、HSK证书（复印件）或汉语水平证明、个人陈述、两封推荐信（须为中文或英文原件）、护照复印件、护照用照片和报名费。然后把上述申请材料在截止日期前寄到指定地点。

　　If you plan to study at a Chinese university as a degree student or a language student, you should go to the school website, download and complete the application form. Other application materials include your diploma and academic record/transcript (original or notarized copy in English or Chinese), a photocopy of your HSK certificate or other Chinese proficiency certificates, your personal statement, two recommendation letters (original copy in

Chinese or English), a photocopy of passport, passport photos and application fee. Mail the application package to the school before the deadline.

17 申请签证 | Applying for a Chinese Visa

核心句
Key
Sentence

Wǒ xiǎng shēnqǐng xuéshēng qiānzhèng.

我 想 申 请 学 生 签 证 。

I want to apply for a student visa.

句型
与替换
Substitution

gōngzuò
工作
work

lǚyóu
旅游
tourist

tuántǐ
团体
group

shuāngwù
商务
business

扩 展 / Extension

Nǐ yào shēnqǐng shénme qiānzhèng?
1. 你 要 申 请 什 么 签 证 ?

What kind of visa do you apply for?

Nǐ dài hùzhào le ma?
2. 你 带 护 照 了 吗 ?

Do you have your passport with you?

Nǐ dǎsuàn zài Zhōngguó dāi duō jiǔ?
3. 你 打 算 在 中 国 呆 多 久 ?

How long do you plan to stay in China?

Qiānzhèng yí gè xīngqī yǐhòu qǔ.
4. 签 证 一 个 星 期 以 后 取 。

The visa will be ready in a week.

甲：
Xiānsheng, wǒ yào shēnqǐng xuéshēng qiānzhèng.
先生，我要申请学生签证。
Sir, I want to apply for a student visa.

乙：
Qǐng gěi wǒ nǐ de shēnqǐngbiǎo、zhàopiàn、 yāoqǐnghán hé hùzhào.
请给我你的申请表、照片、邀请函和护照。
Please give me your application form, photos, invitation letter and passport.

甲：
Zài zhèlǐ.
在这里。
Here they are.

乙：
Nǐ dǎsuàn zài Zhōngguó dāi duō jiǔ?
你打算在中国呆多久？
How long do you plan to stay in China?

甲：
Liǎng gè bàn yuè.
两个半月。
Two and a half months.

乙：
Hǎo, qǐng dào nàbiān jiāo 140 Měiyuán de shēnqǐngfèi.
好，请到那边交140美元的申请费。
Good. Please pay US$140 application fee over there.

甲：
Hǎo. Qiānzhèng shénme shíhou kěyǐ qǔ?
好。签证什么时候可以取？
Sure. When will it be ready?

乙：
Yí gè xīngqī yǐhòu.
一个星期以后。
In a week.

1	shēnqǐngbiǎo 申请表	application form	5	jiāofèi 交费	to pay	
2	zhàopiàn 照片	photo	6	shēnqǐngfèi 申请费	application fee	
3	yāoqǐnghán 邀请函	invitation letter	7	qǔ 取	to pick up	
4	hùzhào 护照	passport				

文化导航
Cultural Navigation

　　无论你到中国留学还是工作，都要拥有有效的签证。对外国人有几种签证类型，分别是旅游探亲签证（L）、访问签证（F）、学习签证（X）、工作签证（Z）和过境签证（G）等。办理签证时要持有效护照、两张护照照片和签证费到所在国的中国大使馆或领事馆办理。若在中国境内办理签证延期，应到当地公安局出入境管理部门办理。

　　You must have a valid visa to enter China for study or work. There are several types of visas for foreigners. They are tourist and family visit visa (L), business visa (F), student visa (X), work visa (Z), and transit visa (G), etc. A basic application procedure is that you go to a Chinese embassy or a consulate with your valid passport, two passport photos and visa application fee. If you want to extend your visa inside China, you should go to the Exit and Entry Administration Department of the local public security bureau.

18 入境 | Arriving in China

Wǒ dào Zhōngguó shì lái lǚyóu de.

我到中国是来旅游的。

I come to China to travel.

句型
与替换
Substitution

xuéxí
学习
study

gōngzuò
工作
work

kāihuì
开会
attend a conference

tànqīn
探亲
visit family

扩 展/Extension

1. Wàiguórén zài zhèr bànlǐ
   外国人 在这儿办理
   rùjìng shǒuxù.
   入境 手续。

   Foreigners go through the entry procedure here.

2. Nǐ shì dào Zhōngguó liúxué ma?
   你是 到 中 国 留学吗?

   Are you coming to China to study?

3. Qǐng chūshì nǐ de zhèngjiàn.
   请 出示 你的 证件。

   Please show your credentials.

甲： Wǒmen zài nǎr páiduì rùjìng?
我们在哪儿排队入境？

Which line should we stand in for the entry procedure?

乙： Wǒmen dào nàbiān qù, zhè shì Zhōngguó gōngmín rùjìngchù.
我们到那边去，这是中国公民入境处。

We should go there. This is for Chinese citizens.

甲： Nǐ de rùjìngkǎ tiánhǎo le ma?
你的入境卡填好了吗？

Did you fill out your entry card?

乙： Zài fēijī shang jiù tiánhǎo le.
在飞机上就填好了。

Yes. I did it on the plane.

甲： Gāi wǒmen le.
该我们了。

It is our turn.

(护照检查处　Passport Control Immigration)

丙： Nǐ dào Zhōngguó shì lái xuéxí de ma?
你到中国是来学习的吗？

Are you coming to China to study?

甲： Bú shì, wǒ shì lái lǚyóu de.
不是，我是来旅游的。

No. I am here to travel.

丙： Hǎo, bǎ hùzhào hé rùjìngkǎ gěi wǒ.
好，把护照和入境卡给我。

Give me your passport and entry card.

1	páiduì 排队	to line up	5	lǚyóu 旅游	to travel
2	rùjìng 入境	to enter a country	6	hùzhào 护照	passport
3	gōngmín 公民	citizen	7	wàiguórén 外国人	foreigner
4	tián 填	to fill out (a form)			

文化导航
Cultural Navigation

外国人进入中国时要经过健康检查、边境检查、报关和安全检查。检查时要出示有效护照、签证、入境卡和报关卡。为了节省时间，入境卡和报关卡一般在飞机上都应填好。

The procedures for foreigners entering China are health check, frontier inspection, custom declaration and security check, when they should present their valid passports, visas, entry cards and custom declaration forms. The latter two are provided on the airplanes for the passengers to fill out prior to the arrival to China to facilitate the entry.

核心句 Key Sentence

Huānyíng nín dào Zhōngguó lái.
欢迎您到中国来。
Welcome to China.

句型与替换 Substitution

wǒ jiā
我家
my home

Běijīng
北京
Beijing

wǒ xiào
我校
my school/university

wǒmen gōngsī
我们公司
our company

扩展／Extension

Xièxie nín lái jīchǎng jiē wǒ.
1. 谢谢您来机场接我。

Thank you for meeting me at the airport.

Lùshang xīnkǔ le ba?
2. 路上辛苦了吧？

Did you have a good trip?

Gěi nín tiān máfan le.
3. 给您添麻烦了。

Sorry for the trouble.

Chē zài wàimiàn děngzhe ne.
4. 车在外面等着呢。

The car is waiting outside.

(乙举着接人牌　B is holding a sign with A's name on it)

Qǐngwèn, nín shì Zhāng xiānsheng ba?

甲：请问，您是 张 先生 吧？

Excuse me. Are you Mr. Zhang?

Shì. Nín shì Wēilián xiānsheng. Hānyíng nín dào Zhōngguó lái.

乙：是。您是威廉先生。欢迎您到 中 国来。

Yes, I am. You must be Mr. William. Welcome to China.

Xièxie nín lái jīchǎng jiē wǒ.

甲：谢谢您来机场 接我。

Thank you for meeting me at the airport.

Bié kèqi, lùshang xīnkǔ le ba?

乙：别客气，路上辛苦了吧？

You are welcome. Did you have a pleasant trip?

Hái xíng, bú tài lèi.

甲：还行，不太累。

Yes, pretty good.

Chē zài wàimiàn, wǒ bāng nín ná xíngli.

乙：车在外面，我帮您拿行李。

The car is outside. Let me help you with the luggage.

Xièxie, gěi nín tiān máfan le.

甲：谢谢，给您添麻烦了。

Thank you for the help.

相关词语/Related Words

1	huānyíng 欢迎	to welcome	3	jīchǎng 机场	airport
2	xīnkǔ 辛苦	trouble; hardship	4	jiē 接	to pick up

5	kèrén 客人	guest	7	tiān 添	to add
6	xíngli 行李	luggage	8	máfan 麻烦	trouble; inconvenience

文化导航
Cultural Navigation

在中国期间，如果你不住宾馆，而住在私人居所，就应在到达中国24小时内（农村地区，72小时内）向当地派出所登记。如果你持有的是学生签证或工作签证，应在到达中国30天内到当地公安局出入境管理部门办理居留证。另外，在中国期间，你不得工作，除非有政府发放的工作许可。若在中国遇到紧急情况，可以拨打110寻求警察帮助。

While in China, foreigners who do not lodge at hotels should, within 24 hours (72 hours in rural areas) of entry, go through the accommodation registration at the local police station. If holding visas Z or X you should, within 30 days of entry, apply for residence permits at the exit-entry department of the local public security bureau. Foreigners should not be employed without the work permission from the government. In case of an emergency, please dial 110 to seek help from the police.

[互相了解]
Getting to Know Each Other

谈家庭 | Talking about Family

Wǒ shì dúshēngnǚ.
我是独生女。
I am the only daughter in my family.

句型
与替换
Substitution

dúshēngzǐ
独生子
the only son

jiāli de lǎodà
家里的老大
the eldest child

jiāli zuì xiǎo de
家里最小的
the youngest child

✚ 扩 展/Extension

Nǐ jiā yǒu jǐ kǒu rén?
1. 你家有几口人?

How many people are there in your family?

Nǐ jiā yǒu jǐ gè háizi?
2. 你家有几个孩子?

How many children are there in your family?

Nǐ fùmǔ shì zuò shénme gōngzuò de?
3. 你父母是做什么工作的?

What do your parents do?

Wǒ méiyǒu xiōngdì jiěmèi.
4. 我没有兄弟姐妹。

I have no brothers and sisters.

甲：
Nǐ jiā yǒu jǐ kǒu rén?
你家有几口人？
How many people are there in your family?

乙：
Sān kǒu, bàba, māma hé wǒ.
三口，爸爸、妈妈和我。
Three. Father, mother and me.

甲：
Nǐ shì dúshēngnǚ a?
你是独生女啊？
You are the only daughter in the family, aren't you?

乙：
Shì a, Zhōngguó jiātíng chàbuduō dōu shì yí gè háizi. Nǐ jiā ne?
是啊，中国家庭差不多都是一个孩子。你家呢？
Yes. Most Chinese families have only one child. How about yours?

甲：
Wǒ shì jiāli de lǎodà, dǐxia yǒu wǔ gè dìdi mèimei ne.
我是家里的老大，底下有五个弟弟妹妹呢。
I am the eldest child in the family and I have 5 younger brothers and sisters.

乙：
Yǒu xiōngdì jiěmèi, duō hǎo!
有兄弟姐妹，多好！
It is nice to have brothers and sisters!

甲：
Wǒ hái xiànmù nǐ ne.
我还羡慕你呢。
Actually I would like to be an only child at home.

相关词语/Related Words

1	dúshēng 独生 zǐnǚ 子女 the only child	2	jiātíng 家庭 family

3	háizi 孩子	child; children	5	xiànmù 羡慕	to be jealous of
4	xiōngdì 兄弟 jiěmèi 姐妹	siblings			

文化导航
Cultural Navigation

中国是世界上人口最多的国家。为了减缓人口增长，中国政府从上世纪七十年代末开始实行独生子女政策，一对夫妇只能生一个孩子。但如果夫妇双方或者有一方是独生子女的话，就可以生两个孩子。由于这些独生子女受到父母和祖父母太多的关爱，被称为"小皇帝"。但这些孩子同时也被寄予太高的希望，压力比较大。

China is the most populous country in the world. To slow down the population growth, China has enforced a family planning policy starting from the end of the 1970s that each couple can only have one child, though some exceptions can be granted, say, to couples to have more than one child if one of them, or both of them is the only child in the family. These only children are called "little emperors" because of the care and love they have received from parents and grandparents. On the other hand, high hopes are placed on them and they usually bear a lot of pressure.

核心句 Key Sentence

Nà shì wǒ de nánpéngyou.
那是我的男朋友。
That is my boyfriend.

句型与替换 Substitution

nǚpéngyou
女朋友
girlfriend

wèihūnfū
未婚夫
fiancé

wèihūnqī
未婚妻
fiancée

zhàngfu
丈夫
husband

qīzi
妻子
wife

扩展/Extension

Wǒ de nánpéngyou hěn shuài.
1. 我的男朋友很帅。 My boyfriend is very handsome.

Wǒmen yào jiéhūn le.
2. 我们要结婚了。 We are about to get married.

Wǒ hěn ài tā.
3. 我很爱他。 I love him a lot.

Tā duì nǐ zěnmeyàng?
4. 他对你怎么样？ Is he nice to you?

甲： Xiǎolì, nà shì shéi? Nàme shuài!
小丽，那是谁？那么帅！
Xiao Li, who is the handsome man?

乙： Shì wǒ nánpéngyou. Wǒmen yào jiéhūn le.
是我男朋友。我们要结婚了。
He is my boyfriend. We are about to get married.

甲： Zhēn de? Nǐmen rènshi duō jiǔ le?
真的？你们认识多久了？
Really? How long have you known each other?

乙： Bù cháng, cái bànnián. Kěshì wǒ zhēn de hěn ài tā.
不长，才半年。可是我真的很爱他。
Not long, about half a year. But I really love him.

甲： Tā duì nǐ zěnmeyàng?
他对你怎么样？
Does he love you?

乙： Tā duì wǒ hěn hǎo, jiùshì píqi yǒudiǎn jí. Shǔ hǔ de dōu zhèyàng.
他对我很好，就是脾气有点急。属虎的都这样。
He is very nice to me. But he is a bit short-tempered. That is what people born in the year of tiger are.

甲： Nà kě bù yídìng, nǐ yào xiǎnghǎo ò.
那可不一定，你要想好哦。
I don't think so. You should give your decision another thought.

相关词语/Related Words

1	shuài 帅	handsome	3	rènshi 认识	to know
2	jiéhūn 结婚	to be married	4	duō jiǔ 多久	for how long

5	ài 爱	to love	7	píqi 脾气	temper
6	duì 对	to	8	bù yídìng 不一定	not necessarily

文化导航
Cultural Navigation

中国人之间常常用"你属什么的"来问彼此的年龄。根据中国传统年历，一共有十二个生肖，分别由鼠、牛、虎、兔、龙、蛇、马、羊、猴、鸡、狗、猪十二个动物代表。有的中国人相信，一个人的性格、秉性跟出生年的动物相关，有时人们还用自己的生肖动物来预测自己的未来、爱情、事业、钱财等。

Chinese people often use "你属什么的？" (Which animal year were you born in?) to ask about one's age. There are twelve animal signs in the Chinese zodiac, including the rat, the ox, the tiger, the hare, the dragon, the snake, the horse, the sheep, the monkey, the rooster, the dog and the boar, with each representing one year in a twelve-year cycle. Some Chinese people believe, scientifically or not, that one's personality and temperament have much to do with the animal that represents the year of one's birth. People sometimes use one's animal to predict their future, love, career, fortune, etc.

22 谈家乡 | Talking about Hometown

Nǐ shì nǎr rén?
你是哪儿人?
Where are you from?

句型
与替换
Substitution

nǎ guó rén
哪国人
which country

cóng nǎr lái
从哪儿来
which place

nánfāngrén ma
南方人吗
from the South

扩 展/Extension

Wǒ shì Měiguórén.
1. 我是美国人。
I am American.

Wǒ de guójí shì Měiguó.
2. 我的国籍是美国。
My nationality is American.

Wǒ de jiāxiāng shì Guǎngdōng Shùndé.
3. 我的家乡是广东顺德。
My hometown is Shunde, Guangdong Province.

Jiāxiāng hái yǒu shénme rén?
4. 家乡还有什么人?
Are there any relatives living in your hometown?

甲： Nǐ shì Zhōngguórén ma?
你是中国人吗?

Are you Chinese?

乙： Wǒ de guójí shì Měiguó, dàn wǒ fùmǔ chūshēng zài Zhōngguó,
我的国籍是美国，但我父母出生在中国，
suǒyǐ wǒ yě suàn shì Zhōngguórén.
所以我也算是中国人。

My nationality is American. But my parents were born in
China so I should be considered Chinese.

甲： Nǐ shì Zhōngguó nǎge dìfang de rén?
你是中国哪个地方的人?

Which part of China are you from?

乙： Wǒ de jiāxiāng shì Guǎngdōng Shùndé.
我的家乡是广东顺德。

My hometown is Shunde, Guangdong Province.

甲： Zhēn de, nǐ huíquguo ma?
真的，你回去过吗?

Really. Have you been back?

乙： Méiyǒu, wǒ zhè cì dǎsuàn qù.
没有，我这次打算去。

No. I plan to visit there this time.

甲： Jiāxiāng hái yǒu shénme rén?
家乡还有什么人?

Are there any relatives living in your hometown?

乙： Wǒ shūshu yì jiā, dàn wǒ cónglái méi jiànguo tāmen.
我叔叔一家，但我从来没见过他们。

My uncle's family is there but I have never seen them.

1	guójí 国籍	nationality	5	jiāxiāng 家乡	hometown
2	chūshēng 出生	to be born	6	jīngcháng 经常	often
3	suǒyǐ 所以	therefore	7	dǎsuàn 打算	to plan
4	dìfang 地方	place; region	8	shūshu 叔叔	uncle on father's side

文化导航
Cultural Navigation

　　中国人有很强的家乡观念，对来自同一个地方的人有强烈的认同感。"家乡"这个词中文和英文的含义是不太一样的。英文的家乡是指一个人出生、长大的地方，而中国人的家乡是指祖先生活的地方，那个地方你可能从没去过。出于家乡观念，海外华人有很多同乡会，比如福建同乡会、温州同乡会，目的就是在异国他乡，同乡之间能互相帮助、互相支持。

Chinese people have a strong sense of attachment to their hometown and a feeling of affinity with people who share the same hometown. Actually "hometown" in Chinese is different from what is meant in English. In English, it refers to where a person was born and grew up. Hometown to Chinese is a place from which your family originally came though you may never get a chance to go back. Among overseas Chinese, there are always townsman societies such as the Fujian Townsman Society or the Wenzhou Townsman Society. Their major goal is to help each other and support each other in a place that is not their hometown.

谈心情 | Talking about Moods

核心句 / Key Sentence

Wǒ jīntiān xīnqíng bù hǎo.
我今天心情不好。
I am in a bad mood today.

句型与替换 / Substitution

xīnqíng hěn chà
心情很差
very bad mood

qíngxù dīluò
情绪低落
low in spirit

fēicháng gāoxìng
非常高兴
very happy

zhēn kāixīn
真开心
truly happy

扩 展 / Extension

Nǐ zhè jǐ tiān zěnme la?
1. 你这几天怎么啦？
What has happened to you these days?

Shénme shì ràng nǐ bù kāixīn le?
2. 什么事让你不开心了？
What has made you unhappy?

Zhè shì tǐng yǐngxiǎng wǒ xīnqíng de.
3. 这事挺影响我心情的。
This influences my mood badly.

Ràng zìjǐ xīnqíng hǎo qǐlai.
4. 让自己心情好起来。
Cheer yourself up.

甲： Zěnme la?　Liǎnsè zhème bù hǎo.
怎么啦？脸色这么不好。

What happened? You don't look good.

乙： Bù zhī wèi shénme,　wǒ jīntiān xīnqíng bù hǎo.
不知为什么，我今天心情不好。

I don't know why but just in a bad mood today.

甲： Gēn nánpéngyou chǎojià le?
跟男朋友吵架了？

Did you quarrel with your boyfriend?

乙： Méiyǒu.　Búguò zuótiān kǎoshì méi kǎohǎo.
没有。不过昨天考试没考好。

No. But I didn't do well in the test yesterday.

甲： Zhè yǒu shénme,　xià cì kǎohǎo bú jiù xíng le?
这有什么，下次考好不就行了？

That is nothing. Do well next time.

乙： Chéngjì bù hǎo,　míngnián jiǎngxuéjīn jiù ná bú dào le.
成绩不好，明年奖学金就拿不到了。

I cannot get the scholarship if my grade is not good.

甲： Yǐjīng zhèyàng le,　shēngqì yě méi yòng.
已经这样了，生气也没用。

It happened already. It is useless to be angry with yourself.

相关词语/Related Words

1	xīnqíng 心情	mood; feeling	3	xiǎng jiā 想家	to miss home
2	chǎojià 吵架	to quarrel	4	yǐngxiǎng 影响	to influence

5	zhòngyào 重要	important	7	shēngqì 生气	angry; anger
6	jiǎngxuéjīn 奖学金	scholarship	8	méi yòng 没用	useless

文化导航
Cultural Navigation

　　当你和中国人闲谈时，会发现话题可以很私人，可以是年龄、婚姻、收入等。这并不是表示中国人喜欢打听别人隐私，而是他们想了解你，想跟你交朋友，因此你不必为怎么回答这类问题感到尴尬，回答时也不必非常精确。

When you chat with Chinese people, you may find that topics can be quite personal. They can be about your age, marriage status, and income. This does not show that they are interested in your personal life but an indication that they want to show their real interest in you. Therefore you don't have to feel embarrassed and don't have to be precise in your answer.

核心句 Key Sentence

Wǒ zài yīyuàn gōngzuò.
我在医院工作。
I am working in a hospital.

句型与替换 Substitution

yínháng
银行
bank

zhèngfǔ bùmén
政府部门
government

wàiqǐ
外企
foreign company

guóyǒu qǐyè
国有企业
state-owned company

扩展/Extension

Nín zài nǎr gōngzuò?
1. 您在哪儿工作？ — Where do you work?

Nín zuò shénme gōngzuò?
2. 您做什么工作？ — What do you do for a living?

Nín xǐhuan zhè fèn gōngzuò ma?
3. 您喜欢这份工作吗？ — Do you like your work?

Shōurù zěnmeyàng?
4. 收入怎么样？ — How about the income?

甲：
Nín zài nǎr gōngzuò?
您在哪儿工作?

Where do you work?

乙：
Zài yīyuàn dāng zhōngyī dàifu.
在医院 当 中医大夫。

In a hospital. I am a traditional Chinese medicine practitioner.

甲：
Xǐhuan ma? Shōurù zěnmeyàng?
喜欢吗? 收入 怎么样?

Do you like it? How about the income?

乙：
Hěn xǐhuan. Shōurù zhōngděng ba. Nǐ ne?
很 喜欢。收入 中 等 吧。你呢?

I like it a lot. The income is in the medium range. How about you?

甲：
Wǒ zài yì jiā wàiguó yínháng zuò tóuháng.
我在一家外国 银行做投行。

I am working in a foreign bank, doing investment banking.

乙：
Zhè kě shì niánqīngrén shǒuxuǎn de gōngzuò. Zěnmeyàng?
这可是年轻人 首选 的 工作。 怎么样?

It is No. 1 choice among young people today. How do you like it?

甲：
Shōurù shì búcuò, dàn yālì hěn dà, gōngzuò shíjiān yě cháng.
收入是不错，但压力很大，工作时间也长。

It is a well-paid job. But there is a lot of pressure and long working hours.

1	yīyuàn 医院	hospital	6	yínháng 银行	bank
2	zhōngyī 中医	Chinese medicine practitioner	7	tóuháng 投行	investment banking
3	shōurù 收入	income	8	shǒuxuǎn 首选	first choice
4	zhōngděng 中 等	medium	9	yālì 压力	pressure
5	wàiguó 外国	foreign			

文化导航
Cultural Navigation

　　西医是17世纪由传教士介绍到中国来的，在此之前中国人完全依靠传统中医治病，中医包括针灸、草药、拔罐、按摩等治疗手段。在现代社会，很多中国人依然使用中医中药配合西医治病，他们认为，只有中医才能根治病症。

Before Western medicine was first introduced to China during the 17th century by European missionaries, the Chinese relied exclusively on traditional Chinese medicine, a system including acupuncture, herbal medicine, cupping, massage and other therapies. Nowadays many people still use Chinese medicine to treat various ailments along with Western medicine believing only the Chinese medicine can eliminate the root of the illness.

核心句 Key Sentence

Wǒ xǐhuan dǎ wǎngqiú.
我喜欢打网球。
I like playing tennis.

句型与替换 Substitution

chànggē
唱歌
singing

tiàowǔ
跳舞
dancing

yóuyǒng
游泳
swimming

kàn diànyǐng
看电影
watching movies

huàhuà
画画
painting

jiāoyóu
郊游
outing

dúshū
读书
reading books

扩展／Extension

Nǐ yèyú shíjiān dōu zuò xiē shénme?
1. 你业余时间都做些什么？

What do you do in your spare time?

Wǒ xǐhuan zàijiā dúshū, kàn
2. 我喜欢在家读书，看
diànshì.
电视。

I like to stay home reading books or watching TV.

Wǒ xǐhuan hùwài huódòng.
3. 我喜欢户外活动。

I like outdoor activities.

Jīntiān wǎnshang wǒmen qù kǎlā
4. 今天 晚 上 我们去卡拉
zěnmeyàng?
OK，怎么样？

Let's go to Karaoke tonight,
shall we?

对话实例／Dialogue

Nǐ yèyú shíjiān xǐhuan zuò xiē shénme?
甲： 你业余时间喜欢做些什么？

What do you do in your spare time?

Wǒ hěn xǐhuan yùndòng， tèbié xǐhuan dǎ wǎngqiú。 Nǐ ne?
乙： 我很喜欢运动，特别喜欢打网球。你呢？

I like sports, especially tennis. How about you?

Wǒ bǐjiào xǐhuan zàijiā dúshū， kàn diànshì。
甲： 我比较喜欢在家读书，看电视。

I like to stay home reading books and watching TV.

Nǐ xǐhuan chànggē、 tiàowǔ ma?
乙： 你喜欢唱歌、跳舞吗？

Do you like singing and dancing?

Xǐhuan shì xǐhuan， jiùshì dōu bù hǎo。
甲： 喜欢是喜欢，就是都不好。

I like both, but not good at either of them.

Nà jīntiān wǎnshang wǒmen qù kǎlā tīng liànlian， zěnmeyàng?
乙： 那今天 晚 上 我们去卡拉OK厅 练练，怎么样？

Then let us go to Karaoke tonight, shall we?

Hǎo a.
甲： 好啊。

It sounds good.

Wǒmen jiù qù Nánmén nà jiā， xiàwǔ yǒu xuéshēng yōuhuì chǎng。
乙： 我们就去南门那家，下午有 学生 优惠场。

Let's go to the one next to the Southern Gate. They have
student discount in the afternoon.

相关词语/Related Words

1	yèyú shíjiān 业余时间	spare time	5	kǎlā OK 卡拉OK	Karaoke
2	xǐhuan 喜欢	to like	6	liàn 练	to practice
3	yùndòng 运动	sport	7	yōuhuì 优惠	discount
4	wǎngqiú 网球	tennis			

文化导航
Cultural Navigation

　　卡拉OK厅是中国人娱乐休闲常去的地方。一群亲朋好友可以在卡拉OK厅预订一个包间，在里面唱歌、跳舞、聊天，还可以喝酒、吃饭。很多人周末都选择到卡拉OK厅预订一个单间放松一下，或者到那里聚会，庆祝生日、升学、升职等。卡拉OK厅晚上和周末的价钱比较贵，下午比较便宜。

Karaoke bars are one of the most popular places for entertainment and relaxation in China. There people can entertain themselves on weekends, or have a party to celebrate one's birthday, acceptance to the top-choice college, or promotion in the workplace. Besides singing and chatting, people can order food and beverages and reserve a private room. Prices in the evenings and on weekends are much higher than in the afternoons.

学校生活
School Life

核心句 Key Sentence

Qǐng chūshì nǐ de lùqǔ tōngzhīshū.
请出示你的录取通知书。
Please show me your admission letter.

句型与替换 Substitution

hùzhào
护照
passport

xuéfèi shōujù
学费 收据
tuition receipt

jiànkāng dēngjì biǎo
健康登记表
health form

扩 展/Extension

Wǒ shì lái bàodào de.
1. 我是来报到的。

I am here to register (for the program).

Zhè shì nǐ de xuéshēngzhèng.
2. 这是你的学生证。

This is your student ID.

Qǐng tián yíxià zhùcè dēngjì biǎo.
3. 请填一下注册登记表。

Please complete the registration form.

Zhè shì shǔqībān de zīliào.
4. 这是暑期班的资料。

Here is the package for the summer program.

甲:
Wǒ shì shǔqī Hànyǔbān de xīnshēng, shì lái bàodào de.
我是暑期汉语班的新生，是来报到的。

I am a new student of the Summer Chinese Program. I am here to register.

乙:
Huānyíng nǐ. Qǐng chūshì yíxià nǐ de lùqǔ tōngzhīshū, hùzhào hé jiāofèi shōujù.
欢迎你。请出示一下你的录取通知书、护照和交费收据。

Welcome. May I see your admission letter, passport and receipt?

甲:
Zài zhèr ne.
在这儿呢。

Here they are.

乙:
Hǎo. Zhè shì liúxuéshēng dēngjìbiǎo hé jiànkāng dēngjìbiǎo, qǐng tián yíxià.
好。这是留学生 登记表和健康 登记表，请填一下。

Great! Here are the foreign student registration form and health form. Please complete them.

……

甲:
Tiánhǎo le.
填好了。

I am done with the forms.

乙:
Xièxie. Zhè shì shǔqībān de zīliào, Zhè shì nǐ de xuéshēngzhèng.
谢谢。这是暑期班的资料，这是你的学 生 证。

Thanks. Here is the package for the summer program and here is your student ID.

甲:
Wǒ shàng nǎge bān?
我 上 哪个班？

Which class should I go to?

乙:
Nǐ děi xiān cānjiā fēnbān kǎoshì zài juédìng shàng nǎge bān.
你得先参加分班考试再决定 上 哪个班。

You have to take the test before we decide which class you will attend.

1	shǔqī 暑期	summer vacation	6	tián biǎo 填 (表)	to complete (a form)
2	bàodào 报到	registration; to register	7	xuéshēngzhèng 学 生 证	student ID
3	lùqǔ 录取 tōngzhīshū 通知书	admission letter	8	fēnbān 分班	class division
4	jiāofèi shōujù 交费收据	receipt	9	qiánghuàbān 强 化 班	intensive class
5	dēngjìbiǎo 登记表	registration form			

文化导航
Cultural Navigation

汉语是中国人口最多的汉民族的语言。汉族约占全国人口的90%，而其他10%的人说藏语、蒙语、苗语等少数民族语言。世界上有13亿人说汉语，差不多每五个人就有一个人说汉语。说汉语的人主要集中在中国，除此之外，还有东南亚的新加坡、印度尼西亚、马来西亚和泰国。另外，在欧美等地区也分布着很多汉语社区。

The Chinese language is the language of the Han people, the major ethnic group of China. About 1.3 billion people, or one-fifth of the world's population, speak Chinese all over the world. In

China, approximately 90% of the population speak the language, as opposed to the non-Chinese languages such as Tibetan, Mongolian and Miao, etc., which are spoken by different ethnic groups. Besides China, Chinese is also spoken by a large population in Southeast Asia, especially in Singapore, Indonesia, Malaysia, and Thailand. Chinese-speaking communities can also be found in many other parts of the world, including Europe, North and South America, and the Hawaiian Islands.

27 选专业 | Major Selection

核心句 Key Sentence

Wǒ duì Zhōngguó zhéxué gǎn xìngqù.
我对中国哲学感兴趣。
I am interested in Chinese philosophy.

句型与替换 Substitution

lìshǐ
历史
history

wénhuà
文化
culture

fǎlù
法律
law

jīngjì
经济
economy

zhèngzhì
政治
political science

扩展/Extension

Nǐ xiǎng xuǎn shénme zhuānyè?
1. 你想选什么专业？
Which major are you going to choose?

Nǐ duì shénme lǐngyù gǎn xìngqù?
2. 你对什么领域感兴趣？
What is your most interested area?

Wǒ xiǎng yánjiū rújiā xuéshuō.
3. 我想研究儒家学说。
I plan to study Confucianism.

Nǐ dú de liǎo yuánwén ma?
4. 你读得了原文吗？
Can you read the original text?

甲： Yào xuǎn zhuānyè le.　nǐ yǒu shénme dǎsuàn?
要 选 专业 了，你 有 什么 打算？
You have to make a decision about your major. Do you have any plans?

乙： Wǒ duì Zhōngguó zhéxué gǎn xìngqù.
我 对 中国 哲学 感 兴趣。
I am interested in Chinese philosophy.

甲： Néng jùtǐ　yìdiǎnr ma?
能 具体一点儿 吗？
Can you be more specific?

乙： Wǒ xiǎng yánjiū　rújiā xuéshuō.
我 想 研究 儒家 学说。
I am particularly interested in Confucius thoughts.

甲： Wèi shénme?
为 什么？
Why?

乙： Yàyì　jiātíng dōu fēicháng zhòngshì jiàoyù,　zhèlǐ kěndìng yǒu rújiā
亚裔 家庭 都 非常 重视 教育，这里 肯定 有 儒家
xuéshuō de yǐngxiǎng.
学说 的 影响。
Asian families attach importance to education and this must be the influence of Confucius thoughts.

甲： Wǒ tóngyì zhège shuōfǎ.　Nǐ dú de liǎo yuánwén ma?
我 同意 这个 说法。你 读得了 原文 吗？
I agree. Can you read the original text in Chinese?

乙： Dú bù liǎo,　suǒyǐ yào hǎohǎo xué Zhōngwén.
读不了，所以 要 好好 学 中文。
Not yet. That is why I am studying Chinese very hard.

相关词语/Related Words

1	xuǎn 选	to select	3	dǎsuàn 打算	to plan; to intend
2	zhuānyè 专业	major	4	duì······ gǎn xìngqù 感兴趣	to be interested in

5	rúxué 儒学	Confucianism	8	shòu…… 受…… yǐngxiǎng 影响	under the influence of
6	xuéshuō 学说	thoughts	9	zhòngshì 重视	to attach importance to
7	yánjiū 研究	to study; to do research	10	yuánwén 原文	the original text

文化导航
Cultural Navigation

中国哲学家孔子（公元前551－公元前479）是儒家学说创始人，他的思想几千年来影响着中国乃至亚洲很多国家。孔子是一个教育家，非常重视教育，认为只有认真学习、认真思考才能懂得事情的真谛。他的很多语录都跟教育有关。在他的思想影响下，很多中国人认为，认真读书、获得优秀成绩是改变人生命运的唯一途径。

Confucius (551 BC-479 BC) was the founder of Confucianism that has influenced China and many other countries in Asia for thousands of years. As an educator, Confucius highly valued education and study believing that real understanding of something comes only from serious study and reflection. There are quite a few of his quotations related to the importance of education, which are deeply rooted in the mind of Chinese people who believe that education is the only way to move up on the social ladder.

28 选课 | Course Selection

核心句 Key Sentence

Nǐ bìxū shàng yì mén bìxiūkè.

你必须上一门必修课。

You have to take one core course.

句型与替换 Substitution

xuǎnxiū 选修 elective	zhuānyè 专业 major
xiězuò 写作 writing	yuèdú 阅读 reading
kǒuyǔ 口语 conversation	jīngdú 精读 intensive reading
fàndú 泛读 extensive reading	tīnglì 听力 listening

扩展/Extension

Wǒ xiǎng gēn nín tǎolùn yíxià
1. 我想跟您讨论一下
xuǎnkè wèntí.
选课问题。

I want to talk with you about my course selection.

Nǐ zhìshǎo yào shàng wǔ mén kè.
2. 你至少要上五门课。

You have to take at least five courses.

Wǒ shàng shénme xuǎnxiūkè,
3. 我上什么选修课，
nín yǒu shénme jiànyì?
您有什么建议?

Do you have any suggestions about the elective course I will take?

Xuǎn yì mén nǐ zuì gǎn xìngqù
4. 选 一门 你 最 感 兴趣　　　Choose one course you are most
de kè.　　　　　　　　　　　interested in.
　　的课。

对话实例/Dialogue

Wáng lǎoshī,　　wǒ xiǎng gēn nín tǎolùn yíxià xuǎnkè wèntí.
甲: 王 老师，我 想 跟 您 讨论 一下 选课 问题。
Professor Wang, I would like to talk with you about my
course selection.

Hǎo.　Jīnnián shì nǐ yánjiūshēng de dì-yī nián,　zhìshǎo yào shàng wǔ
乙: 好。今年 是 你 研究生 的 第一 年，至少 要 上 五
mén kè.
　　门 课。
Good. This is your first year as a graduate student and you
have to take five courses at least.

Méi wèntí.
甲: 没 问题。
No problem.

Nǐ děi shàng liǎng mén bìxiūkè hé yì mén zhuānyè xiězuò kè.
乙: 你 得 上 两 门 必修课 和 一门 专业 写作 课。
You have to take two core courses and one writing course.

Nà qítā liǎng mén nín yǒu shénme jiànyì?
甲: 那 其他 两 门 您 有 什么 建议？
Do you have any suggestions about the other two courses?

Nǐ duì Zhōngguó zōngjiào gǎn xìngqù,　jiù shàng yì mén Zhōngguó
乙: 你 对 中国 宗教 感兴趣，就 上 一 门 "中国
zōngjiào rùmén ba,　lìngwài yì mén nǐ zìjǐ xuǎn.
宗教 入门" 吧，另外 一门 你 自己 选。
You are interested in religions of China. Why not take
"Introduction to Chinese Religions"? You can choose the
other one yourself.

Nà wǒ shàng wényánwén yuèdú,　nín kàn xíng ma?
甲: 那 我 上 "文言文 阅读"，您 看 行 吗？
Then I will choose "Classic Chinese Reading". What do you think?

Fēicháng hǎo.
乙: 非常 好。
(It) sounds perfect.

1	gēn 跟······ tǎolùn 讨论	to discuss with...; to talk with...	4	mén 门	the measure word for courses
2	xuǎnkè 选课	to select a course	5	jiànyì 建议	suggestion; to suggest
3	zhìshǎo 至少	at least	6	rùmén 入门	introduction to

文化导航
Cultural Navigation

　　中国传统宗教是道教和佛教。也有人把儒家学派称作"儒教"。但对大多数中国人来说，它们更像是教导人们为人处世、建国立业的指导思想，而不是像西方社会无处不在的宗教信仰。除了道教和佛教外，中国还有一小部分人信伊斯兰教、天主教和基督教。

　　The traditional religions of China are Daoism and Buddhism. Sometimes the Confucian school is called "Confucianism". But for most Chinese people they are more like philosophies of life that influence the behaviors and beliefs of individuals and of the state rather than institutionalized belief systems as religions are in the West. Other institutionalized religions besides Daoism and Buddhism in the country include Islam, Catholicism and Christianity, representing a small part of the population respectively.

核心句
Key Sentence

Jiàoxuélóu zài shítáng hé túshūguǎn zhōngjiān.
教学楼在食堂和图书馆中间。
The classroom building is between the dining hall and the library.

句型与替换
Substitution

liúxuéshēnglóu qiánmiàn
留学生楼前面
in front of the foreign student building

xíngzhènglóu hòumiàn
行政楼后面
behind the administration building

sùshèlóu zuǒbian
宿舍楼左边
on the left of the student dormitory

扩 展/Extension

Láojià, jiàoxuélóu zěnme zǒu?
1. 劳驾，教学楼怎么走？

Excuse me. How to get to the classroom building?

Xíngzhènglóu lí zhèr bù yuǎn.
2. 行政楼离这儿不远。

The administration building is not far from here.

Yìzhí wǎng qián zǒu.
3. 一直往前走。

Go straight.

Kànjiàn sùshèlóu wǎng zuǒ guǎi.
4. 看见宿舍楼往左拐。

Turn left at the student dormitory.

甲：
Láojià, jiàoxuélóu zěnme zǒu?
劳驾，教学楼怎么走？
Excuse me, do you know how to get to the classroom building?

乙：
Jǐ hào jiàoxuélóu?
几号教学楼？
Which classroom building?

甲：
Wǒ lái kàn yí kàn, ò, shì wǔ hào jiàoxuélóu.
我来看一看，哦，是五号教学楼。
Let me see. Oh, it is No. 5.

乙：
Wǔ hào jiàoxuélóu zài shítáng hé túshūguǎn zhōngjiān.
五号教学楼在食堂和图书馆中间。
No. 5 Classroom Building is between the dining hall and the library.

甲：
Lí zhèlǐ yuǎn bù yuǎn?
离这里远不远？
Is it far from here?

乙：
Bù yuǎn. Nǐ yìzhí wǎng qián zǒu, kànjiàn xíngzhènglóu wǎng zuǒ guǎi,
不远。你一直往前走，看见行政楼往左拐，
zài zǒu guò liǎng gè lóu jiù dào le.
再走过两个楼就到了。
No. You walk straight until you see the administration building. Turn left, pass two buildings and you will be there.

甲：
Xièxie nǐ.
谢谢你。
Thank you.

乙：
Wǒ yě wǎng nàge fāngxiàng qù, nǐ gēn wǒ yìqǐ zǒu ba.
我也往那个方向去，你跟我一起走吧。
I am also going to that direction. You may follow me.

1	láojià 劳驾	Excuse me.	2	zěnme zǒu 怎么走	How to get to...?

3	zài 在 …… hé 和 …… zhījiān 之间	between...and...	8	xíngzhèng- 行 政 lóu 楼	administration building
4	yìzhí zǒu 一直走	to go straight	9	túshūguǎn 图书馆	library
5	wǎng zuǒ guǎi 往 左 拐	to turn left	10	shítáng 食堂	dining hall
6	fāngxiàng 方 向	direction	11	sùshèlóu 宿舍楼	dormitory building
7	jiàoxuélóu 教学楼	classroom building			

文化导航
Cultural Navigation

　　美国很多大学都跟周围社区融合在一起，分不清彼此。但中国的大学都有自己的校园、围墙和大门，是一个独立的社区。中国的大学生一般要求住在学校宿舍里，吃在学校食堂，由此形成了一种特殊的中国校园文化，出现了一批校园文学、校园歌曲等。

Most universities in China have their exclusive land and buildings, bounded by high walls. This is different from the United States where a lot of universities are integrated into the surrounding communities. Chinese college students are required to live in dorms on campus and eat in on-campus dining halls which are subsided so that students can eat at a relatively lower price. University life in China is highly valued by students, some of whom share their experience in writing and songs called campus literature and campus songs.

30 一天安排 | Daily Schedule

Zhè shì wǒmen de yí rì ānpái.
这是我们的一日安排。
This is our daily schedule.

句型
与替换
Substitution

kèchéng jìndùbiǎo
课程进度表
course schedule

xiàolì
校历
school calendar

rìchéng
日程
daily schedule

扩展/Extension

Shíjiān pái de zhème mǎn.
1. 时间排得这么满。 (You've got) such a tight schedule.

Nǐmen měi tiān dōu hěn máng ba?
2. 你们每天都很忙吧? You should be very busy every day.

Wǒmen měi tiān shàng liù jié kè.
3. 我们每天上六节课。 We have six classes every day.

Zhōumò kěyǐ fàngsōng yíxià.
4. 周末可以放松一下。 (We) can relax a bit on weekends.

甲：
Lái Zhōngguó yí gè xīngqī le, máng bù máng?
来中国一个星期了，忙不忙？

You have been here for a week. Are you busy?

乙：
Kànkan, zhè shì wǒmen de yí rì ānpái.
看看，这是我们的一日安排。

Look, this is our daily schedule.

甲：
Wa, shíjiān pái de zhème mǎn.
哇，时间排得这么满。

Wow, you have such a tight schedule.

乙：
Shì a, wǒmen měi tiān shàng liù jié kè, cóng zǎochen 8 diǎn jiù kāishǐ.
是啊，我们每天上六节课，从早晨8点就开始。

Yes. We have six classes every day, starting at 8:00 am.

甲：
Liù jié kè yǐhòu ne?
六节课以后呢？

What do you do after the sixth period?

乙：
Shàng yī duì yī de dānbānkè hé fǔdǎokè.
上一对一的单班课和辅导课。

We have one-on-one sessions and tutoring hours.

甲：
Wǎnshang zuò shénme?
晚上做什么？

What do you do in the evening?

乙：
Zuò zuoyè, zhǔnbèi měi rì yì kǎo.
做作业，准备每日一考。

I do homework and prepare for the daily quiz.

甲：
Zhème xué, nǐ de Zhōngwén jìnbù hěn dà ba?
这么学，你的中文进步很大吧？

You study so hard. You must have made a lot of progress with your Chinese.

乙：
Nà dào shì, gēn Zhōngguórén duìhuà jīběn méi wèntí le.
那倒是，跟中国人对话基本没问题了。

That is right. I can talk with Chinese people without much difficulty.

1	ānpái 安排	plan		5	zhǔnbèi 准备	to prepare
2	dānbānkè 单班课	one-on-one session		6	jìnbù 进步	progress; improvement
3	fǔdǎo 辅导	to tutor		7	duìhuà 对话	conversation
4	měi rì yì kǎo 每日一考	daily quiz		8	jīběn 基本	basically; almost

文化导航
Cultural Navigation

中国大学生的生活比较有规律，典型的一天时间安排是学生早上7点起床，吃早饭，然后从8点开始上四节课。12点左右是午饭时间，然后是午休时间。中午不上课。下午一般上两节课，之后是一小时或两小时的课余活动时间，晚饭之后是晚自习，就寝时间一般在10点到12点。

A typical daily schedule for a college student in China is to get up at 7:00 and have breakfast. There are four class periods in the morning starting at 8:00. Lunch time is around 12:00 followed by a nap time. There are usually two class periods in the afternoon and one or two hours for extra curriculum activities. Evening is the time for self-study. Bed time is about 10:00 to 12:00.

核心句 Key Sentence

Lǎoshī tài yán le.

老师太严了。

The teacher is too strict with us.

句型与替换 Substitution

fùzé
负责
responsible

hǎo
好
nice

lìhai
厉害
tough

扩展/Extension

1. Nǐmen lǎoshī zěnmeyàng?
   你们老师怎么样？

   How about your teacher?

2. Lǎoshī duì wǒmen yāoqiú hěn yán.
   老师对我们要求很严。

   The teacher is very strict with us.

3. Wǒ pà Wáng lǎoshī.
   我怕王老师。

   I am afraid of Professor Wang.

4. Yánshī chū gāotú.
   严师出高徒。

   A strict teacher brings up better students.

甲： Lǐ lǎoshī duì wǒmen tài yán le.
李老师对我们太严了。

Professor Li is too strict with us.

乙： Zěnme la?
怎么啦？

What's up?

甲： Měi tiān dōu jiūzhèng wǒmen fāyīn, zài tā miànqián, wǒ dōu bù gǎn
每天都纠正我们发音，在他面前，我都不敢
shuōhuà le.
说话了。

He corrects our pronunciation every day. I dare not speak in front of him.

乙： Tā duì xiězì yāoqiú yán ma?
他对写字要求严吗？

How about character writing?

甲： Yán! Zì yídìng yào xiě gōngzhěng, luàn yìdiǎn tā jiù dǎ hóngchā.
严！字一定要写工整，乱一点他就打红叉。

Sure. We must write neat and tidy. He will mark red if there is any messy part.

乙： Yě tài lìhai le ba.
也太厉害了吧。

He is very tough.

甲： Wǒ guòqù xiě fántǐzì, xiànzài xué jiǎntǐzì, yǒushí zài yì piān
我过去写繁体字，现在学简体字，有时在一篇
wénzhāng li liǎng zhǒng dōu yòng, tā jiù shuō bù xíng.
文章里两种都用，他就说不行。

I wrote traditional Chinese characters before and now switch to simplified. If I use both in one piece of writing, he will say "not acceptable".

乙：
Wèi shénme?
为 什么？

Why?

甲：
Tā shuō, yàobù yòng fántǐzì, yàobù yòng jiǎntǐzì, bù néng hùn
他说，要不用繁体字，要不用简体字，不能混
zài yìqǐ yòng.
在一起用。

He said, "You can use either one but not both at the same time."

乙：
Yánshī chū gāotú, nǐ yǐhòu kěnéng huì gǎnxiè tā ne.
严师出高徒，你以后可能会感谢他呢。

A strict teacher brings up better students. You may appreciate his strictness in the future.

相关词语/Related Words

1	yángé 严格	strict	5	luàn 乱	messy
2	jiūzhèng 纠正	to correct	6	dǎ hóngchā 打红叉	to mark red
3	fāyīn 发音	to pronounce; pronunciation	7	fántǐzì 繁体字	traditional Chinese characters
4	gōngzhěng 工整	neat and tidy	8	jiǎnhuàzì 简化字	simplified Chinese characters

文化导航
Cultural Navigation

汉字分为繁体字和简化字。繁体字也称正体字，形成的时间是汉朝末年，现在香港、台湾、澳门等地使用。简化字是1956年中国政府为扫盲普及文化教育而推出来的，目的是把笔画多的字简化下来，让人们好读好认。一般认为，会认2000字就算脱盲，认识3000字就可以读报，而受过良好教育的人要认识6000−7000字。

There are two systems for Chinese characters. The traditional system, used in Hong Kong, Taiwan and Macao, takes its form from standardized character forms dating back from the late Han Dynasty. The simplified Chinese character system, developed by the PRC in 1956 to promote mass literacy, simplifies most complex traditional glyphs to fewer strokes so that it is easier to write and master. It is believed that a well-educated Chinese can recognize approximately 6,000-7,000 characters. With 3,000 characters people can read newspaper. The government defines literacy as the knowledge of 2,000 characters.

32 借书 | Borrowing Books

Túshū kěyǐ jiè liǎng gè yuè.
图书可以借两个月。
You can keep books for two months.

句型 与替换 Substitution

yīnxiàng zhìpǐn
音像制品
audio and video products

lùxiàngdài
录像带
video tapes

lùyīndài
录音带
audio tapes

gōngjùshū
工具书
reference books

扩 展/Extension

Zhōngwén diànyǐng zài jǐ lóu?
1. 中文电影在几楼？ On which floor are Chinese movies?

Wàiwénshū zài èr lóu, H qū.
2. 外文书在二楼，H区。 Foreign books are on the second floor in Section H.

Kěyǐ xùjiè jǐ cì?
3. 可以续借几次？ How many times can I renew?

Yí cì kěyǐ jiè jǐ běn?
4. 一次可以借几本？ How many books can I borrow one time?

Gōngjùshū bú wài jiè.
5. 工具书不外借。 Reference books cannot be taken out.

甲:
Yīnxiàng zhìpǐn kěyǐ jiè duō cháng shíjiān?
音像制品可以借多 长 时间？

How long can audio and video products be kept?

乙:
Liǎng gè xīngqī.
两 个星期。

Two weeks.

甲:
Kěyǐ xùjiè ma?
可以续借吗？

Can they be renewed?

乙:
Zhǐ néng xùjiè yí cì.
只 能 续借一次。

You can only renew once.

甲:
Túshū yí cì kěyǐ jiè jǐ běn?
图书一次可以借几本？

How many books can I borrow one time?

乙:
Zuì duō jiè shí běn, dàn gōngjùshū bú wài jiè.
最多借十本，但工具书不外借。

Ten at most. But reference books can only be used in library.

甲:
Nà wǒ jiè zhè pán hé zhè sān běn shū.
那我借这盘DVD和这三本书。

Then I will borrow this DVD and these three books.

乙:
Bǎ nǐ de túshūzhèng gěi wǒ.
把你的图书证给我。

Please give me your library card.

1	xùjiè 续借	to renew	5	wàiwénshū 外文书	book of the foreign language
2	gōngjùshū 工具书	reference book	6	zìdiǎn 字典	dictionary
3	túshūzhèng 图书证	library card	7	wénxiàn 文献	document; literature
4	zūqī 租期	lease term			

文化导航
Cultural Navigation

汉语有很多地方方言，主要有吴、粤、闽、湘等。这些方言之间的差异，特别是语音之间的差异很大，讲不同方言的人几乎听不懂对方说的话。为解决此问题，中国政府大力推广普通话。普通话是全国通用的标准话。现在学校教的是普通话，政府部门、新闻媒体也都使用普通话。

The Chinese language comprises many regional language varieties, or dialects, the primary ones being Wu, Cantonese, Min, Xiang and so on. Great differences exist between these dialects, especially in pronunciation. As a result, speakers of different dialects usually cannot understand each other. To resolve the problem, the government has promoted "common speech" or *putonghua* across regions. Nowadays, *putonghua* is taught in schools and used by mass media and government offices.

33 考试 | Taking Tests

核心句
Key Sentence

Qīmò kǎoshì kǎo de zěnmeyàng?
期末考试考得怎么样?
How did you do on your final examination?

句型与替换
Substitution

shēngcí xiǎokǎo
生词小考
vocabulary quiz

dānyuán cèyàn
单元测验
unit test

qīzhōng kǎoshì
期中考试
mid-term examination

shuǐpíng kǎoshì
水平考试
proficiency test

扩 展/Extension

Jīntiān de kǎoshì tèbié nán.
1. 今天的考试特别难。 The test today is extremely hard.

Yuèdú bùfen tǐng róngyì de.
2. 阅读部分挺容易的。 The reading part is pretty easy.

Tā kǎole bān li dì-yī.
3. 他考了班里第一。 He did best on the test in class.

Tā de píngjūn chéngjì shì 91 fēn.
4. 他的平均成绩是91分。 His average score is 91.

对话实例/Dialogue

Qīmò kǎoshì nǐ kǎo de zěnmeyàng?
甲: 期末考试你考得怎么样?
How did you do on the final examination?

乙：Bú tài hǎo, tèbié shì yuèdú bùfen.
不太好，特别是阅读部分。
Not very well, especially the reading part.

甲：Nà tīnglì bùfen ne?
那听力部分呢？
How about the listening part?

乙：Tīnglì bùfen hái xíng, dáduìle 85%.
听力部分还行，答对了85%。
Listening comprehension is all right. I got 85% correct.

甲：Tīngshuō nǐ de píngjūn chéngjì shì bān li dì-yī.
听说你的平均成绩是班里第一。
I am told that you are the top one in class in terms of the average score.

乙：Wǒ yě méi xiǎngdào.
我也没想到。
I didn't expect it.

甲：Xià gè yuèkǎo HSK, nǐ zhǔnbèi de zěnmeyàng?
下个月考HSK，你准备得怎么样？
We are going to take the HSK next month. How is your preparation for that?

乙：Zhèng zuòtí ne. Xīwàng néng kǎoguò.
正做题呢。希望能考过。
I am working on it. I hope I can pass the test.

相关词语/Related Words

1	yuèdú 阅读	reading comprehension	3	xiězuò 写作	writing; composition
2	tīnglì 听力	listening comprehension	4	píngjūn chéngjì 平均成绩	average score

5	dì-yī 第一	the first; the best	7	jiǎndān 简单	easy
6	róngyì 容易	easy	8	nán 难	difficult; hard

文化导航
Cultural Navigation

中国汉语水平考试（HSK）是为测试母语非汉语者（包括外国人、华侨和中国少数民族考生）的汉语水平而设立的国家级标准化考试。由国家汉办组织设计，共分为四级：基础汉语水平考试、初等汉语水平考试、中等汉语水平考试、高等汉语水平考试。中国汉语水平考试每年定期在中国国内和海外举办，凡考试成绩达到规定标准者，可获得相应等级的《汉语水平证书》。

The *Hanyu Shuiping Kaoshi*, abbreviated as HSK, is a standardized test of Modern Standard Chinese Language Proficiency for non-native speakers, namely foreign students, overseas Chinese, and members of ethnic groups in China. It translates literally to "Chinese Proficiency Test". The China National Office for Teaching Chinese as a Foreign Language (Hanban) is currently responsible for the HSK exams, which are comprised of Basic, Elementary, Intermediate, and Advanced Tests. The HSK is held on the designated test dates in China and abroad. Those who pass the test will receive a certificate.

核心句
Key
Sentence

Wǒmen yào fàng jià le.
我们要放假了。
We are about to start the break.

句型
与替换
Substitution

shǔjià
暑假
summer break (vacation)

chūnjià
春假
spring break

hánjià
寒假
winter break (vacation)

cháng zhōumò
长周末
long weekend

扩 展/Extension

Chūnjià yǒu shénme dǎsuàn?
1. 春假 有 什么 打算?

What is your plan for the coming spring break?

Ànzhào xiàolì, xià gè yuè fàng
2. 按照 校历, 下个 月 放
hánjià.
寒假。

The winter break starts next month according to the school calendar.

Wǒ fàngjià qījiān cānjiā yánjiū
3. 我 放假 期间 参加 研究

I will participate in a research

xiàngmù.
项目.

Wǒ shēnqǐng shǔjià jiǎngxuéjīn le.
4. 我 申 请 暑期 奖学金 了。

project during the break.

I have applied for the summer
scholarship.

对话实例/Dialogue

Mángle yì xuéqī,　zǒngsuàn yào fàngjià le.
甲: 忙了一学期，总算 要 放假 了。

After a busy semester, the summer vacation finally comes.

Yǒu shénme dǎsuàn?
乙: 有 什么 打算?

Do you have any plans?

Wǒ yào cānjiā yí gè yánjiū xiàngmù,　hái shēnqǐngle jiǎngxuéjīn.
甲: 我 要 参加 一个 研究 项目，还 申请了 奖学金。

I plan to participate in a research project. I have applied for
a scholarship.

Xīwàng dà ma?
乙: 希望 大 吗?

What is the chance?

Bù zhīdào,　ná bú dào jiù huíguó kàn fùmǔ.　　Nǐ ne?
甲: 不知道，拿 不 到 就 回国 看 父母。 你呢?

I don't know. If I cannot get it, I will go back home to visit
my parents. What is your plan?

Wǒ yào cānjiā yí gè wénhuà lǚyóu xiàngmù.
乙: 我 要 参加 一个 文化 旅游 项目。

I plan to participate in a cultural trip.

Zhōngguó dōu wánr biàn le ba?
甲: 中 国 都 玩儿 遍 了 吧?

You have been to everywhere in China, right?

Chà de yuǎn ne,　zhǐ qùle jǐ gè dìfang, Zhōngguó zhème dà.
乙: 差 得 远 呢，只 去了 几 个 地方，中 国 这么 大。

Far from it. I've only been to several places. China is so big.

1	zǒngsuàn 总算	finally	6	fùmǔ 父母	parents
2	dǎsuàn 打算	plan; to plan	7	lǚyóu 旅游	to travel; tour
3	cānjiā 参加	to participate in; to attend	8	dìfang 地方	place
4	xiàngmù 项目	project; program	9	chà de yuǎn 差得远	far from it
5	jiǎngxuéjīn 奖学金	scholarship			

文化导航
Cultural Navigation

中国各级学校年度安排大致相同。秋季学期九月一号开学，一月放假，放假时间大约是春节前十天。寒假一般为一个月左右。春季学期七月初结束，然后是两个月的暑假。除了寒暑假之外，公共假期学生也不上课，公共假期有十一国庆节、五一劳动节、元旦等。

Chinese schools including universities and grade schools across the country follow almost the same calendar. The fall semester starts on September 1st and ends in January about 10 days before the Spring Festival. The winter break usually lasts one month before the spring semester starts. It comes to a close in early July when the two-month summer vacation begins. There is no school during the public holidays including the National Day of China that falls on October 1st, the Labor Day on May 1st, and the New Year's Day on January 1st.

[住宿
Lodging]

核心句 Key Sentence

Wǒ yào zū yí tào yì jūshì de gōngyù.

我要租一套一居室的公寓。

I want to rent a one-bedroom apartment.

句型与替换 Substitution

dài wèishēngjiān
带卫生间
with bathroom

dài chúfáng
带厨房
with kitchen

dài jiājù
带家具
furnished

扩 展/Extension

Nǐ yào zū shénmeyàng de gōngyù?
1. 你要租什么样的公寓？

What kind of apartment do you want to rent?

Zūjīn duōshao qián?
2. 租金多少钱？

How much is the rent?

Dài jiājù de gōngyù yuèzūjīn duōshao qián?
3. 带家具的公寓 月租金 多少钱？

How much is a furnished apartment a month?

Zūjīn bāokuò shuǐfèi, diànfèi ma?
4. 租金包括水费、电费吗？

Does the rent include water and electricity fees?

甲: Wǒ yào zū yí tào yì jūshì de gōngyù, zūjīn duōshao qián?
我要租一套一居室的公寓，租金多少钱？

I want to rent a one-bedroom apartment. How much is the rent?

乙: Dài jiājù de 2500 yuán, bú dài jiājù de 2000 yuán.
带家具的2500元，不带家具的2000元。

A furnished one is ¥2,500 a month and a non-furnished one is ¥2,000.

甲: Gōngyù dài chúfáng hé wèishēngjiān ma?
公寓带厨房和卫生间吗？

Is it with kitchen and bathroom?

乙: Dài, hái dài yí gè 10 píngmǐ de kètīng.
带，还带一个10平米的客厅。

Yes, and it has a 10 m² living room.

甲: Zūjīn bāokuò shuǐfèi, diànfèi ma?
租金包括水费、电费吗？

Does the rent include water and electricity fees?

乙: Zhǐ bāo diànfèi, bù bāo shuǐfèi.
只包电费，不包水费。

It only includes electricity but not water.

甲: Wǒ kěyǐ kànkan dài jiājù de gōngyù ma?
我可以看看带家具的公寓吗？

Can I take a look at a furnished one?

乙: Dāngrán kěyǐ, wǒmen xiànzài jiù zǒu.
当然可以，我们现在就走。

Sure. Let's go now.

1	jūshì 居室	bedroom	7	píngmǐ 平米	square meter
2	gōngyù 公寓	apartment	8	kètīng 客厅	living room
3	zūjīn 租金	rent	9	bāokuò 包括	to include
4	jiājù 家具	furniture	10	shuǐfèi 水费	cost for water
5	chúfáng 厨房	kitchen	11	diànfèi 电费	cost for electricity
6	wèishēngjiān 卫生间	bathroom			

文化导航
Cultural Navigation

从中华人民共和国成立的1949年到上世纪九十年代初，中国城市住房由政府分配，分配通过个人所在单位实施，是政府提供的一种福利，房租只是象征性的。自上世纪九十年代初，中国开始实施住房私有化改革，自此房屋市场迅速发展，拥有自己的一套住房成为大多数城市居民生活中的首要目标。

From 1949 when the People's Republic of China was founded to the early 1990s, China implemented a policy of allocating houses to urban residents as a benefit. Residents only paid a monthly fee for maintenance. China started its housing reform of privatization in the early 1990s. Since then the Chinese housing market has developed rapidly. For many Chinese, their No. 1 wish is to own an apartment of their own.

核心句 Key Sentence

Zhège xiǎoqū yǒu huāyuán.
这个小区有花园。
This community has its own garden.

句型与替换 Substitution

értóng lèyuán
儿童乐园
children's playground

lǎorén huódòng zhōngxīn
老人活动中心
activity center for the old people

tíngchēchǎng
停车场
parking lot

扩展/Extension

1. Zhège xiǎoqū shèshī hěn quán.
这个小区设施很全。
This community has great facilities.

2. Dìtiězhàn lí xiǎoqū dàmén hěn jìn.
地铁站离小区大门很近。
The subway station is very near to the community entrance.

3. Xiǎoqū měi tiān 24 xiǎoshí dōu yǒu ménwèi zhíbān.
小区每天24小时都有门卫值班。
The security guards are on duty 24 hours a day.

Chū wèntí jiù gěi wùyè dǎ
4. 出问题就给物业打
diànhuà.
电话。

Call the property management whenever in need.

Xiǎoqū fùjìn yǒu jiā chāoshì.
5. 小区附近有家超市。

There is a supermarket close to the community.

对话实例/Dialogue

Zhège xiǎoqū shèshī hěn quán a.
甲: 这个小区设施很全啊。

This community has great facilities.

Shì a,   yǒu huāyuán,   értóng lèyuán,   tíngchēchǎng,   lǎorén huódòng
乙: 是啊，有花园、儿童乐园、停车场、老人活动
zhōngxīn.
中心。

Yes. It has public gardens, children's playgrounds, parking lots and an activity center for the old people.

Fùjìn gōnggòng jiāotōng zěnmeyàng?
甲: 附近公共交通怎么样？

How about the public transportation nearby?

Dìtiězhàn   lí xiǎoqū dàmén jiù   yí gè lùkǒu.
乙: 地铁站离小区大门就一个路口。

The subway station is one block away from the community entrance.

Ānquán zěnmeyàng?
甲: 安全怎么样？

How about the safety here?

Xiǎoqū 24 xiǎoshí yǒu bǎo'ān zhíbān,   fēicháng ānquán.
乙: 小区24小时有保安值班，非常安全。

The security guards are on duty 24 hours a day. It is very safe.

甲: Mǎi dōngxi fāngbiàn ma?
买 东西 方便 吗？
How about shopping?

乙: Xiǎoqū li jiù yǒu xiǎomàibù, bù yuǎn hái yǒu yì jiā chāoshì.
小区 里 就 有 小卖部， 不远 还有 一家 超市。
There is a store in the community and a supermarket close by.

相关词语/Related Words

1	shèshī 设施	facilities	7	zhíbān 值班	on duty
2	fùjìn 附近	nearby	8	suíshí 随时	any time
3	gōnggòng jiāotōng 公共交通	public transportation	9	wùyè guǎnlǐ 物业管理	property management
4	dìtiězhàn 地铁站	subway station	10	xiǎomàibù 小卖部	store
5	ānquán 安全	safety	11	chāoshì 超市	supermarket
6	ménwèi 门卫	security guard			

文化导航
Cultural Navigation

　　有的中国人买房、为店铺选址、安排屋内摆设时，会讲究风水。风水泛指附近的山、水、树木等自然环境。风水来自阴阳学说，核心是结合各方面相关信息，对空间安排进行整体协调，以达到天人合一、自然和谐的目的。比如说看一个人的办公室风水是不是好，要看这个办公室的用途是什么，在此办公的人跟周围的环境是否和谐等。

When some Chinese people buy houses, look for business locations or decorate houses, they would follow *Fengshui*. *Fengshui* refers to the natural surroundings such as mountains, water, trees and so on. *Fengshui* derives from yin and yang principle and is literally translated as "wind-water". It is the ancient Chinese practice of placement and arrangement of space to achieve harmony with the environment. For example, one may hire a Practitioner of *Fengshui* to determine whether an office is in harmony with the universe according to the function of the room and the person who will use the room.

核心句 Key Sentence

Yùpén lòushuǐ le.

浴盆漏水了。

The bathtub is leaking.

句型与替换 Substitution

bīngxiāng
冰箱
refrigerator

shuǐlóngtóu
水龙头
faucet

mǎtǒng
马桶
toilet

kōngtiáo
空调
air conditioner

扩展/Extension

Wǒ zhǎo wùyè guǎnlǐ.
1. 我找物业管理。

I am here for the property management.

Kōngtiáo huài le.
2. 空调坏了。

The air conditioner is broken.

Wǒ míngtiān shàngwǔ pài rén xiū.
3. 我明天上午派人修。

I will have it fixed tomorrow morning.

Xūyào fùfèi ma?
4. 需要付费吗?

Do I have to pay?

Rúguǒ shì yònghù de wèntí,
5. 如果是用户的问题,

jiù fù cáiliàofèi.
就付材料费。

The tenant should pay for the material if he/she broke it.

甲： Wèi, wùyè guǎnlǐ bàngōngshì ma?
喂，物业管理办公室吗？

Hello, is it the property management office?

乙： Shì. Yǒu shì ma?
是。有事吗？

Yes, it is. What can I do for you?

甲： Wǒ gōngyù de yùpén lòushuǐ le, wèishēngjiān dì shang dōu shì shuǐ.
我公寓的浴盆漏水了，卫生间地上都是水。

My bathtub is leaking with water all over the floor in the bathroom.

乙： Nǐ zhù jǐ lóu jǐ hào?
你住几楼几号？

Which apartment?

甲： 15 hào lóu 3 mén 302.
15号楼3门302。

It is 3-302 in Building 15.

乙： Míngtiān shàngwǔ jiāli yǒu rén ma? Wǒmen pài rén xiū.
明天上午家里有人吗？我们派人修。

Is there anybody home tomorrow morning? I will have it fixed.

甲： Yǒu rén. Xūyào fùfèi ma?
有人。需要付费吗？

Yes, I am home. Do I have to pay?

乙： Shì yònghù de wèntí, jiù fù cáiliàofèi. Bú shì, jiù búyòng fùfèi.
是用户的问题，就付材料费。不是，就不用付费。

You need to pay for the material if you broke it. Otherwise, it is free.

1	wùyè guǎnlǐ 物业管理	property management	6	xūyào 需要	to need
2	lòushuǐ 漏水	leaking	7	fù 付	to pay
3	wèishēngjiān 卫生间	bathroom	8	fèi 费	fee
4	pài 派	to assign; to send	9	yònghù 用户	tenant
5	xiū 修	to repair; to fix	10	cáiliào 材料	material

文化导航
Cultural Navigation

　　中文地址和英文地址的表达顺序正好相反。英文地址是从小到大，从门牌号到小区、城市，最后才是国家；而中文地址是从大到小，基本顺序是国家名－省－市－区－街道－楼名和公寓号。比如说：中国北京东城区王府井大街5号楼301室。

　　Unlike an address in English that starts with the number of the apartment or houses and ends with the name of the state and country, Chinese addresses are arranged in a descending order from country, province/city, county/district, street, unit of the building, and the number of the apartment. For example, 中国北京东城区王府井大街5号楼301室.

核心句 Key Sentence

Wǒmen xiǎng qǐng yí gè xiǎoshígōng.
我们 想 请一个 小时工。
We want to hire an hourly worker.

句型与替换 Substitution

jiājiào
家教
private tutor

bǎomǔ
保姆
nanny

qīngjié nǚgōng
清洁 女工
cleaning lady

wéixiūgōng
维修工
repairman

扩展/Extension

1. Wǒ kěyǐ bāng nǐ jièshào.
我可以 帮 你介绍。
I can help you find a suitable one.

2. Xiǎoshígōng děi bāng wǒ dǎsǎo fángjiān、xǐ yīfu、zuòfàn.
小时工 得 帮 我打扫 房间、洗 衣服、做饭。
The hourly worker should help me clean the room, do the laundry and cook meals.

3. Měi zhōu zuò sān tiān, měi tiān sì gè xiǎoshí.
每 周 做三 天，每 天 四 个小时。
He/She should work four hours a day, three days a week.

4. Shìchǎngjià duōshao qián?
市场价 多少 钱?
What is the market rate?

甲: Wǒmen xiǎng qǐng yí gè xiǎoshígōng, nǐ néng bāngmáng zhǎo yí gè ma?
我们 想 请一个小时工, 你 能 帮 忙 找 一个吗?
We want to hire an hourly worker. Can you help us find one?

乙: Wǒ kěyǐ bāng nǐ wènwen, nǐ zhǎo xiǎoshígōng zuò shénme?
我可以 帮 你 问问, 你 找 小时工 做 什么?
I can ask round. What do you want the person to do?

甲: Bāng wǒ dǎsǎo fángjiān, xǐ yīfu, yì tiān zuò liǎng dùn fàn.
帮 我 打扫 房间、 洗衣服、 一天 做 两 顿 饭。
Help clean the room, do the laundry, and cook two meals a day.

乙: Yì xīngqī jǐ gè xiǎoshí?
一星期几个小时?
How many hours a week?

甲: Měi zhōu wǔ tiān, měi tiān sì gè xiǎoshí.
每 周 五天, 每 天 四个小时。
Five days a week and four hours a day.

乙: Nà wǒ bāng nǐ zhǎo gè sì-wǔshí suì de tuìxiū nǚgōng ba.
那我帮你找个四五十岁的退休女工吧。
I will find you a retired woman in her 40s or 50s.

甲: Hǎo a. Nǐ zhīdào yí gè yuè dàyuē duōshao qián ma?
好啊。 你知道一个月大约多少 钱吗?
It sounds great. Do you know how much I should pay a month?

乙: 2000 dào 3000 kuài qián ba.
2000到3000块 钱吧。
It should be between ¥2,000 and ¥3,000.

相关词语/Related Words

1	jièshào 介绍	to introduce; to recommend	3	xǐ yīfu 洗衣服	to do the laundry
2	dǎsǎo 打扫	to clean	4	zuòfàn 做饭	to cook

5	tuìxiū nǚgōng 退休女工	retired woman worker	8	zhàogù értóng 照顾儿童	to look after the child
6	shìchǎngjià 市场价	market price	9	bìngrén 病人	patient
7	fǔdǎo gōngkè 辅导功课	to tutor with the homework			

文化导航
Cultural Navigation

在日常生活中，中国人若有需要或碰到麻烦时，首先想到的是找家人、朋友及朋友的朋友出主意，想办法，找关系。在中国人的观念里，家人和朋友是自己人，远比不相干的人值得信赖。所以当有中国朋友让你帮忙时，别觉得不舒服，其实这是不把你当外人的表现。如果你帮不上忙，可以婉转地说出来，还可以提一些建议。

Chinese people rely more on personal networks of friends and family members. They turn to networks for help, suggestion and support when in need or in difficulty. In their belief, friends and family members are more trustworthy. Therefore, when your Chinese friends ask you for help, please don't feel uncomfortable. Actually it is a sign that you are considered as a friend instead of an outsider. In a situation that you cannot help, you can let them know in a polite way and put forward some suggestions if possible.

39 找室友 | Looking for a Roommate

核心句
Key Sentence

Zhǎo shìyǒu kěyǐ zài wǎngshang fā gè guǎnggào.
找室友可以在网上发个广告。
You can post an advertisement on the web to look for a roommate.

句型与替换
Substitution

xiàobào
校报
school newspaper

bùgàolán
布告栏
bulletin board

bàozhǐ
报纸
newspaper

扩 展/Extension

Wǒ yào zhǎo yí gè xīn shìyǒu.
1. 我要找一个新室友。

I am looking for a new roommate.

Nǐ yào zhǎo shénmeyàng de shìyǒu?
2. 你要找什么样的室友?

What kind of roommate are you looking for?

Xīn shìyǒu zuìhǎo gēn wǒ shēnghuó xíguàn chàbuduō.
3. 新室友最好跟我生活习惯差不多。

I prefer a roommate whose life style is similar to mine.

4. Guǎnggào xiěshang zūjīn hé nǐ
de liánxì fāngshì.
广告 写上租金和你
的联系方式。

The advertisement should include the rent and your contact information.

对话实例/Dialogue

甲: Wǒ de shìyǒu huíguó le, děi zhǎo yí gè xīn shìyǒu.
我的室友回国了，得找一个新室友。
My roommate went back to her home country and I need to find a new roommate.

乙: Xiǎng zhǎo shénmeyàng de?
想找什么样的?
What kind of person are you looking for?

甲: Zuìhǎo yě shì liúxuéshēng, shēnghuó xíguàn hé wǒ chàbuduō.
最好也是留学生，生活习惯和我差不多。
I prefer a foreign student. We may have a similar life style.

乙: Wǒ dào rènwéi Zhōngguó xuésheng gèng hǎo, kěyǐ liànxí shuō Zhōngwén.
我倒认为中国学生更好,可以练习说中文。
But I think a Chinese student is better. You can practice Chinese with her.

甲: Nǐ shuō de yě duì.
你说得也对。
You are right.

乙: Yào wǒ bāngmáng ma? Wǒ kěyǐ wènwen wǒ de péngyou.
要我帮忙吗? 我可以问问我的朋友。
Do you need my help? I can ask my friends and find one for you.

甲: Búyòng le. Wǒ zài wǎngshang fā gè guǎnggào, yīnggāi néng zhǎodào.
不用了。我在网上发个广告，应该能找到。
No, thanks. I can post an advertisement on the Internet and should find one.

乙: Zhēnde búyòng wǒ bāngmáng?
真的不用我帮忙?
Are you sure you don't need my help?

1	shēnghuó 生活 xíguàn 习惯	life style; life habits	5	shìyǒu 室友	roommate; housemate
2	chàbuduō 差不多	similar	6	tiáojiàn 条件	condition
3	yìxìng 异性	the opposite sex	7	zūjīn 租金	rent
4	guǎnggào 广告	advertisement	8	liánxì fāngshì 联系方式	contact information

文化导航
Cultural Navigation

有时你主动帮助朋友时，朋友可能会说：不用，不用。实际上，这样说并不表示朋友在拒绝你的帮助，而是不想麻烦你。如果你真的想帮忙，可以多问几次，让朋友知道你是真心想帮忙，而且能帮上忙。在你的坚持下，他可能就会接受，并说"不好意思"或者"麻烦了"。

When you offer help to your friend, he/she may say " 不用 ". This expression is mostly not a refusal to your offering; instead, your friend may not want to bother you or cause your inconvenience. If you sense the situation and really want to help, you can ask again to make your friend know that you can and are willing to be of some help. With your insistence, he or she may accept it by saying " 不好意思 " or " 麻烦了 ".

40 公寓转租 | Subleasing the Apartment

Wǒ dǎsuàn bǎ gōngyù duǎnqī chūzū chuqu.
我打算把公寓短期出租出去。
I plan to temporarily rent the apartment out.

zhuǎnzū
转租
sublease

chángqī chūzū
长期出租
lease on a long-term basis

fēnzū
分租
rent a room in my apartment

扩 展/Extension

Wǒ zhǎo fángchǎn zhōngjiè gōngsī.
1. 我 找 房产 中介 公司。
I am looking for the property intermediary agency.

Zūjīn nǐ yào duōshao qián?
2. 租金你要 多少 钱?
How much do you want for the rent?

Wǒmen bāng nǐ zhǎo zūhù, shōu zūjīn.
3. 我们 帮 你 找 租户, 收 租金。
We will help you find a tenant and collect the rent.

Wǒmen tíchéng bǎi fēn zhī èrshí.
4. 我们 提成 百分之二十。
Our commission is 20%.

（在房产中介公司 At a property intermediary agency）

甲： Shǔjià wǒ yào huíguó, xiǎng bǎ gōngyù duǎnqī chūzū.
暑假我要回国，想把公寓短期出租。

I will go back to my country for the summer and want to sublease my apartment on a short-term basis.

乙： Shénmeyàng de gōngyù?
什么样的公寓？

What kind of apartment?

甲： Yí shì yì tīng, dài jiājù, lí dìtiězhàn、 chāoshì dōu hěn jìn.
一室一厅，带家具，离地铁站、超市都很近。

It is a one-bedroom furnished apartment, close to the subway station and the supermarket.

乙： Nà yí gè yuè nǐ yào duōshao zūjīn?
那一个月你要多少租金？

How much do you want for the rent?

甲： Yīnwèi shì duǎnqī chūzū, 2000 kuài jiù xíng.
因为是短期出租，2000块就行。

Since I sublease it for a short term, ¥2,000 is fine.

乙： Rúguǒ wěituō wǒmen, tíchéng bǎi fēn zhī èrshí.
如果委托我们，提成百分之二十。

If you entrust us, we will charge 20% of the rent as a commission.

甲： Yào zhǎo bú dào zūhù ne?
要找不到租户呢？

How about if you cannot find a tenant?

乙： Xiànzài shì wàngjì, zhǎo zūhù bú shì wèntí.
现在是旺季，找租户不是问题。

It is a busy season now and it should not be a problem to find a tenant.

相关词语/Related Words

1	fángchǎn 房产	property	6	tíchéng 提成	to collect commission
2	zhōngjiè 中介	intermediary	7	wàngjì 旺季	busy season
3	wěituō 委托	to entrust	8	dànjì 淡季	off season
4	zūhù 租户	tenant	9	shǒuxùfèi 手续费	service charge
5	zūjīn 租金	rent			

文化导航
Cultural Navigation

　　由于中国房地产市场的快速发展和城市化的进程加快，房屋租借市场发展也很迅速。人们求租或出租房屋都很方便，可以在网上、报纸上，也可以到中介公司查找信息。中介公司根据双方条件牵线搭桥，收取一定的佣金。

Because of the rapid development of housing market and urbanization, renting and leasing an apartment has witnessed a rapid growth and become quite convenient in China now. You can look for listings online, in the local newspaper or simply go to seek the service at intermediary agencies who will match apartment owners and potential tenants on a commission basis.

核心句
Key Sentence

Měi gè fángjiān dōu pèi yǒu diànhuà.
每个房间都配有 电话。
Every room has a telephone.

句型与替换
Substitution

chuáng
床
bed

shūzhuō
书桌
desk

shūjià
书架
bookshelf

yīguì
衣柜
wardrobe

kuāndài shàngwǎng
宽带上网
broadband connection

扩展／Extension

Jǐ gè rén yì jiān?
1. 几个人一间？ — How many people are there in a room?

Wǒ zhù de shì liǎng rén yì jiān.
2. 我住的是两人一间。 — Mine is double occupancy.

Yǒu rén dǎsǎo fángjiān ma?
3. 有人打扫房间吗？ — Is there anybody cleaning the room?

Sān tiān huàn yí cì chuángdān.
4. 三天换一次床单。 — The linen is changed every three days.

甲： Zhè jiù shì liúxuéshēng sùshèlóu,　　wǒ zhù zài wǔ lóu 503 shì.
这就是留学生宿舍楼，我住在五楼503室。
This is the foreign student dormitory. I live in Room 503 on the 5th floor.

乙： Zhēn búcuò,　　gānjìng zhěngqí.
真不错，干净 整齐。
It is really nice, clean and tidy.

甲： Shì a,　　hái yǒu shítáng,　xiǎomàibù,　diànnǎofáng,　yuèlǎnshì.
是啊，还有食堂、小卖部、电脑房、阅览室。……
Zhè jiù shì wǒ de fángjiān.
这就是我的房间。
Yes. We have a canteen, a convenience store, a computer room and a reading room. Oh, this is my room.

乙： Tǐng kuānchang de,　guāngxiàn hěn hǎo.　　Jǐ gè rén yì jiān?
挺 宽 敞 的，光线 很 好。几个人一间？
It is spacious, sunny and bright. How many people are there in the room?

甲： Wǒ zhù de shì liǎngrénjiān.　　Yě yǒu dānrénjiān,　　dànshì jiàqián
我住的是两人间。也有单人间，但是价钱
yǒudiǎnr guì.
有点儿贵。
Mine is double occupancy. There are single occupancy rooms but the rate is higher.

乙： Jiājù dōu shì pèi de ba?
家具都是配的吧？
The furniture comes with the room, right?

甲： Shì,　měi gè fángjiān dōu pèiyǒu diànhuà, kuāndài, shūzhuō, shūjià, yīguì.
是，每个房间都配有电话、宽带、书桌、书架、衣柜。
Yes. There is a telephone, broadband connection, a desk, bookshelves and a wardrobe in each room.

乙： Yǒu rén dǎsǎo fángjiān ma?
有人打扫房间吗？
Is there anybody cleaning the room?

甲： Yǒu.　　Sān tiān huàn yí　cì chuángdān.
有。三 天 换 一 次 床单。
Yes. The linen is changed every three days.

1	shuāngrénjiān 双人间	double room; double occupancy	7	diànnǎofáng 电脑房	computer room
2	dānrénjiān 单人间	single room; single occupancy	8	yuèlǎnshì 阅览室	reading room
3	gānjìng 干净	clean	9	dānrénchuáng 单人床	single bed
4	zhěngqí 整齐	tidy	10	dǎsǎo 打扫	to clean
5	kuānchang 宽敞	spacious	11	chuángdān 床单	bed linen
6	xiàngyáng 向阳	sunny			

文化导航
Cultural Navigation

　　尽管中国大学生可以到校外租房，但出于安全、方便的考虑大多数学生都选择住在学校宿舍。由于学生宿舍没有厨房，学生都会到学校食堂吃饭。各校留学生一般都有单独的留学生宿舍楼，条件比其他学生宿舍要好，设施齐备，实施公寓化管理，因此更像旅馆。

Most college students in China choose to live in student dormitories on campus though they are allowed to rent apartments off campus due to the consideration of safety and convenience. As there is no place to cook in the dorm, they usually eat in the dining hall on campus. Foreign students generally live in separate foreign student dormitory buildings with better conditions. These dormitories have great facilities, thus more like a hotel than a dorm.

核心句 / Key Sentence

Shìyǒu tài chǎo le.
室友太吵了。
My roommate is too loud.

句型与替换 / Substitution

huílai tài wǎn
回来太晚
come back too late

qǐ de tài zǎo
起得太早
get up too early

shuì de tài wǎn
睡得太晚
stay up too late

yǒu tài duō láifǎngzhě
有太多来访者
have too many visitors

扩展 / Extension

Wǒ yāoqiú huàn shìyǒu.
1. 我要求换室友。
I request to change a roommate.

Tā měi tiān huílai tài wǎn.
2. 她每天回来太晚。
She comes back too late every day.

Wǒ xiǎng gēn ānjìng yìdiǎn de rén
3. 我想跟安静一点的人
zuò shìyǒu.
做室友。
I want to have a quiet roommate.

Yǒu héshì de, mǎshàng tōngzhī
4. 有合适的，马上通知
nǐ.
你。
I will let you know as soon as I find one.

对话实例/Dialogue

甲: Zhāng lǎoshī, kěyǐ yāoqiú huàn shìyǒu ma?
张 老师，可以要求换室友吗？

Mr. Zhang, can I ask to change a roommate?

乙: Wèi shénme?
为 什么？

Why?

甲: Tā tài chǎo le, měi tiān bànyè 12 diǎn cái huílai, nòng de wǒ dōu shuì bù hǎo.
她太吵了，每天半夜12点才回来，弄得我都睡不好。

She is too loud. She comes back at 12 every day, and I cannot sleep well.

乙: Nǐ gēn tā tán le ma?
你跟她谈了吗？

Did you speak to her about it?

甲: Bù hǎoyìsi zhíjiē shuō.
不好意思直接说。

No. I feel embarrassed to say it directly to her.

乙: Nà wǒmen zhǎozhao tā.
那我们 找 找 她。

We will speak to her about it.

甲: Háishi gěi wǒ huàn gè shìyǒu ba, yào zǎoshuì zǎoqǐ, ānjìng yìdiǎn de.
还是给我换个室友吧，要早睡早起，安静一点的。

Please find me a new roommate. I want someone who is a quiet and early person.

乙: Wǒmen shìshi ba, yǒu héshì de, mǎshàng tōngzhī nǐ.
我们 试试吧，有合适的，马上 通知你。

We will try. If there is someone, we will let you know.

1	yāoqiú 要求	to ask for; to request	6	zǎoshuì 早睡 zǎoqǐ 早起	to go to bed early and get up early
2	huàn 换	to change	7	ānjìng 安静	quiet
3	chǎo 吵	loud; noisy	8	héshì 合适	suitable
4	shuì bù hǎo 睡不好	unable to sleep well	9	tōngzhī 通知	to notify
5	xíguàn 习惯	habit			

文化导航
Cultural Navigation

　　有人说美国人说话直来直去，在大多数情况下 "行"就是"行"，"不行"就是"不行"，不太会拐弯抹角。但中国人一般不会直接对别人说"不"，因为这样说会得罪人，伤别人的面子，甚至会引起争执。中国人把面子看得很重，因为它涉及到个人尊严的问题，因此在人际交往中一定要顾及对方，给人留面子。

　　Some people say the American style of communication is direct, candid, straightforward and to the point. In most cases, "yes" means yes and "no" means no. The Chinese do not say "no" directly to anyone in many cases or he will feel offended and lose face. Face, which represents self-dignity, is very much concerned by the Chinese when they communicate with each other. By saying "no" directly, you will make the other party lose face and may lead to a direct confrontation.

就餐
Dining

核心句
Key Sentence

Nà shì yì jiā lǎozìhào kǎoyādiàn.
那是一家老字号烤鸭店。
That is a roast duck restaurant with a long-standing name.

句型与替换
Substitution

jiācháng fànguǎn
家常饭馆
home-style restaurant

xiǎochīdiàn
小吃店
snack store

huǒguōdiàn
火锅店
hot pot restaurant

扩 展/Extension

Jīntiān wǒmen dào wàimiàn qù chī ba?
1. 今天我们到外面去吃吧？

Shall we go out for dinner today?

Wǒmen jīntiān dào nǎr qù chī ne?
2. 我们今天到哪儿去吃呢？

Which restaurant should we go for dinner today?

Nà jiā kǎoyādiàn hěn yǒumíng.
3. 那家烤鸭店很有名。

The Peking Roast Duck House is very well-known.

Nàr de cài wèidào búcuò, jiàqián yě gōngdao.
4. 那儿的菜味道不错，价钱也公道。

The food there is very delicious and the price is reasonable.

甲: Jīntiān shì nǐ de shēngrì, Wǒmen dào wàimiàn qù chī ba?
今天是你的生日，我们到外面去吃吧？

It is your birthday today. Shall we go out for dinner?

乙: Hǎo, wǒmen qù nǎr? Xiànzài fànguǎn dàochù dōu shì.
好，我们去哪儿？现在饭馆到处都是。

Good. Where should we go with so many restaurants around?

甲: Wǒmen qù qiánmén nà jiā lǎozìhào kǎoyādiàn ba?
我们去前门那家老字号烤鸭店吧？

Shall we go to the Peking Roast Duck House in Qianmen with a long-standing name?

乙: Nàr lù yuǎn rén duō, xià cì yǒu péngyou zài qù ba.
那儿路远人多，下次有朋友再去吧。

It is too far and too crowded. Let's go there when we have friends visiting us.

甲: Nà jiù qù Tiānxīn Jiǔdiàn, nà shì yì jiā tèsè càiguǎn, hěn yǒu qíngdiào.
那就去天心酒店，那是一家特色菜馆，很有情调。

Then let us go to Tianxin Restaurant. It is a specialty restaurant with a tasteful decoration.

乙: Yě xíng, búguò yǒudiǎnr guì.
也行，不过有点儿贵。

A good choice but it is still a bit too expensive.

甲: Zhōngguó Jiǔdiàn zěnmeyàng? Gǔsè-gǔxiāng de.
中国酒店怎么样？古色古香的。

How about China Restaurant? It has the classic Chinese beauty.

乙: Tài guì le. Wǒmen háishi qù jiēkǒu nà jiā xiǎochīdiàn, cài de
太贵了。我们还是去街口那家小吃店，菜的
wèidào búcuò, Jiàqián yě gōngdao.
味道不错，价钱也公道。

It is too expensive. Let's go to the snack store around the street corner. Its food is delicious and the price is reasonable.

1	fànguǎn 饭馆	restaurant	6	gǔsè-gǔxiāng 古色古香	classic
2	jiǔdiàn 酒店	(high-end) restaurant	7	jiēkǒu 街口	street corner
3	càiguǎn 菜馆	restaurant	8	xiǎochī 小吃	snack
4	Běijīng 北京 kǎoyā 烤鸭	Peking Roast Duck	9	wèidao 味道	taste (of the food)
5	qíngdiào 情调	flavor	10	gōngdao 公道	reasonable

文化导航
Cultural Navigation

　　稍微了解一点中国的外国人都知道北京烤鸭。北京烤鸭被称为世界最好吃的菜之一，吃烤鸭是到北京必做的两件事之一，另一件是爬长城。北京有两个烤鸭店最有名，一是便宜坊，一是全聚德，两家饭馆都有上百年的历史，代表着两种不同的烤鸭风格。

Peking Roast Duck is known to almost all the people who know something about China for its reputation as one of the most delicious food in the world. It is one of the two things you should absolutely try if you go to Beijing. The other is to climb the Great Wall. The most famous Peking Roast Duck restaurants are Bianyifang Roast Duck Restaurant and Quanjude Roast Duck Restaurant, both of which have a history of over one hundred years, and represent two different schools of roasting duck.

44 订位 | Reserving Seats

Wǒ xiǎng yùdìng yì zhāng bārénzhuō.
我想预订一张八人桌。
I want to reserve a table for eight.

yí gè dānjiān
一个单间
a private room

yí gè kàochuāng de liǎngrénzhuō
一个靠窗的两人桌
a table for two by the window

扩展/Extension

Shì dìngcān zhuānxiàn ma?
1. 是订餐专线吗?　　Is it the reservation line?

Wǒ xiǎng dìng yí gè bāojiān.
2. 我想订一个包间。　I want to reserve a private room.

Gěi wǒmen ānpái zài ānjìngdiǎnr
3. 给我们安排在安静点儿　Please find us a quiet place.
de dìfang.
的地方。

Wǎnshang 6 diǎn de dōu dìngmǎn le.
4. 晚上 6 点的都订满了。There is no vacancy at 6 pm.

对话实例/Dialogue

Nín hǎo. Tiānxīn Jiǔlóu dìngcān zhuānxiàn.
甲: 您好。天心酒楼订餐专线。
Hello, this is the reservation line of Tianxin Restaurant.

乙: Nín hǎo. Qǐng gěi wǒ yùdìng yì zhāng bārénzhuō. Kěyǐ bāojiān ma?
您好。请给我预订一张八人桌。可以包间吗？

Hello. I want to reserve a table for eight. Can we have a private room?

甲: Duìbuqǐ, bāojiān zhìshǎo shí rén.
对不起，包间至少十人。

Sorry. We will give a private room to a group of 10 at least.

乙: Nà gěi wǒmen ānpái zài yí gè ānjìngdiǎnr de dìfang.
那给我们安排在一个安静点儿的地方。

Please find us a quiet corner then.

甲: Jǐnliàng ba. Shénme shíjiān?
尽量吧。什么时间？

I will try. What time?

乙: Míngtiān wǎnshang 6 diǎn.
明天晚上6点。

Tomorrow evening at 6 o'clock.

甲: Zěnme chēnghu nín?
怎么称呼您？

How should I address you?

乙: Wǒ xìng Wáng.
我姓王。

My last name is Wang.

相关词语／Related Words

1	dìngcān 订餐	to reserve meals	5	ānpái 安排	to arrange
2	zhuānxiàn 专线	special line	6	ānjìng 安静	quiet
3	yùdìng 预订	to reserve	7	dìfang 地方	place
4	bārénzhuō 八人桌	a table for eight	8	jǐnliàng 尽量	to try one's best

中国菜世界闻名。但中国幅员辽阔，不同地区的饮食都带有自己的地区特色。中国菜大致来说有八大菜系，最著名的是川菜、鲁菜、粤菜和淮扬菜。一般来说，北方菜味重，以咸味为主，多葱蒜；东部菜味淡、微辣（但无锡菜味甜，上海菜多油）；西部菜（四川、湖南）多花椒、辣椒；南方菜清淡，注重食材的原味。

Chinese cuisine is well-known all over the world. Since China is so vast, each region has its own unique local flavor. Generally, Chinese food can be roughly divided into eight types of regional cuisine, with the most known being Sichuan, Shandong, Cantonese, and Huaiyang. Northern dishes tend to be strong-flavored, with spring onions or garlic in charge, while eastern food is more delicate and lightly spiced, with a hint of spring onion or ginger, except in the city of Wuxi, where sweetness can overwhelm the other flavors, or Shanghai, where dishes can be very oily. Western (Sichuan or Hunan) meals can be entirely dominated by the strong tastes of brown peppercorns (*huajiao*) and chilies (*lajiao*), while southerners prefer complex and subtle sauces which accentuate the fresh flavors of the ingredients.

公司聚餐 | Company Party

Měi zhuō yào sì gè lěngpán.
每桌要四个冷盘。
There are four cold dishes for each table.

bā gè rèchǎo
八个热炒
eight hot dishes

yí gè tāng
一个汤
one soup

yí gè shuǐguǒpán
一个水果盘
one fruit platter

yì pán diǎnxin
一盘点心
one dessert platter

扩展/Extension

1. Wǒmen gōngsī míngtiān jùcān.
我们公司明天聚餐。
We will have a company party tomorrow.

2. Wǒmen xiǎng zài nín nàr yùdìng shí zhuō jiǔxí.
我们想在您那儿预订十桌酒席。
We want to reserve 10 tables at your restaurant.

3. Kěyǐ gěi wǒ yí gè yùsuàn ma?
可以给我一个预算吗?
Can you give me an estimate?

4. Bāozhuō wǒmen fēn 2000 yuán hé 3000 yuán liǎng gè dàngcì.
包桌我们分2000元和3000元两个档次。
We have two types for set table meals: ¥2,000 and ¥3,000.

5. Jiǔshuǐ lìng suàn, búguò kěyǐ zì dài jiǔshuǐ.
酒水另算,不过可以自带酒水。
Drinks are excluded but you can bring your own drinks.

甲：
Wǒmen gōngsī zhōumò jùcān, xiǎng zài nín nàr yùdìng shí zhuō jiǔxí.
我们 公司 周末聚餐，想在您那儿预订十 桌 酒席。

We will have a company party this weekend and want to
reserve 10 tables at your restaurant.

乙：
Méi wèntí. Wǒmen gěi nín yùdìng èr lóu yànhuìtīng.
没问题。我们 给您预订二楼宴会厅。

No problem. We will reserve for you the Feast Hall on the
second floor.

甲：
Kěyǐ gěi wǒ yí gè yùsuàn ma?
可以给我一个预算 吗?

Can you give me an estimate?

乙：
Bāozhuō wǒmen fēn 2000 yuán hé 3000 yuán liǎng gè dàngcì. Jiǔshuǐ
包桌 我们 分2000元和3000元 两个档次。酒水
lìng suàn.
另算。

We have two types for set table meals: ¥2,000 and ¥3,000.

Drinks are not included.

甲：
Yǒu duōshao dào cài?
有多少道菜?

How many courses?

乙：
Sì gè lěngpán, bā gè rèchǎo, yí gè tāng, yí gè shuǐguǒpán.
四个冷盘、八个热炒、一个汤、一个水果盘。

Four cold dishes, eight hot dishes, one soup and one fruit platter.

甲：
Wǒ míngtiān xiān guòlai kànkan càidān zài dìng, hǎo ma?
我明天 先过来看看菜单再订，好 吗?

Can I take a look at the menu first tomorrow?

乙：
Hǎo, míngtiān jiàn.
好，明天见。

Sure, see you tomorrow.

1	jùcān 聚餐	party; get-together	6	lìng suàn 另 算	exclusive; not included
2	yànhuìtīng 宴会厅	feast hall	7	zì dài 自带	to bring your own
3	yùsuàn 预算	estimate	8	dào 道	course (of dishes)
4	bāo 包	to include	9	càidān 菜单	menu
5	jiǔshuǐ 酒水	drinks			

文化导航
Cultural Navigation

　　在比较高档的中式宴会上，上菜是有一定顺序的：先上冷盘，一般是四个或八个，然后是装饰漂亮的主菜热炒，热炒的菜式一般包括鸡、肉、鱼、虾，味道也是甜、酸、苦、咸、辣都有。在两道菜之间一般会上一些小点心。最后一道菜一般是汤。

A typical Chinese banquet dinner for special guests usually starts with an even-numbered selection of cold dishes, four or eight being traditionally served. This is followed by a variety of hot dishes that usually cover the gamut of the five basic tastes – sweet, sour, salty, spicy and bitter – which consist of exquisite meat dishes, fish, prawns and chicken. Between the courses, a variety of sweets are served. Soup is usually the last course to conclude the dinner.

核心句 Key Sentence

Zhè shì chúshī de náshǒucài.
这是厨师的拿手菜。
This is the chef's specialty.

句型与替换 Substitution

zhèngzōng de Guǎngdōng míngcài
正宗的广东名菜
authentic Cantonese dish

dìdao de Huáiyángcài
地道的淮扬菜
authentic Huaiyang dish

fànguǎn de tèsècài
饭馆的特色菜
specialty dish of the restaurant

jīntiān de tuījiàncài
今天的推荐菜
dish of the day

扩 展/Extension

1. Càishì tài fēngshèng le, xièxie
   菜式太丰盛了，谢谢
   nín de kuǎndài.
   您的款待。

   There are so many dishes. Thank you for your hospitality.

2. Wèi nǐ de chénggōng, gānbēi.
   为你的成功，干杯。

   For your success, bottoms up.

3. Wǒ jìng nín yì bēi.
   我敬您一杯。

   Let me propose a toast to your health.

4. Wǒ zìjǐ lái.
   我自己来。

   Let me help myself.

甲：
Wáng chùzhǎng, zhè shì shàngzuò, nín qǐng zuò.
王 处长，这是上座，您请 坐。
Director Wang, this is the upper (honored) seat. Please be seated.

乙：
Bié kèqi. Wǒmen yìqǐ zuò.
别客气。我们一起坐。
Thank you. Let's sit here together.

······

甲：
Wáng chùzhǎng, zhè cì de shìqing duōkuī nín bāngmáng, wǒ jìng nín yì bēi.
王 处长，这次的事情多亏您帮忙，我敬您一杯。
Director Wang, thank you for your help. I would like to propose a toast to your health.

乙：
Yīnggāi de, nín tài kèqi le. Wéi nín de chénggōng, gānbēi.
应该的，您太客气了。为您的成功，干杯。
You are welcome. To your success, bottoms up.

······

甲：
Wáng chùzhǎng, nín chángchang zhège cài, zhè shì chúshī de náshǒu-
王 处长，您尝 尝 这个菜，这是厨师的拿手
cài, wèidào fēicháng zhèngzōng.
菜，味道非常 正宗。
Director Wang, please try this dish. This is the chef's specialty and very authentic.

乙：
Xièxie, wǒ zìjǐ lái.
谢谢，我自己来。
Thank you. Let me help myself.

甲：
Zhège cài hěn qīngdàn, nín chángchang.
这个菜很清淡，您尝尝。
This dish is very light and you should try it.

乙：
Càishì tài fēngshèng le, xièxie nín de kuǎndài.
菜式太丰 盛了，谢谢您的款待。
It is such a rich banquet. Thank you for your hospitality.

甲：
Nín de dàolái shì wǒmen de róngxìng.
您的到来是我们的荣幸。
It is our honor to have you here.

相关词语／Related Words

1	shàngzuò 上座	upper (honored) seat	6	náshǒucài 拿手菜	specialty
2	gānbēi 干杯	to drink this toast; bottoms up	7	wèidào 味道	taste
3	jìngjiǔ 敬酒	to propose a toast	8	qīngdàn 清淡	light in taste
4	cháng 尝	to taste	9	fēngshèng 丰盛	rich; sumptuous
5	chúshī 厨师	chef	10	kuǎndài 款待	generous treatment

文化导航
Cultural Navigation

在中国的酒宴上，酒扮演着重要角色，互相敬酒是必不可少的。通常的顺序是，主人在宴会开始时用白酒向来宾敬酒，敬酒会有敬酒词，当说到"干杯"时，在座的应喝尽自己杯里的酒。之后，在座的主宾互相敬酒。在每上一道新菜的时候，一般都伴随着一轮敬酒。

Drinking plays an important role in Chinese banquets. Toasting is necessary, and the drinking of wine starts only after the host has made a toast at the beginning of the meal. It is possible that he will stand and hold his glass out with both hands while saying a few words. When he says the words "干杯", which means bottoms up, all the people present should drain their glasses. After this initial toast, drinking and toasting are open to all. It is also a custom for toasts to be proposed between courses.

核心句 Key Sentence

Wǒ yào yí fèn bāozi.
我要一份包子。
I want a combo of steamed stuffed buns.

句型与替换 Substitution

liángmiàn
凉面
cold noodles

jiǎozi
饺子
dumplings

chǎofàn
炒饭
fried rice

扩展/Extension

1. Nǐ jīntiān xiǎng chī shénme zhǔshí?
你今天想吃什么主食？
What staple food do you want to eat today?

2. Wǒ zuì xǐhuan chī jiǎozi le.
我最喜欢吃饺子了。
I like dumplings best.

3. Gěi wǒ yí fèn liángmiàn hé yì wǎn jīdàntāng.
给我一份凉面和一碗鸡蛋汤。
Give me the cold noodles and a bowl of egg soup.

4. Bāozi zhēn xiāng, nǐ cháng yí gè ba?
包子真香，你尝一个吧？
The steamed stuffed buns are so tasty. Would you like to try one?

甲: Zhème duō zhǒng, nǐ xiǎng chī shénme?

这么多种，你想吃什么？

There are so many different kinds. What do you want to eat?

乙: Kànzhe dōu tǐng hǎochī de, yàobù wǒ chī bāozi ba.

看着 都挺 好吃的，要不我吃包子吧。

They all look good. I think I will have the steamed stuffed buns.

甲: Wǒ zuì xǐhuan chī miàntiáo, nàge liángmiàn kànzhe búcuò.

我最喜欢吃 面条，那个凉面 看着不错。

I like noodles most and the cold noodles look good.

乙: Shīfu, wǒ yào yí fèn bāozi hé yì wǎn mǐzhōu, gěi tā yí fèn

师傅，我要一份包子和一碗 米粥，给他一份

liángmiàn hé yì wǎn jīdàntāng.

凉 面和一碗鸡蛋汤。

Sir, I want a combo of steamed stuffed buns and a bowl of rice

porridge, and give him the cold noodles and a bowl of egg soup.

师傅: Dōu shì wǔ kuài.

都是五块。

Five yuan each.

......

乙: Bāozi zhēn xiāng, nǐ cháng yí gè ba.

包子真香，你尝一个吧。

The steamed stuffed buns are so delicious. Try one.

甲: Hǎo, lái yí gè. Nǐ yě chángchang zhè liángmiàn, xiàtiān chīle

好，来一个。你也尝尝这凉面，夏天吃了

zhēn liángkuai.

真凉快。

Give me one. You try the cold noodles. It is so cool to eat it

in the summer.

乙: Shì búcuò, jiàqián hái piányi, yǐhòu wǒmen tiāntiān lái.

是不错，价钱还便宜，以后我们天天来。

It is really good and cheap. Let's come here every day.

1	bāozi 包子	steamed stuffed bun		5	liángkuai 凉快	cool
2	zhōu 粥	rice porridge		6	chǎomiàn 炒面	fried noodles
3	jīdàntāng 鸡蛋汤	egg soup		7	cōngyóubǐng 葱油饼	Chinese pizza
4	xiāng 香	tasty; delicious				

文化导航
Cultural Navigation

中国饭分为主食和菜。主食由粮食或淀粉制成，例如面条和米饭。菜一般指肉食和蔬菜，在一顿饭里处于陪衬角色。中国南方的主要农作物是米，因此米饭是南方饭桌上的主食。而在北方小麦是主要农作物，因此面食是主食，如面条、饺子、馒头等。

Chinese food is categorized into "主食" and "菜". "主食", the staple or principal food of a meal, is made with grain or starch such as noodles or rice. "菜" made with meat and vegetables is considered a minor portion of a meal. In the southern part of China where rice is the main crop, rice is the main staple. The main crop in the northern part of China is wheat thus flour-based food is the main staple including noodles, dumplings and steamed buns.

核心句
Key Sentence

Zuótiān chīle Rìshì zìzhùcān.
昨天 吃了 日式 自助餐。
We ate at a Japanese buffet restaurant yesterday.

句型 与替换
Substitution

Zhōngshì
中式
Chinese

xīshì
西式
Western

Hánshì
韩式
Korean

扩 展／Extension

1. Zìzhùcān chéngniánrén měi wèi jiǔshí
自助餐 成 年 人 每位九十
yuán, sān suì yǐxià értóng miǎnfèi.
元，三岁以下儿童 免费。

For the buffet, each adult is ¥90, and children under three are free.

2. Jiàqián bù bāokuò jiǔshuǐ.
价钱 不 包括 酒水。

Drinks are not included in the price.

3. Zhè jiā zìzhù cāntīng yǒu sìshí duō
这 家自助餐厅 有四十多
zhǒng càishì.
种 菜式。

There are over 40 items of dishes in this buffet restaurant.

4. Rìshì kǎoròu dāngchǎng zuò.
日式 烤肉 当 场 做。

Hibachi is cooked on the spot.

甲: Wǒmen zuótiān qù chī Rìshì zìzhùcān le.
我们 昨天 去 吃 日式 自助餐 了。
We went to eat at a Japanese buffet restaurant yesterday.

乙: Zěnmeyàng?
怎么样?
How was it?

甲: Hěn búcuò, yǒu sìshí duō zhǒng shòusī.
很 不错, 有 四十多 种 寿司。
Pretty good. There are over 40 kinds of sushi.

乙: Duōshao qián?
多少 钱?
How much is it?

甲: Chéngniánrén měi wèi jiǔshí yuán, sān suì yǐxià értóng miǎnfèi.
成年人 每 位 九十 元, 三 岁 以下 儿童 免费。
For adults it's ¥90 each and children under three are free.

乙: Chīdào Rìshì kǎoròu le ma?
吃到 日式 烤肉 了 吗?
Did you eat hibachi?

甲: Chī le, dāngchǎng zuò de.
吃了, 当场 做 的。
Yes, and it was cooked on the spot.

乙: Tīngzhe búcuò, nǎ tiān wǒ yě qù chángchang.
听着 不错, 哪 天 我 也 去 尝 尝。
It sounds really good. I will try it myself.

1	zìzhùcān 自助餐	buffet	6	jiǔshuǐ 酒水	drinks
2	zhǒng 种	kind	7	lìngshōu 另收	not included
3	shòusī 寿司	sushi	8	kǎoròu 烤肉	barbecue
4	chéngniánrén 成年人	adult	9	dāngchǎng zuò 当场做	to make on the spot
5	miǎnfèi 免费	free of charge			

文化导航
Cultural Navigation

中国菜的核心是平衡协调。多数中国菜里都有一种主要成分，再配上其他一些次要成分，使整个菜肴色味俱佳。拿炒肉片来说，它的颜色是粉红色，吃起来很嫩滑，跟它相配的菜一般是绿色的蔬菜，比如青椒、芹菜，吃起来很爽脆。另外，一餐饭不应只有一个菜，菜的数量应该是偶数，比如说四个。

Harmonization is the key word in Chinese dishes. Most of Chinese dishes have one main ingredient plus a number of supplementary ingredients to keep the dish harmonized in color and taste. Take meat for example. Its color is pink and texture tender. It is most likely to be found with a green vegetable which is either crispy or crunchy such as celery (crunchy) or green peppers (crispy). In addition, meals should not be made up of a single dish, which is monotonous, but be served in pairs, and often in fours.

核心句 Key Sentence

Nín yào shénme zhǔcài?

您要什么主菜?

What main dish do you want to order?

句型与替换 Substitution

kāiwèipǐn
开胃品
appetizer

tāng
汤
soup

shālā tiáoliào
沙拉调料
salad dressing

fàn hòu tiánshí
饭后甜食
dessert

扩展/Extension

1. Nín xiān diǎn diǎnr shénme kāiwèipǐn?
   您先点点儿什么开胃品? What appetizer do you want to order first?

2. Wǒ yào yí fèn niúpái, wǔ fēn shú jiù kěyǐ.
   我要一份牛排, 五分熟就可以。 I want a beefsteak, medium.

3. Niúpái dài tāng hé shālā.
   牛排带汤和沙拉。 Beefsteak comes with soup and salad.

4. Shālā yào shénme tiáoliào?
   沙拉要什么调料? What salad dressing do you want?

甲： Nín xiān diǎn diǎnr shénme kāiwèipǐn?
您 先 点点儿什么 开胃品?

What appetizer do you want to order first?

乙： Gěi wǒ yí fèn zhá yángcōngquān ba.
给我一份炸 洋 葱 圈 吧。

Please give me fried onion rings.

甲： Nín yào shénme zhǔcài?
您 要 什么 主菜?

What main dish do you order?

乙： Wǒ yào yí fèn niúpái, wǔ fēn shú jiù kěyǐ.
我 要 一份牛排,五分熟就可以。

Beefsteak, medium.

甲： Niúpái dài tāng hé shālā, nín yào shénme tāng?
牛排带汤和沙拉, 您要什么 汤?

Beefsteak comes with soup and salad. What soup do you want?

乙： Nǎiyóu mógu tāng.
奶油蘑菇汤。

Cream mushroom soup.

甲： Shālā yào shénme tiáoliào?
沙拉要什么 调料?

What salad dressing do you want?

乙： Yìshì de. Tiándiǎn yíhuìr zài diǎn.
意式的。甜点一会儿再点。

Italian. I will order dessert later.

1	kāiwèipǐn 开胃品	appetizer	3	zhǔcài 主菜	main dish
2	zhá yángcōngquān 炸洋葱圈	fried onion rings	4	wǔ fēn shú 五分熟	medium (cooked)

5	shālā 沙拉	salad	9	miànbāo 面包	bread
6	nǎiyóu 奶油	cream	10	hújiāo 胡椒	pepper
7	tiáoliào 调料	dressing	11	dāo 刀	knife
8	tiándiǎn 甜点	dessert	12	chā 叉	fork

文化导航
Cultural Navigation

中国人在家里请客，通常是最尊贵的客人坐在主人的对面，而主人坐在离门最近的地方，方便上菜。在正式宴会上，座位是按照参加者的级别、年龄、职位安排的。中国人视右为大，左为小，因此在宴会上或正式招待会上，最重要的客人通常被安排坐在主人的右边。

At a banquet, seating is arranged based on rank, age, and title. At home, the guest of honor usually sits directly across from the host, who takes the least honorable seat near the serving door. Traditionally, the Chinese regard the right side as the superior and the left side as the inferior. Therefore on formal occasions, including meetings and banquets, the host invariably arranges for the main guests to sit on his right side.

50 快餐 | Fast Food

核心句 Key Sentence

Wǒmen qù chī Kěndéjī.

我们去吃肯德基。

Let's go and eat at KFC.

句型与替换 Substitution

Màidāngláo
麦当劳
McDonald's

bǐsàbǐng
比萨饼
pizza

Hànbǎobāo
汉堡包
hamburger

niúpái
牛排
beefsteak

扩展 / Extension

1. Wǒ xiǎng chī Měiguófàn le.
   我想吃美国饭了。
   I want to eat American food.

2. Kěndéjī yǒu bù shǎo Zhōngshì shípǐn.
   肯德基有不少中式食品。
   KFC has quite a few Chinese-style items.

3. Gěi wǒ yí fèn jīròu hànbǎo tàocān,
   给我一份鸡肉汉堡套餐、
   zhōngbēi kělè.
   中杯可乐。
   Please give me a set meal of Chicken Hamburger and one medium cola.

4. Mǎshàng jiù hǎo.
   马上就好。
   It will be ready in a moment.

甲：
Zuìjìn měi tiān dōu chī Zhōngguófàn, xiǎng chī Měiguófàn le.
最近 每 天 都吃 中国饭，想吃 美国饭了。

I have been eating Chinese food every day recently and want to have some American food.

乙：
Nà hǎo, wǒmen qù chī Kěndéjī, qiánmiàn jiù yǒu yì jiā.
那好，我们去吃肯德基，前面就有一家。

We can go and eat at KFC. There is one not far from here.

甲：
Kěndéjī yě yǒu bù shǎo Zhōngshì shípǐn, nàr de mǐzhōu jiù búcuò.
肯德基也有不少 中式食品，那儿的米粥就不错。

KFC has quite a few Chinese-style items and its rice porridge is pretty good.

乙：
Shì ma? Wǒ qù chángchang.
是吗? 我去尝尝。

Really? I will try it.

......

甲：
Fúwùyuán, gěi wǒ yí fèn jīròu hànbǎo tàocān, zhōngbēi kělè.
服务员，给我一份鸡肉汉堡 套餐、中杯可乐。

Waitress, please give me a set meal of Chicken Hamburger and a medium cola.

服务员：
25 kuài 7 máo, mǎshàng jiù hǎo.
25块7毛，马上就好。

25.7 yuan. It will be ready in a moment.

乙：
Fúwùyuán, gěi wǒ yí fèn xiǎotǒng làwèi zhájī hé yì wǎn mǐzhōu.
服务员，给我一份小桶辣味炸鸡和一碗 米粥。

Waitress, please give me a bucket of spicy fried chicken and a bowl of rice porridge.

服务员：
Zhájī 18 kuài, zhōu 5 kuài, yígòng 23 kuài.
炸鸡18块，粥5块，一共23块。

Fried chicken 18 yuan and rice porridge 5 yuan, altogether 23.

	Zhōngshì 中式	Chinese-style		zhōngbēi 中杯	medium size
1	中式	Chinese-style	6	中杯	medium size
2	shípǐn 食品	food	7	kělè 可乐	cola
3	mǐzhōu 米粥	rice porridge	8	tǒng 桶	bucket
4	yí fèn 一份	a set; a portion	9	làwèi 辣味	spicy
5	tàocān 套餐	set meal	10	zhájī 炸鸡	fried chicken

文化导航
Cultural Navigation

　　西式快餐连锁店是上世纪80年代开始进入中国的。当时中国改革开放已经开始，西式快餐店的开业吸引了很多想要体验西方生活方式的中国消费者。但到了20世纪90年代后期，中国的餐饮业已经快速发展起来了。面对来自中国本土餐饮同行的竞争以及越来越多的西式快餐、正餐店的进入，早期进入中国市场的西式快餐连锁店巨头肯德基和麦当劳不得不改变菜单，增加中式食品，比如面条、米饭、粥等。

　　Western fast-food chains came to China in the 1980s when China had started its economic reform several years before. These Western chains attracted a large number of Chinese consumers who wished to experience Western life style through tasting its food. By the late 1990s, the food industry in China began to flourish. With an intense competition from both local and foreign chains, Western fast-food giants such as KFC and McDonald's began to make their menus more Chinese by adding typical Chinese food such as noodles, cooked rice, and porridge, etc.

核心句 Key Sentence

Jīntiān wǒ zuòdōng.
今天我做东。
I will be the host today.

句型与替换 Substitution

Wǒ qǐngkè.
我请客。
I'll check out. It's on me.

Wǒ fùzhàng.
我付账。
I pay for the meal.

Wǒmen AA zhì.
我们AA制。
Let's go Dutch.

Wǒmen gè fù gè de.
我们各付各的。
Let's pay our own separately.

扩 展/Extension

Jīntiān wǒ qǐngkè, bié gēn wǒ zhēng.
1. 今天我请客，别跟我争。 Let me play the host. Please don't argue with me.

Zhè cì gāi wǒ le.
2. 这次该我了。 It is my turn this time.

Wǒmen gè fù gè de.
3. 我们各付各的。 Let's go Dutch today.

^{Kěyǐ yòng xìnyòngkǎ jiézhàng ma?}
4. 可以用 信用卡 结账吗？　Can we pay with a credit card?

^{Wǒmen zhǐ shōu xiànjīn.}
5. 我们只 收 现金。　We only accept cash.

对话实例/Dialogue

甲：^{Shuōhǎo le,　jīntiān wǒ zuòdōng,　bié gēn wǒ zhēng.}
说好了，今天我做东，别跟我争。

Let me say that I will play the host today. Please don't argue with me.

乙：^{Nà bù xíng, shàng cì　jiùshì　nǐ qǐngkè,　zhè cì gāi wǒ le.}
那不行，上次就是你请客，这次该我了。

It is not right. You treated me last time and it is my turn this time.

甲：^{Yàoburán,　wǒmen gè fù gè de.}
要不然，我们各付各的。

Or let's go Dutch.

乙：^{Nà　…　yě xíng.　Fúwùyuán,　jiézhàng.}
那……也行。服务员，结账。

That ... sounds good. Miss, bill please.

甲：^{Kěyǐ yòng xìnyòngkǎ jiézhàng ma?}
可以用 信用卡 结账吗？

Can we pay with the credit card?

服务员：^{Duìbuqǐ,　wǒmen zhǐ shōu xiànjīn.}
对不起，我们只 收 现金。

Sorry, we only accept cash.

乙：^{Kěshì wǒ méi dài xiànjīn.}
可是我没带现金。

But I don't have cash with me.

甲：^{Suàn le,　jīntiān háishi wǒ fùzhàng ba.}
算了，今天还是我付账吧。

Let it go. Let me pay the meal today.

1	zuòdōng 做东	to play the host	5	xìnyòngkǎ 信用卡	credit card
2	zhēng 争	to fight for; to argue	6	xiànjīn 现金	cash
3	qǐngkè 请客	to treat somebody	7	suàn le 算了	to let it go
4	jiézhàng 结账	to pay the bill			

文化导航
Cultural Navigation

在饭馆吃饭时，常常会看见中国人在抢着付账。你跟朋友吃饭时，他也会主动付账。这是中国人好客和友谊的表示，也是建立关系的一种方式。在这种情况下，你可以建议自己付自己的那一份。如果朋友坚持替你付账，你可以找机会回请。另外在中国吃饭不用付小费。

When dining at a restaurant, you can often see a scene that some Chinese fight over the check at the end of a meal. If you have dinner with a Chinese friend at a restaurant, he or she often offers to pay for your meal. This is a Chinese tradition to show hospitality and friendship and a way to establish a network. In this kind of situation, you can suggest that you go Dutch and pay your own. If your friend insists, you should offer to treat him/her to another dinner. In addition, tipping is not a common practice at Chinese restaurants.

核心句 Key Sentence

Jīntiān shì péngyou jùhuì, qǐng dàjiā suíyì.

今天是朋友聚会，请大家随意。

This is a friend get-together. Please feel at home.

句型与替换 Substitution

bié kèqi

别客气

Don't stand on ceremony.

duō chī diǎnr

多吃点儿

eat more

扩展/Extension

1. Zhōumò dào wǒ jiā chīfàn ba.
   周末 到我家吃饭吧。

   Come to eat with us this weekend.

2. Wǒ zuòle jǐ gè jiāchángcài, bù zhī hé bù hé nǐ de kǒuwèi.
   我做了几个家常菜，不知合不合你的口味。

   I cooked some home-style dishes and hope you will like them.

3. Nín zuò de fàn zhēn hǎochī.
   您做的饭 真 好吃。

   It is really delicious.

4. Xièxie nín de zhāodài.
   谢谢您的招待。

   Thank you for your hospitality.

对话实例/Dialogue

甲：
Shì Xiǎo Wáng a,　qǐng jìn,　qǐng jìn.　Huānyíng guānglín.
是 小 王 啊，请 进，请 进。欢迎 光临。

Hello, Xiao Wang. Come on in. Welcome.

乙：
Liú zhǔrèn,　nín hǎo.　Zhīdào nín xǐhuan hē hóngjiǔ,　jiù gěi nín
刘主任，您好。知道您喜欢喝红酒，就给您
mǎile yì píng.
买了一瓶。

How are you, Director Liu? I know you love red wine and bought one bottle for you.

甲：
Tài kèqi le.　Lái,　zuò zhèr,　yíhuìr jiù kāifàn le.
太客气了。来，坐这儿，一会儿就开饭了。

Thank you. Have a seat please. Meal starts in a moment.

乙：
Nín zuò zhème duō de cài,　yídìng mángle bàntiān le ba.
您做这么多的菜，一定忙了 半天了吧。

You have made so many dishes. You must have spent a lot of time on them.

甲：
Jiù zuòle jǐ gè jiāchángcài.　Bù zhī hé bù hé nǐ de kǒuwèi.
就做了几个家常菜。不知合不合你的口味。

I just made some home-style dishes and hope you will like them.

乙：
Kànzhe jiù hǎochī.
看着就好吃。

They look great.

甲：
Nà jiù duō chī diǎnr.　Jīntiān shì péngyou jùhuì,　suíyì.
那就多吃点儿。今天是朋友聚会，随意。

Then eat more. This is a friend get-together. Please feel at home.

乙：
Xièxie nín de zhāodài,　tài hǎochī le.
谢谢您的招待，太好吃了.

Thank you for inviting me. The food is absolutely fantastic.

1	guānglín 光临	visit	5	kǒuwèi 口味	taste
2	hóngjiǔ 红酒	red wine	6	jùhuì 聚会	get-together
3	jiāchángcài 家常菜	home-style dish	7	suíyì 随意	to feel at home
4	hé kǒuwèi 合 （口味）	to fulfill			

文化导航
Cultural Navigation

中国人在家里请客，一般都是主人准备所有的饭菜，并不期待客人带菜。在美国很流行的自带食品朋友聚会，在中国还不太常见。当然客人应该带些礼物，比如说红酒、巧克力、水果、蛋糕等。另外，在席间，主人会说自己准备的饭菜太少，做得不太好等谦虚的话，作为客人应该称赞主人做的饭菜。

When Chinese people invite friends to their home for dinner, they mean it and will prepare all the dishes for the meal. They do not count on the guests for any contributions. Potluck dinner parties are not as popular in China as they are in the United States. But visitors should bring something as a token of appreciation such as a bottle of wine, a box of chocolate, a basket of fruit or a cake. During the meal, the host will say that they have not prepared a lot of dishes and their dishes are not good enough in order to show their modesty. As a guest, you should show your respects by complimenting how delicious the dishes are.

[购物]
Shopping

核心句 Key Sentence

Wǒmen qù guàngjiē ba.
我们去逛街吧。
Let us go shopping.

句型与替换 Substitution

gòuwù zhōngxīn
购物中心
mall; shopping center

chāoshì
超市
supermarket

nóngmào shìchǎng
农贸市场
farmer's market

zǎoshì
早市
morning market

yèshì
夜市
evening market

jiùhuò shìchǎng
旧货市场
flea market

扩展/Extension

Xiǎng qù nǎr guàngjiē?
1. 想去哪儿逛街?

Where do you want to go for shopping?

Wǒmen qù gāng kāi de nà jiā guójì gòuwù zhōngxīn ba.
2. 我们去刚开的那家国际购物中心吧。

Let's go to the international shopping mall that just opened.

Nàr yǒu hěn duō guójì dǐngjí
3. 那儿有 很 多国际顶级
pǐnpái diàn.
品牌店。

There are a lot of international top brand stores.

Nàr de dōngxi wùměi-jiàlián.
4. 那儿的东西 物美价廉。

Things there are cheap and nice.

对话实例/Dialogue

Jīntiān shì xīngqītiān, wǒmen qù guàngjiē ba.
甲: 今天是星期天，我们去逛街吧。

It is Sunday today. Let's go shopping, shall we?

Xiǎng qù nǎr?
乙: 想 去哪儿？

Where do you want to go?

Qù gāng kāi de nà jiā guójì gòuwù zhōngxīn ba.
甲: 去 刚 开的那家国际购物 中心 吧。

I want to go to the newly opened international shopping mall.

Hǎo a. Tīngshuō tèbié dà, yì tiān dōu guàng bù guòlái.
乙: 好啊。听说特别大，一天都逛 不过来。

Sounds good. I heard it is so huge that you cannot visit all the stores in a day.

Nàr yǒu hěn duō guójì dǐngjí pǐnpái diàn.
甲: 那儿有 很 多国际顶级品牌店。

There are many international top brand stores.

Kě tīngshuō nàr de dōngxi dōu hěn guì, dǎzhé yǐhòu hái yào jǐqiān yuán.
乙: 可听说那儿的东西都很贵，打折以后还要几千元。

But things there are very expensive, about several thousand yuan even after discount.

Zhǐshì kànkan, héshì cái mǎi.
甲: 只是看看，合适才买。

Just window shopping. We only buy things we need.

Mǎi dōngxi háishi qù Yǎxiù,　　yòu hǎo yòu piányi.
乙: 买东西还是去雅秀，又好又便宜。

If we want to buy something, go to Yaxiu where things are good and cheap.

相关词语/Related Words

1	guójì 国际	international	4	diàn 店	store
2	dǐngjí 顶级	top class	5	dǎzhé 打折	to discount
3	pǐnpái 品牌	brand	6	piányi 便宜	cheap in price

文化导航
Cultural Navigation

　　中国有很多不同的购物场所，可以满足人们不同的消费目的和需要，比如说有超大型购物中心、百货商店、超级市场，也有很多规模不大但很方便的社区商店。除此之外，还有农贸市场、古玩市场、早市、夜市等各种各样的自由市场。

There are different places you can shop at in China for different shopping purposes. There are malls or shopping centers, department stores, and supermarkets. Besides, there are neighborhood/community stores, small in size, but very convenient for people in the community. There are also a lot of flea markets including farmer's markets, antique markets, morning markets and evening markets, etc.

核心句 Key Sentence

Nǎizhìpǐn qū zài nǎr?
奶制品区在哪儿？
Where is the section for dairy products?

句型与替换 Substitution

ròulèi
肉类
meat and meat products

dòuzhìpǐn
豆制品
bean products

shuǐchǎnpǐn
水产品
seafood

tiáowèipǐn
调味品
seasoning

shúshí
熟食
cooked food

yǐnliào
饮料
soft drinks

扩 展／Extension

Nín děi xiān cún yíxià bāo.
1. 您得先存一下包。

You have to put your bag in the locker first.

Zài nǎr néng zhǎodào shālājiàng
2. 在哪儿能找到沙拉酱
hé xiāngcháng?
和香肠？

Where can I find salad dressing and sausage?

3. Shālājiàng zài tiáowèipǐnqū,
   沙拉酱 在调味品区，
   zài dì-èr pái.
   在第二排。

   Salad dressing is in the seasoning section in the second row.

4. Huòjià hàomǎ shì duōshao?
   货架号码是多少？

   What is the number of the shelf?

对话实例/Dialogue

甲: Duìbuqǐ, nín děi cún yíxià bāo.
对不起，您得存一下包。
Excuse me. You have to put your bag in the locker first.

乙: Hǎo. Nà shì cúnbāochù ba?
好。那是存包处吧？
Sure. It is the locker place, isn't it?

……

乙: Láojià, wǒ xiǎng mǎi shālājiàng hé xiāngcháng, zài nǎr néng zhǎo de dào?
劳驾，我想买沙拉酱和香肠，在哪儿能找得到？
Excuse me, I want to buy salad dressing and sausage. Where can I find them?

甲: Shālājiàng zài tiáowèipǐnqū, zài dì-èr pái zhōngjiān de nàge huòjià.
沙拉酱在调味品区，在第二排中间的那个货架。
Salad dressing is in the seasoning section. The shelf is in the middle of the second row.

乙: Huòjià hàomǎ shì duōshao?
货架号码是多少？
What is the number of the shelf?

甲: 15 hào.
15号.
Number 15.

乙: Shúshíqū zài nǎr?
熟食区在哪儿？
Where is the cooked food section?

甲: Nín yìzhí wǎng qián zǒu, zǒudào tóu wǎng zuǒ guǎi, zài wǎng qián zǒu
您一直往前走，走到头往左拐，再往前走
jiùshì shúshíqū.
就是熟食区。
Go straight to the end, turn left, and then you can see the cooked food section.

1	cúnbāo 存包	to place the bag in the locker	5	qū 区	section
2	cúnbāochù 存包处	locker section	6	huòjià 货架	shelf
3	shālājiàng 沙拉酱	salad dressing	7	hàomǎ 号码	number
4	xiāngcháng 香肠	sausage			

文化导航
Cultural Navigation

　　超级市场是很多中国消费者购物的首选场所之一。中国大城市里有很多超市，其中不少是连锁店。超级市场受欢迎的原因有：商品齐全，质量有保障，价钱公道，日用商品（如食品、日用品、服装、书籍、家用电器）应有尽有。很多商店实行会员制，定期推出优惠活动，接受信用卡消费。北京最受欢迎的超级市场有沃尔玛、家乐福、欧尚等。

　　Supermarkets are very popular around China. There are many big supermarkets in large cities and some of them are chain stores. Your eyes will be dazzled by the great variety of goods in different brands and you can have more choices. Furthermore, the supermarkets sell good-quality products which can be cheaper than other shopping centers in most cases. Commonly, food, commodities, clothes, books and household electric appliances are all available. Many supermarkets periodically have promotions to their members and credit cards are welcome. Well-received supermarkets in Beijing include Wal-Mart, Carrefour and Auchan.

Wǒ xiǎng mǎi yì běn Hànyǔ kǒuyǔ shǒucè.

我想买一本汉语口语手册。

I want to buy a handbook of conversational Chinese.

句型与替换 Substitution

zìdiǎn
字典
dictionary

jiàocái
教材
textbook

zázhì
杂志
magazine

xiǎoshuō
小说
novel

扩 展/Extension

Nǐ zhǎo shénme shū?
1. 你找 什么书？

What books are you looking for?

Zhè tào shǒucè shì gāng chūbǎn de.
2. 这套手册是 刚 出版的。

This series of handbooks is just published.

Mǎi de rén duō ma?
3. 买的人多吗？

Did a lot of people buy it?

Zhè běn shū hǎo xiédài, dài CD,
4. 这本书好携带，带CD，
jiàqián yě bú guì.
价钱也不贵。

This book is portable with CD and the price is reasonable.

甲: Wǒ xiǎng mǎi yì běn Hànyǔ kǒuyǔ shǒucè, yǒu shénme jiànyì ma?
我 想 买 一 本 汉语 口语 手册, 有 什么 建议 吗?

I am looking for a handbook of conversational Chinese. Do you have any recommendations?

乙: Xuéle jǐ nián Zhōngwén le?
学了 几 年 中文 了?

How many years have you studied Chinese?

甲: Chàbuduō yì nián.
差不多 一 年。

About a year.

乙: Dào Zhōngguó shì lǚyóu háishi xuéxí a?
到 中国 是 旅游 还是 学习 啊?

You came to China to travel or to study?

甲: Xuéxí, dàn wǒ xiǎng yǒu shíjiān dàochù zǒuzou, liǎojiě Zhōngguó.
学习, 但 我 想 有 时间 到处 走走, 了解 中国。

To study. But I also plan to find time to travel a bit, understanding China better.

乙: Nǐ kànkan zhè tào kǒuyǔ xìliè shǒucè, gāng chūbǎn de.
你 看看 这 套 口语 系列 手册, 刚 出版 的。

You can take a look at this series of conversational Chinese handbooks. They are just published.

甲: Kànzhe búcuò, mǎi de rén duō ma?
看着 不错, 买 的 人 多 吗?

They look really good. Did a lot of people buy the series?

乙: Tǐng chàngxiāo de, hǎo xiédài, dài CD, jiàqián yě bú guì.
挺 畅 销 的, 好 携带, 带 CD, 价钱 也 不 贵。

They sell fast. They are portable with CD and the price is reasonable.

1	jiànyì 建议	recommendation; suggestion	7	liǎojiě 了解	to understand
2	xìliè 系列	series (of books)	8	tào 套	set (of books)
3	shǒucè 手册	handbook	9	jiāo qián 交钱	to pay for
4	chūbǎn 出版	to publish	10	zuòzhě 作者	author
5	hǎo xiédài 好携带	portable	11	chàngxiāo 畅销	to sell well
6	jiàqián 价钱	price			

文化导航
Cultural Navigation

对于母语是英语的人来说，住在国外的不便之一是很难找到英文书店。但住在北京情况要好些。北京最有名的要属坐落在王府井商业区的"外文书店"，那里有很多用英文写的关于中国各个方面的书籍，大部分是中国出版的。离此不远的"王府井新华书店"二楼也出售很多英文原版小说。其他出售外文书籍的还有北京图书大厦、中关村图书大厦、海淀外文书店、友谊商店英文书店、外研书店等。

For the native speakers of English, one of the drawbacks living in a foreign country including China is the difficulty to find a good English bookstore. If you live in Beijing, you are very lucky since there are quite a few English bookstores there. For example, the Foreign Languages Bookstore which sells a large collection of books on Chinese culture, all in English, the majority of which are published by Chinese publishing houses. The second one in line is the Wangfujing Xinhua Bookstore. Its second floor contains a large collection of classic British and American novels. The others are Beijing Book Center, Zhongguancun Book Center, Haidian Foreign Languages Bookstore, the English Bookstore in the Friendship Store, and Foreign Language Teaching and Research Press Bookstore.

核心句 / Key Sentence

Nǐ kěyǐ mǎi xiē Zhōngguó chuántǒng gōngyìpǐn.

你可以买些中国 传统工艺品。

You can buy some traditional Chinese handicrafts.

句型与替换 / Substitution

sīchóu
丝绸
silk

nírén
泥人
clay figure

jiǎnzhǐ
剪纸
paper-cut

shānshuǐhuà
山水画
landscape painting

扩展 / Extension

Wǒ xiǎng huíguó mǎi xiē lǐwù,
1. 我 想 回国买些礼物，
yǒu shénme jiànyì?
有 什么 建议？

I want to buy some gifts to take back home. Do you have any suggestions?

Sīchóubèi tèbié piàoliang,
2. 丝绸被特别漂亮，
yòu qīng yòu nuǎn.
又 轻 又 暖。

Silk quilts are very pretty, light and warm.

Yàoshi xǐhuan huà,   jiù mǎi fú
3. 要是喜欢画，就买幅
Zhōngguóhuà.
中 国 画。

If (you) like paintings, you can buy a piece of Chinese painting.

Wǒ sònggěi péngyou, tóngshì
4. 我送给朋友、同事
Zhōngguó jiǎnzhǐ hé nírén.
中 国 剪纸和泥人。

I will buy my friends and colleagues some Chinese papercuts and clay figures.

Qù Wénhuàjiē mǎi zuìhǎo.
5. 去文化街 买最好。

The best place to buy these goods is the Cultural Street.

对话实例/Dialogue

甲： Wǒ yào huíguó le, xiǎng mǎi xiē lǐwù, yǒu shénme jiànyì?
我要回国了，想买些礼物，有什么建议？
I will go back soon and want to buy some gifts. Do you have any suggestions?

乙： Nǐ kěyǐ mǎi xiē Zhōngguó chuántǒng gōngyìpǐn.
你可以买些中 国 传 统 工艺品。
You can buy some traditional Chinese handicrafts.

甲： Gěi wǒ māma mǎi shénme ne?
给我妈妈买什么呢？
What should I buy for my mother?

乙： Wǒ jiànyì nǐ mǎi yì chuáng sīchóubèi, tèbié piàoliang, yòu qīng yòu nuǎn.
我建议你买一 床 丝绸被, 特别漂亮，又 轻 又 暖。
I suggest you buy a silk quilt, very beautiful, light and warm.

甲： Hǎo. Wǒ bàba ne?
好。我爸爸呢？
Sounds good. How about my father?

乙： Nǐ bàba yàoshi xǐhuan huà, jiù mǎi fú zìhuà. Péngyou, tóngshì
你爸爸要是喜欢画，就买幅字画。朋友、同事
kěyǐ mǎi xiē jiǎnzhǐ, nírén.
可以买些剪纸、泥人。
If your father likes paintings, you can buy a piece of calligraphy or Chinese painting. You can buy some papercuts and clay figures for friends and colleagues.

甲： Hǎo zhǔyi. Qù nǎr mǎi zuìhǎo ne?
好主意。去哪儿买最好呢？
Good idea. Where can I buy them for the best deal?

     Wénhuà jiē.   Míngtiān shì xīngqītiān.   wǒ péi nǐ qù.

乙：文化街。明天是星期天，我陪你去。

The Cultural Street. It is Sunday tomorrow and I can go with you.

相关词语／Related Words

1	lǐwù 礼物	gift	4	yòu qīng 又 轻 yòu nuǎn 又 暖	light and warm
2	gōngyìpǐn 工艺品	handicraft	5	zìhuà 字画	calligraphy and painting
3	piàoliang 漂 亮	pretty	6	tóngshì 同事	colleague

文化导航
Cultural Navigation

　　很多外国人回国的时候都买一些中国字画带回去送给亲友。中国字画被认为是中国传统艺术的最高境界，表现了中国哲学的精髓：中庸、和谐。用来写字、画画的工具被称为文房四宝，即纸、墨、笔、砚，也是回国送给朋友的好礼物。

A lot of foreigners love to buy some pieces of Chinese calligraphy and painting as gifts when they go back to their own country. Actually Chinese calligraphy and painting are considered the highest form of art in China. They are the best embodiment of Chinese philosophy: balance and harmony. The writing tools are the so-called four treasures of the study room: paper, writing brush, ink slab and ink stick. They are also good gifts for friends in your home country.

核心句
Key
Sentence

Xīhóngshì zěnme mài?
西红柿怎么卖？
How much are the tomatoes?

句型
与替换
Substitution

Duōshao qián yì jīn?
多少钱一斤？
How much per *jīn*?

Zěnme zhème guì?
怎么这么贵？
Why so expensive?

Piányidiǎnr ba.
便宜点儿吧。
Can I buy them cheaper?

扩 展／Extension

Jīntiān de cài tèbié xīnxiān.
1. 今天的菜特别新鲜。

The vegetables today are very fresh.

Nǐ de zěnme bǐ biéde tānr guì?
2. 你的怎么比别的摊儿贵？

Why are yours more expensive than those in other stands?

Néng zài piányidiǎnr ma?
3. 能再便宜点儿吗？

Can you lower the price a bit?

Yì fēn qián yì fēn huò.
4. 一分钱一分货。

You get what you pay for.

对话实例/Dialogue

甲：Xīhóngshì zěnme mài?
西红柿怎么卖？

How much are the tomatoes?

乙：Liǎng kuài qián yì jīn.
两块钱一斤。

Two yuan per *jin* (half a kilogram).

甲：Zěnme bǐ nàge tānr guì liǎng máo qián ya?
怎么比那个摊儿贵两毛钱呀？

Why do you charge twenty fen more than the other stand?

乙：Wǒ de xīhóngshì shì jīntiān xīn zhāi de, tèbié xīnxiān.
我的西红柿是今天新摘的，特别新鲜。

My tomatoes were newly picked today and very fresh.

甲：Néng zài piányidiǎnr ma?
能再便宜点儿吗？

Can I buy them cheaper?

乙：Zhēnde bù néng le, zhè xīhóngshì yòu dà yòu hóng, fēicháng xīnxiān.
真的不能了，这西红柿又大又红，非常新鲜。

You really cannot. My tomatoes are big and red and very fresh.

甲：Nà gěi wǒ liǎng jīn ba.
那给我两斤吧。

Give me one kilogram.

乙：Yì fēn qián yì fēn huò.
一分钱一分货。

You get what you pay for.

1	Zěnme mài? 怎么卖?	How much is it?	4	guì 贵	expensive
2	jīn 斤	half a kilogram (basic unit in the Chinese old weight system)	5	xīnxiān 新鲜	fresh
3	tānr 摊儿	stand; stall			

文化导航
Cultural Navigation

　　中国官方使用的度量衡是十进制的"公制"，但很多人还是习惯使用中国传统的度量衡，即"市制"。市制的长度基本单位是"里"，相当于二分之一公里或0.311英里。重量基本单位是"斤"，等于0.5公斤或1.102磅。

　　For measuring length, weight, and liquid/volume, China officially uses metric system called "公制". But many people still use the traditional measurement system called "市制". The basic unit of the length of distance in the traditional system is "里", which equals half a kilometer, or 0.311 mile. The basic unit of weight in the system is "斤", which equals half a kilogram, or 1.102 pounds.

核心句
Key Sentence

Wǎngshang gòuwù *hěn ānquán.*
网 上 购物 *很安全*。
Online shopping is very safe.

句型与替换
Substitution

hěn fāngbiàn
很方便
very convenient

piányi de duō
便宜得多
much cheaper

xuǎnzé duō
选择多
have a lot of options

扩 展/Extension

1. Nǐ cháng zài wǎngshang mǎi dōngxi ma?
你 常 在 网 上 买东西吗? Do you often do online shopping?

2. Wǎnggòu kěyǐ huò dào fùkuǎn.
网 购可以 货 到 付款。 By online shopping, you can pay when receiving the goods.

3. Wǎngshang tuìhuò yǒudiǎnr máfan.
网 上 退货有点儿麻烦。 It is a bit complicated if you return the goods you bought online.

4. Zhème guì de dōngxi yīnggāi dào
这么贵的东西 应该 到 You should buy the expensive
shāngdiàn mǎi.
商 店 买。 goods in stores.

甲： Xiǎo Wáng, wǒ zài wǎngshang kànshàng yí kuài jìnkǒubiǎo.
小王，我在网上看上一块进口表。
Xiao Wang, I saw an imported watch sold in an online store.
I like it very much.

乙： Shāngdiàn méi mài de ma?
商店没卖的吗？
Can you buy it in a store?

甲： Yǒu, dànshì guì hǎo duō.
有，但是贵好多。
Yes, but much more expensive.

乙： Kěshì wǎngshang kàn bú jiàn shíwù a. Wànyī mǎidào jiǎhuò ne?
可是网上看不见实物啊。万一买到假货呢？
But you cannot see the real things online. How can you guarantee
it is not a fake one?

甲： Xiànzài wǎnggòu hěn ānquán.
现在网购很安全。
It is safe to purchase things online.

乙： Nà méi jiàndào huò jiù jiāoqián yě bùxíng a.
那没见到货就交钱也不行啊。
But you cannot pay it without seeing the real goods first.

甲： Kěyǐ huò dào fùkuǎn.
可以货到付款。
I can pay it when receiving the goods.

乙： Nà fùqián yǐhòu shāngpǐn yǒu wèntí ne? Zhème guì de dōngxi háishi
那付钱以后商品有问题呢？这么贵的东西还是
dào shāngdiàn mǎi fàngxīn.
到商店买放心。
But if there is a problem after you pay? I think you should buy
expensive goods like this in stores.

1	jìnkǒu 进口	imported	3	shāngdiàn 商店	store
2	shāngpǐn 商品	goods	4	shíwù 实物	real object

5	bǎozhèng 保 证	guarantee	8	tuìhuò 退货	to return goods
6	jiǎhuò 假货	fake goods	9	máfan 麻烦	troublesome
7	jiāoqián 交钱	to pay money (for...)			

文化导航
Cultural Navigation

　　现在中国网上购物很火，最受欢迎的网站是"淘宝网"。网购给生活在中国的外国人带来了极大的方便，他们可以很容易地买到在本国用惯了的东西，比如说大尺码的衣服、咖啡、某个品牌的奶酪、婴儿配方奶，而这些商品在中国的一般商店很难买到。在中国网上购物，要到当地银行开一个网上账户，很多网站也接受Visa卡，还有的网站可以货到付款，极大降低了购物风险。

Online shopping has taken China by storm, and the most popular site is Taobao. Online stores offer great convenience to foreigners living in China who can easily buy Western brand stuff they are used to, such as large-sized clothes, coffee, cheese and formula, which can hardly be bought in most Chinese stores. All of these are available online, and can be delivered straight to your door. In order to set up for online shopping, you'll need an online banking account that can be easily opened up in your local Chinese bank. Most sites also accept Visa cards. Some sites collect charges upon delivery, which reduces purchasing risks greatly.

核心句
Key Sentence

Kěyǐ dǎdiǎnr zhé ma?
可以打点儿折吗?
Can you give me some discount?

句型与替换
Substitution

piányidiǎnr
便宜点儿
a bit cheaper

jiǎndiǎnr jià
减点儿价
reduce the price a bit

yōuhuìdiǎnr
优惠点儿
give a better price

dǎ qī zhé
打七折
30% off the original price

扩展/Extension

Zhè jiàn yīfu kěyǐ dǎzhé ma?
1. 这件衣服可以打折吗?

Can you give me some discount on this dress?

Zài piányidiǎnr, wǒmen jiù mǎi
2. 再便宜点儿，我们就买
xialai.
下来。

We will buy it if you give us a better price.

Zài gěi nǐ jiǔ wǔ zhé de yōuhuì.
3. 再给你九五折的优惠。

I will give you a further 5% discount.

Zhè jiàn shuìyī shì qīngcāng chǔlǐpǐn.
4. 这件睡衣是清仓处理品。This pajama is one clearance item.

Zhè jiàn chènshān yǒudiǎnr guòshí le.
5. 这件衬衫有点儿过时了。This shirt is a bit out of fashion.

对话实例/Dialogue

Zhè tiáo qúnzi tǐng xīncháo de,   jiùshì tài guì le.
甲: 这条裙子挺新潮的，就是太贵了。

This dress is very trendy but a bit too expensive.

Fúwùyuán,   zhè jiàn yīfu   kěyǐ dǎzhé ma?
乙: 服务员，这件衣服可以打折吗？

Miss, can you give us some discount on this dress?

Zhè yǐjīng shì dǎzhé le de.
丙: 这已经是打折了的。

This is on sale already.

Zài piányidiǎnr,   wǒmen jiù mǎi xialai.
乙: 再便宜点儿，我们就买下来。

We will buy it if you give us a better price.

Hǎo,   zài gěi nǐ 5% de yōuhuì.   Jīntiān hěn duō shāngpǐn qī zhé,
丙: 好，再给你5%的优惠。今天很多商品七折，
nǐmen mǎi,   dōu zài gěi nǐmen jiǎn 5%.
你们买，都再给你们减5%。

OK. I will give you a further 5% discount. There are many
goods with 30% off the original price. If you buy any of these,
I will give you a further 5% discount.

Zhēn de?
乙: 真的？

Really?

……

Zhè jiàn shuìyī búcuò,   shì qīngcāng chǔlǐ,   zài jiǎn 5%,   jiù tài
甲: 这件睡衣不错，是清仓处理，再减5%，就太
piányi le.
便宜了。

This pajama is pretty good. It is one clearance item. If we get a further 5% off, it is really a good deal.

Nà jiù yào zhè tiáo qúnzi hé zhè jiàn shuìyī ba.

乙：那就要这条裙子和这件睡衣吧。

Then let's buy this dress and this pajama.

相关词语／Related Words

1	qúnzi 裙子	dress; skirt	7	shuìyī 睡衣	pajama
2	xīncháo 新潮	trendy; fashionable	8	qīngcāng 清仓 chǔlǐ 处理	clearance
3	shímáo 时髦	fashionable	9	chènshān 衬衫	shirt; blouse
4	dǎzhé 打折	discount	10	kùzi 裤子	trousers
5	yōuhuì 优惠	discount	11	dàyī 大衣	overcoat
6	jiǎnjià 减价	price reduction	12	xīfú 西服	suit

文化导航
Cultural Navigation

　　当看到一家商店打折出售商品，你应该明白打折的商品价格是原价的百分之多少。比如广告上说"打八折"，也就是优惠，按原价的出售。有时你还可以进一步讨价还价。在农贸市场和自由市场，商贩们已经抬高了要价，留给了你讲价的空间，有时你的出价可以到要价的甚至更低。但大型商店都是固定价格，一般没有讲价的余地。

If you see a store that sells at a discounted price, you should understand the percentage of the original price you should pay. For example, if the sign says "八折", it means giving 20% discount and charging 80% of the original price. Sometimes, you can ask for a further discount by bargaining. Usually you can bargain at farmer's markets and street markets where sellers often ask for a higher price and leave room for you to bargain. You can even start from the half of the asking price or lower. Most department stores use fixed prices and you cannot bargain.

60 换衣服 | Changing Clothes

核心句
Key
Sentence

Néng gěi wǒ huàn jiàn xiǎo yí hào de ma?
能 给 我 换件 小一号 的吗？
Can I change it for a smaller size?

句型
与替换
Substitution

dà	30 hào	dà yí hào
大	30号	大一号
large	Size 30	one size larger
cháng	duǎn	biéde yánsè
长	短	别的颜色
long	short	different color

扩 展/Extension

Zhè shì wǒ zuótiān mǎi de, yǒu-
1. 这是我昨天买的，有
diǎnr dà.
点儿大。

I bought it yesterday but it's a bit too large.

Yǒu fāpiào ma?
2. 有发票吗？

Do you have the receipt?

Nín shì xiǎng huàn háishi tuì?
3. 您是想 换还是退？

Do you want to change it for another one or just return this one?

Wǒ gěi nín ná yí jiàn shìshi.
4. 我给您拿一件试试。

I will get you one to try.

Dàxiǎo, yánsè dōu héshì.
5. 大小、颜色都合适。

Both size and color are good.

甲：
Zhè shì wǒ zuótiān mǎi de, yǒudiǎnr dà.
这是我昨天买的，有点儿大。

I bought it yesterday but it's a bit too large.

乙：
Yǒu fāpiào ma?
有发票吗？

Do you have the receipt?

甲：
Yǒu, zài zhèr ne.
有，在这儿呢。

Yes. Here it is.

乙：
Èng, nín shì xiǎng huàn háishi tuì?
嗯，您是想换还是退？

Good. Do you want to change it or just return it?

甲：
Néng gěi wǒ huàn jiàn xiǎo yí hào de ma?
能给我换件小一号的吗？

Can you change it for one of the smaller size for me?

乙：
Xíng dàoshì xíng, jiùshì méiyǒu lǜsè de le.
行倒是行，就是没有绿色的了。

I can do it but there are no green ones.

甲：
Nà yǒu lánsè de ma?
那有蓝色的吗？

Do you have blue ones?

乙：
Yǒu, wǒ gěi nín ná yí jiàn shìshi.
有，我给您拿一件试试。

Yes. I will get one for you to try.

甲：
Hǎo. Èng. Dàxiǎo, yánsè dōu héshì, jiù yào zhè jiàn le.
好。嗯。大小、颜色都合适，就要这件了。

Good. The size and color are both good. I just want this one.

1	fāpiào 发票	receipt		7	héshì 合适	fit
2	huàn 换	to exchange		8	hóng 红	red
3	tuì 退	to return		9	lǜ 绿	green
4	shìshi 试试	to try		10	lán 蓝	blue
5	dàxiǎo 大小	size		11	hēi 黑	black
6	yánsè 颜色	color		12	bái 白	white

文化导航
Cultural Navigation

　　中国传统服饰中最具代表意义的是女式旗袍。高档旗袍的面料一般是丝绸，图案大都是条、格或素色绣花，与西式裙装相比，看上去不那么拘谨。旗袍的剪裁很简洁，很能突出女性的线条，穿起来既高雅又大方。现在，平常很少有人穿旗袍，只有在节日、庆祝会等特殊场合才穿。

　　One of the most typical and representative items of traditional Chinese clothing is the *qipao* for women. The material is silk with either patterned or picturesque embroidery on it. At first glance these designs look alive when compared to Western dress. It is this simplicity that accents the shape of the body to create an elegant and neat look. Today Western style clothing is much more common and Chinese *qipao* can only be seen during the special events such as festivals and celebrations.

61 退货 | Returning Goods

核心句 Key Sentence

Gāng mǎi de diànshì huài le.

刚 买 的 电视 坏 了。

The TV I recently bought is broken.

句型 与替换 Substitution

zhìliàng yǒu wèntí

质量 有 问题

quality problem

huàmiàn bù qīngchu

画面 不 清楚

poor image

bù chū túxiàng

不 出 图像

no image

扩 展/Extension

Zhège páizi de dōngxi zhìliàng hěn hǎo.

1. 这个 牌子 的 东西 质量 很 好。

This brand is good in quality.

Wǒ gěi nǐ huàn yì tái.

2. 我 给 你 换 一台。

I will change a new one for you.

Wǒ xiān ràng rén gěi nín xiūxiu.

3. 我 先 让 人 给 您 修修。

I will have somebody fix it for you first.

Zhè shì tuìkuǎn, nín diǎndian.

4. 这 是 退款，您 点点。

This is your refund. Please check.

甲: Láojià, wǒ gāng mǎi de diànshì huài le.
劳驾，我刚买的电视坏了。
Excuse me, the TV I bought not long ago is broken.

乙: Zhège páizi de diànshì hěn hǎo a, zhìliàng méiyǒu wèntí.
这个牌子的电视很好啊，质量没有问题。
This brand of TV is very good in quality.

甲: Zhè shì wǒ shàng gè yuè mǎi de, kāishǐ hái tǐng hǎo de, cóng shàng
这是我上个月买的，开始还挺好的，从 上
gè xīngqī kāishǐ bù chū túxiàng le.
个星期开始不出图像了。
I bought it last month. It was good at the beginning but from last week there are no images.

乙: Bǎ fāpiào gěi wǒ. Wǒ xiān ràng rén gěi nín xiūxiu.
把发票给我。我先让人给您修修。
Show me the receipt. I will have somebody fix it for you first.

甲: Háishi tuì le ba, xīn diànshì jiù xiū, duō bièniu a.
还是退了吧，新电视就修，多别扭啊。
I want to return it. I don't feel comfortable to have my new TV fixed.

乙: Nà wǒ gěi nín huàn yì tái.
那我给您换一台。
Then I will change a new one for you.

甲: Tuì le ba, wǒ zuòzuo shìchǎng diàochá zài mǎi.
退了吧，我做做市场调查再买。
Please return it for me. I will buy a new one after doing some market research.

乙: Yě xíng. Zhè shì tuìkuǎn, nín diǎndian.
也行。这是退款，您点点。
No problem. This is your refund. Please check.

相关词语/Related Words

1	páizi 牌子	brand	2	zhìliàng 质量	quality

3	túxiàng 图像	image	6	diàochá 调查	to investigate; investigation
4	xiū 修	to repair	7	tuìkuǎn 退款	money for the returned goods
5	shìchǎng 市场	market	8	diǎn qián 点（钱）	to count the money

文化导航
Cultural Navigation

　　对中国人来说，不同的颜色具有不同的象征意义。红色表示幸福、喜庆。春节很多女士都穿红色，房间也用红色来装饰，结婚时红色是主要的颜色。绿色象征着健康、成长、生命、兴旺等正面意义，也是中国人喜欢的颜色。黑色、白色都是跟死亡相关的颜色，葬礼上花圈是用白、黄色的鲜花或纸花扎起来的。但在西方文化的影响下，现在越来越多的年轻人结婚时穿白色婚纱，把白色视为纯洁的颜色。

Different colors have different implications for Chinese people. Red stands for joy and happiness. During holiday seasons and at weddings, most women wear red, and the houses are decorated in red. Green is a wonderful color, meaning health, growth, birth, life, youth, prosperity and harmony. Both black and white are the universal funeral colors, not except Chinese. The Chinese use white and yellow fresh or paper flowers for funeral floral sprays and wreaths. However, young people nowadays like to wear white wedding dresses on their wedding day under the influence of the Western culture and they believe white stands for purity and innocence.

娱乐休闲
Entertainment

核心句 Key Sentence

Gěi wǒ yì bēi pǔtōng kāfēi.
给我一杯普通咖啡。
Please give me a cup of regular coffee.

句型与替换 Substitution

bīngkāfēi
冰咖啡
ice coffee

nátiě
拿铁
latte

kǎbùqínuò
卡布奇诺
cappuccino

mókǎ
摩卡
mocha

hóngchá
红茶
black tea

扩 展 / Extension

Nǐ yào shénme hào bēi de?
1. **你要什么号杯的?**
What size of cup do you want?

Kāfēi jiā nǎi jiā táng ma?
2. **咖啡加奶加糖吗?**
Do you want your coffee with milk and sugar?

Hóngchá jiā nǎi bù jiā táng.
3. **红茶加奶不加糖。**
I want the black tea with milk but without sugar.

Qǐng gěi wǒ yí gè kěsòng miànbāo.
4. **请给我一个可颂面包。**
Please give me a croissant.

甲： Wǒ yào yì bēi pǔtōng kāfēi.
我要一杯普通咖啡。
I want a cup of regular coffee.

乙： Shénme hào bēi?
什么号杯?
What size?

甲： Zhōngbēi.
中杯。
Medium.

乙： Kāfēi jiā nǎi jiā táng ma?
咖啡加奶加糖 吗?
With milk and sugar?

甲： Jiā nǎi, dàn bù jiā táng.
加奶, 但不加糖。
With milk but no sugar.

乙： Nín hái yào shénme?
您还要什么?
What else do you want?

甲： Zài gěi wǒ yí gè kěsòng miànbāo.
再给我一个可颂 面包。
Please give me a croissant.

乙： Hǎo. Yígòng 45 kuài 3 máo. Nín náhǎo. Xià yí wèi.
好。一共45块3毛。您拿好。下一位。
It is 45.3 yuan. Here you are. Next please.

1	hào bēi 号杯	size of cup	5	kěsòng miànbāo 可颂 面包	croissant
2	zhōngbēi 中杯	medium-sized cup	6	lǜchá 绿茶	green tea
3	jiā nǎi 加奶	with milk	7	kāfēidòu 咖啡豆	coffee bean
4	bīngshā 冰沙	freeze	8	hēikāfēi 黑咖啡	black coffee

文化导航
Cultural Navigation

中国是茶的故乡，但大城市里咖啡馆的数量远远高于茶馆的数量。中国即将超过德国和日本，成为仅次于美国的世界第二大咖啡消费国。尽管如此，很多中国人依然保持每天喝茶的习惯，还有相当一部分人非常讲究喝茶的方式，比如说什么季节喝什么茶，不同的茶如何泡，用什么茶具等。中国茶根据产地和烘制方法分为几大类：绿茶、乌龙、花茶、红茶和砖茶。

China is the homeland of tea and a lot of people drink tea daily. There are different kinds of tea due to different locations and different techniques involved in the making of tea. They are green tea, Wulong tea, scented tea (jasmine tea), black tea and compressed tea. Some people are particular in drinking tea: the time when a certain kind of tea should be drunk, the way of brewing, and the drinking utensils such as tea pots. However, over the past decades, people in China have developed the love in coffee and there are a lot of cafés in big cities. In fact, China is poised to overtake Germany and Japan to become the second largest coffee consumer after the United States.

核心句
Key Sentence

Nà jiā jiǔbā de dēngguāng búcuò.
那家酒吧的灯光不错。
The lighting of the bar is nice.

句型与替换
Substitution

yuèduì 乐队 band	shèjì zhuānghuáng 设计装潢 decoration
yīnxiǎng 音响 sound system	wǔchí 舞池 dancing floor

扩展／Extension

Nà jiā jiǔbā yǒudiǎnr chǎo.
1. 那家酒吧有点儿吵。

That bar is a bit too loud.

Zhè jiā jiǔbā de yīnyuè róuhé,
2. 这家酒吧的音乐柔和，
wǔchí yě dà.
舞池也大。

The music of the bar is soft and its dancing floor is spacious.

Nà jiā jiǔbā tiáo de jiǔ kǒugǎn
3. 那家酒吧调的酒口感
hěn hǎo.
很好。

The drinks mixed at the bar taste great.

Wǒ yàole yì bēi cǎoméi kǒuwèi
4. 我要了一杯草莓口味
de Mǎgélìtǎ.
的玛格丽塔。

I ordered a margarita with strawberry flavor.

甲: Tīngshuō Hòuhǎi de jiǔbā búcuò.
听说后海的酒吧不错。

I hear that the bars at Houhai are very good.

乙: Shì búcuò, wǒ qùguo liǎng jiā.
是不错，我去过两家。

They are good indeed. I've been to two of them.

甲: Zěnmeyàng?
怎么样？

How are they?

乙: Dì-yī jiā yǒudiǎnr chǎo, dàn dēngguāng, shèjì zhuānghuáng
第一家有点儿吵，但灯光、设计装潢
búcuò, hěn yǒu qíngdiào.
不错，很有情调。

The first one is a bit too loud but its lighting and decorations are
very tasteful.

甲: Dì-èr jiā ne?
第二家呢？

How about the second one?

乙: Dì-èr jiā de yīnyuè róuhé duō le, wǔchí yě dà. Liǎng jiā tiáo
第二家的音乐柔和多了，舞池也大。两家调
de jiǔ dōu búcuò.
的酒都不错。

The music of the second one is much softer and its dancing
floor is spacious. Both bars make very good drinks.

甲: Kànlái nǐ zài nàr tǐng kāixīn de.
看来你在那儿挺开心的。

Sounds that you had a very good time there.

乙: Biān hējiǔ, biān tīng yīnyuè, biān liáotiān, hěn fàngsōng.
边喝酒、边听音乐、边聊天，很放松。

Yes, we were drinking, listening to music, and chatting,
very relaxed.

1	chǎo 吵	noisy; loud	6	fàngsōng 放松	relaxed
2	róuhé 柔和	soft; mild	7	Báilándì 白兰地 (酒名)	brandy
3	qíngdiào 情调	taste	8	píjiǔ 啤酒	beer
4	tiáo jiǔ 调酒	to stir a drink	9	Mǎtíní 马提尼 (酒名)	martini
5	kāixīn 开心	happy	10	Mǎgélìtǎ 玛格丽塔 (酒名)	margarita

文化导航
Cultural Navigation

　　自改革开放以来，酒吧文化进入了中国，且发展迅速。目前北京有400余家酒吧，酒吧文化已成为时尚文化的标志，到酒吧坐坐也成为到北京的旅游项目之一。北京有几个地方以酒吧闻名。首屈一指的要数三里屯酒吧一条街，它坐落在北京市区的东部，与众多外国使馆为邻，包括加拿大、澳大利亚、法国、比利时以及德国使馆。另一个著名的酒吧集中地是后海，坐落在湖边，胡同密集，那里还有很多珠宝店和礼品店。如果说三里屯酒吧一条街代表着时尚，后海则充满了中国元素。

Since the reform and opening up of China, bars have gradually entered China, and rapidly developed. At present, there are more than 400 bars in Beijing. Bar culture today has become a symbol of Chinese fashion, and going to the bar is one of the must things to do in Beijing. There are several places that are famous for good bars. One is Sanlitun Bar Street which is located in the east part of Beijing, adjacent to many foreign embassies including Canada Embassy, Australia Embassy, France Embassy, Belgium Embassy and Germany Embassy. Another one is Houhai Bar Street on a beautiful lake. If Sanlitun Bar Street is the trendy route to go, Houhai Bar Street is full of Chinese culture. Houhai Bar Street is with intensive alleys and different customs. There are a variety of jewelry stores and gift shops, enough to make tourists spend time here.

核心句 Key Sentence

Nǐ néng bāng wǒmen pāi zhāng zhàopiàn ma?
你能 帮我们拍张 照片 吗?
Can you help to take a picture of us?

句型与替换 Substitution

bāng wǒmen kànkan zhàoxiàngjī yǒu
帮我们看看照相机有
shénme wèntí
什么问题
take a look at the camera of us

wǎng nàbiān nuónuo
往那边挪挪
move a bit for us

扩 展/Extension

Zhèr de jǐngsè zhēn měi!
1. **这儿的景色 真 美!**　　What beautiful scenery!

Wǒmen qù lǐpǐn shāngdiàn mǎi
2. **我们去礼品 商 店 买**　　Let's go to the gift shop to buy
diǎn dōngxi.
点 东西。　　something.

Wǒmen liǎng gè xiǎoshí yǐhòu
3. **我们 两 个小时以后**　　Please come back here in two hours.
zài zhèr jíhé.
在这儿集合。

Wǒmen zài zhèr xiūxi
4. **我们在这儿休息**　　Shall we take a rest here?
yíhuìr, hǎo ma?
一会儿,好吗?

甲： Wáng Xīn, wǒmen zhōngyú pádào dǐng le.
王 新，我们 终于 爬到 顶 了。
Wang Xin, we finally climbed to the top.

乙： Zhèr de jǐngsè zhēn měi!
这儿的景色真 美!
Wow, what beautiful scenery!

甲： Wǒmen yìqǐ zhào zhāng xiàng ba.
我们一起照 张 相 吧。
Let's take a picture together.

乙： Hǎo, wǒmen zhǎo gè rén bāngmáng.
好，我们 找个人帮忙。
Yes, let's ask someone for help.

甲： Láojià, nín néng bāng wǒmen zhào zhāng xiàng ma?
劳驾，您能 帮 我们 照 张 相 吗?
Excuse me, can you help to take a picture of us?

丙： Méi wèntí. Hǎo ... zhàohǎo le.
没 问题。好……照好了。
Sure. Ready...done.

甲/乙： Xièxie nín.
谢谢您。
Thank you very much.

相关词语／Related Words

1	zhōngyú 终于	finally	5	měi 美	beautiful
2	pá 爬	to climb	6	yìqǐ 一起	together
3	dǐng 顶	top	7	zhàoxiàng 照 相	to take pictures
4	jǐngsè 景色	scene			

文化导航
Cultural Navigation

　　长城是中国古代的军事防御建筑。秦始皇统一中国后，将已有的长城修整，连为一体，以防御北方游牧民族的入侵。现存长城总长约8851千米，因此，在中文里，长城被称为"万里长城"。长城是人类历史上伟大的工程。到北京，一定要去爬长城。

The Great Wall was the military defense construction in ancient China. After the unification of China, Qin Shi Huang, the first emperor of China during the Qin Dynasty (221 BC-206 BC), reconstructed the Great Wall to protect his country from the nomadic groups in the north. The existent Great Wall is about 8851 km in length. Therefore in Chinese, the wall is called "万里长城". The Great Wall is a marvelous project in history. It is a must thing to do to climb the Great Wall when you are in Beijing.

65 看电影 | Seeing a Movie

核心句 Key Sentence

Wǒ zuótiān kànle yí bù xīn diànyǐng.
我昨天看了一部新电影。
I went to see a new movie yesterday.

句型与替换 Substitution

gùshìpiàn
故事片
feature movie

Hǎoláiwù dàpiàn
好莱坞大片
Hollywood big picture

sānwéi dònghuàpiàn
三维动画片
3D cartoon picture

gōngfupiàn
功夫片
martial arts movie

jìlùpiàn
纪录片
documentary

扩展/Extension

1. Zuótiān wǎnshang wǒ kàn diànyǐng qù le.
   昨天晚上我看电影去了。 I went to see a movie last night.

2. Yǎnyuán yǎn de hěn hǎo.
   演员演得很好。 The actors act very well.

3. Nà bù diànyǐng píngjià búcuò.
   那部电影评价不错。 The review on that movie is pretty good.

4. Wǎnchǎng piàojià tài guì.
   晚场票价太贵。 Price for the evening show is too expensive.

甲：
Wǒ zuótiān wǎnshang kànle yí bù xīn diànyǐng.
我 昨天 晚 上 看了 一部 新 电影。
I went to see a new movie last night.

乙：
Zěnmeyàng?
怎么样?
How is it?

甲：
Gùshi tèbié gǎnrén, yě hěn zhēnshí.
故事 特别 感人, 也 很 真实。
The story is very touching and true to life.

乙：
Yǎnyuán zěnmeyàng?
演员 怎么样?
How about the actors?

甲：
Dōu búcuò, tèbié shì nǚzhǔjué, yǎnjì hěn chūsè.
都 不错, 特别 是 女主角, 演技 很 出色。
All are good, especially the leading actress who has
outstanding acting skills.

乙：
Xiànzài hái yǒu shénme xīn diànyǐng?
现在 还 有 什么 新 电影?
Are there any other new movies?

甲：
Míngtiān yǒu yí bù Měiguó sānwéi dònghuàpiàn shàngyìng, yǐngpíng
明天 有 一部 美国 三维 动画片 上映, 影评
búcuò.
不错。
Tomorrow there will be an American 3D cartoon movie. Its
reviews are good.

乙：
Nà wǒmen míngtiān zhōngwǔ yìqǐ qù, wǎnchǎng piàojià tài guì.
那 我们 明天 中 午一起去, 晚场 票价 太贵。
Then let's go to see it at noon tomorrow. Price for the
evening show is too expensive.

1	diànyǐng 电影	movie	7	yǎnjì 演技	acting skill
2	gùshi 故事	story; plot	8	chūsè 出色	outstanding
3	gǎnrén 感人	touching; moving	9	yǐngpíng 影评	movie review
4	zhēnshí 真实	true to life	10	piàojià 票价	ticket price
5	yǎnyuán 演员	actor	11	wǎnchǎng 晚场	evening show
6	zhǔjué 主角	leading role	12	wǔchǎng 午场	noon show

文化导航
Cultural Navigation

　　中国电影大致分为四类：第一类是主旋律电影，这类电影一般由政府出资，主题是中国政治人物和重要历史事件；第二类是文艺片，表现的是当代中国普通人民的生活和思想；第三类是娱乐商业片，主要是贺岁喜剧片和武打功夫片；第四类是新锐电影，由年轻导演执导，表现了思想上的叛逆和艺术上的创新。

　　In China today, movies fall into four categories: 1. mainstream movies which are generally funded by the government and depict political figures and historic events of the country; 2. artistic movies which portray the life and thoughts of ordinary people in contemporary China; 3. entertainment and commercial movies which consist mainly of New Year celebration comedies and martial arts movies; 4. new generation movies directed by young directors emphasizing a rebellious and avant-garde style.

核心句
Key Sentence

Xīnwén jiémù jiùyào kāishǐ le.
新闻节目 就要开始了。

It is about the time for news.

句型与替换
Substitution

guójì xīnwén
国际新闻
international news

zúqiú bǐsài
足球比赛
football games

fǎngtán jiémù
访谈节目
talk show

zōngyì jiémù
综艺节目
variety show

tiānqì yùbào
天气预报
weather forecast

扩 展/Extension

Xiànzài shì guójì xīnwén jiémù.
1. 现在 是 国际新闻节目。

It is now the international news program.

Zhège fǎngtán jiémù méi yìsi.
2. 这个 访谈节目没意思。

The talk show is not interesting.

Zhè shì dìfāngtái běndì xīnwén
3. 这 是 地方台本地新闻
jiémù.
节目。

It is a local news program on the local channel.

Wǒmen huàn yí gè píndào.
4. 我们 换 一个频道。

Let's change to another channel.

甲： Wáng Qiáng, kuài lái, guójì xīnwén jiémù jiùyào kāishǐ le.
王强，快来，国际新闻节目就要开始了。

Wang Qiang, come here. It is about the time for the international news.

乙： Lái le. Zěnme huí shì? Túxiàng bù qīngchu.
来了。怎么回事？图像不清楚。

I am coming. How come? The image is not clear.

甲： Nà huàn yí gè píndào.
那换一个频道。

Let's change to another channel.

乙： Zhè shì liù píndào, kě zhège fǎngtán jiémù méi yìsi.
这是六频道，可这个访谈节目没意思。

This is Channel Six. But this talk show is not good.

甲： Nà wǒmen kàn dìfāngtái, xiànzài shì běndì xīnwén jiémù.
那我们看地方台，现在是本地新闻节目。

We can watch the local news on the local channel now.

乙： Hǎo. Wǒmen kànwán xīnwén, jiù kàn zúqiú bǐsài zěnmeyàng?
好。我们看完新闻，就看足球比赛怎么样？

Good. After the news, can we watch the football game?

甲： Xíng, suíbiàn.
行，随便。

Fine, as you like.

相关词语/Related Words

1	guójì 国际	international	3	jiémù 节目	program
2	xīnwén 新闻	news	4	túxiàng 图像	image

5	qīngchu 清楚	clear	8	běndì xīnwén 本地新闻	local news
6	píndào 频道	channel	9	suíbiàn 随便	as you like
7	dìfāngtái 地方台	local station			

文化导航
Cultural Navigation

中国所有的电视台和其他媒体机构都属于各级政府，分为三层：中央、省（直辖市）级和地方。中央一级主要媒体有：中央电视台、人民日报、新华社、中央人民广播电台、中国国际广播电台、中国新闻社、光明日报和经济日报。收视率最高的电视台当属中央电视台，一些省级地方台的影响也很大，比如湖南卫视、江苏卫视等。

In China, all television stations and media organizations are government-owned. There are three levels sponsored by different levels of government agencies: central, provincial (municipal) and local. At the central government level, the following is a list of media sources: China Central Television (CCTV), People's Daily, Xinhua News Agency, China National Radio, China Radio International, China News Agency, Guangming Daily, and Economic Daily. The most viewed station is CCTV but some provincial stations are also highly rated such as Hunan TV and Jiangsu TV.

核心句
Key Sentence

Wǒ zuótiān qù kàn shèyǐngzhǎn le.
我昨天去看摄影展了。
I went to a photo exhibition yesterday.

句型与替换
Substitution

huàzhǎn
画展
painting exhibition

shūzhǎn
书展
book show

huāzhǎn
花展
flower show

chēzhǎn
车展
auto show

扩展/Extension

Zhǎnlǎn zěnmeyàng?
1. 展览 怎么样?
How is the exhibition?

Yǒu shénme zuòpǐn ràng nǐ
yìnxiàng shēnkè?
2. 有 什么 作品 让 你
印象 深刻?
Which works impressed you most?

Shèyǐngshī de jìqiǎo zěnmeyàng?
3. 摄影师的技巧怎么样?
How is his technique as a photographer?

Zhǎnlǎn miǎnfèi.
4. 展览 免费。
The exhibition is free.

甲: Zuótiān wǒ qù kànle yí gè shèyǐngzhǎn.
昨天我去看了一个摄影展。

I went to a photography exhibition yesterday.

乙: Zěnmeyàng?
怎么样?

How is it?

甲: Búcuò, shì yí gè niánqīng yìshùjiā de zuòpǐn.
不错,是一个年轻艺术家的作品。

It is pretty good. It is for a young artist's works.

乙: Néng jùtǐ shuōshuo ma?
能具体说说吗?

Can you describe it?

甲: Tā de zuòpǐn dàbùfen shì hēibáizhào, fǎnyìng de shì pǔtōngrén
他的作品大部分是黑白照,反映的是普通人
de shēnghuó.
的生活。

Most of his works are black and white focusing on ordinary people.

乙: Jìqiǎo zěnmeyàng?
技巧怎么样?

How about his techniques?

甲: Qǔjǐng, jiǎodù dōu búcuò, guāngxiàn yùnyòng hái kěyǐ gèng
取景、角度都不错,光线运用还可以更
hǎoxiē.
好些。

His scene selection and angles are good but he could improve his use of lighting.

乙: Kànlái nǐ duì shèyǐng hěn zàiháng.
看来你对摄影很在行。

You are quite an expert in photography.

相关词语/Related Words

1	yìshùjiā 艺术家	artist		7	gòusī 构思	design
2	yìnxiàng 印象	impression		8	qǔjǐng 取景	to take image
3	shēnkè 深刻	deep		9	jiǎodù 角度	angle
4	zuòpǐn 作品	works		10	guāngxiàn 光线	lighting
5	hēibái 黑白	black and white		11	zàiháng 在行	to be good at
6	jìqiǎo 技巧	technique				

文化导航
Cultural Navigation

过去，中国的大多数博物馆是不能免费进入的，门票从5元到30元人民币不等。从2011年底开始，中央级和省级艺术博物馆、公共图书馆、公共文化中心及这些场馆的基本服务免费对公众开放，丰富了民众的业余文化生活。

In the past, most public art museums in China charged fees ranging from 5 yuan to 30 yuan a person. China has opened all national and provincial art museums and all public libraries or public cultural centers, as well as the basic services in these places, to the public for free since the end of 2011. This has enriched the life of the Chinese.

68 看京剧 | Watching Peking Opera

核心句
Key
Sentence

Wǒ yuè lái yuè xǐhuan Zhōngguó chuántǒng yìshù.
我越来越喜欢中国 传统艺术。
I like traditional Chinese arts more and more.

句型
与替换
Substitution

jīngjù
京剧
Peking Opera

zájì
杂技
acrobatics

gōngfu
功夫
martial arts

扩 展／Extension

Zhè wèi nányǎnyuán yǎn shénme juésè?
1. 这位男演员演什么角色？   What role does the actor play?

Jīngjù hěn hǎotīng.
2. 京剧 很 好听。   The music of Peking Opera is very beautiful.

Wǒ tīng bù dǒng jīngjù.
3. 我 听不懂京剧。   I cannot understand Peking Opera.

Píngmù shang yǒu Yīngwén fānyì.
4. 屏幕 上 有 英文翻译。   There are English subtitles on the screen.

甲: Zhèxiē yǎnyuán zhuāngbàn zěnme zhème bù yíyàng?
这些 演员 装扮 怎么 这么 不一样?

Why do these actors have such different costumes and make-ups?

乙: Jīngjù fēn bù tóng lèi de juésè, cóng bù tóng de zhuāngbàn jiù kěyǐ
京剧 分不同类的角色, 从不同的 装扮 就可以
zhīdào tāmen yǎn shénme juésè.
知道他们演什么角色。

There are different categories of roles in Peking Opera. From costumes and make-ups, we can tell what role categories they belong to.

甲: Nàge nǚyǎnyuán chuān de xìfú zhēn hǎokàn.
那个女演员 穿 的戏服真 好看。

That actress wears such a beautiful costume.

乙: Tā shì jīntiān yì chū xì li de nǚzhǔjué.
她是今天一出戏里的女主角。

She is the leading actress in one of today's pieces.

甲: Kāishǐ le, wǒmen kuài jìnqu. Nǐ tīng yīnyuè duō hǎotīng.
开始了, 我们 快进去。 你听 音乐多 好听。

It's started already. Let's go in. Listen, what beautiful music it is!

乙: Kěshì wǒ tīng bù dǒng a.
可是我听不懂啊。

But I don't understand it.

甲: Píngmù shang bú shì yǒu Yīngwén fānyì ma?
屏幕 上 不是有 英文翻译吗?

There are English subtitles on the screen, aren't there?

相关词语/Related Words

	zhuāngbàn				juésè	
1	装扮	way to dress		3	角色	role
	xìfú				yīnyuè	
2	戏服	costume		4	音乐	music

5	<ruby>台<rt>tái</rt></ruby>	stage	7	<ruby>翻译<rt>fānyì</rt></ruby>	translation
6	<ruby>屏幕<rt>píngmù</rt></ruby>	screen			

文化导航
Cultural Navigation

京剧是中国传统戏曲形式中最著名的一种。它开始于18世纪，到19世纪发展完善，集唱、舞、打、乐为一身，是中国传统文化的瑰宝。中国主要京剧团体在北方集中于北京和天津，南方在上海。京剧的角色分生、旦、净、丑四种："生"是男性主角，"旦"是女性角色，"净"是脸上涂油彩的男性角色，"丑"是男性丑角。每一种再分为若干类。例如，旦角可分为若干类，包括老旦、武旦、刀马旦、青衣、花旦等。

Peking Opera is a form of traditional Chinese theaters which combines music, vocal performance, mime, dance and acrobatics. It arose in the late 18th century and became fully developed and recognized by the mid-19th century. It is regarded as one of the cultural treasures of China. Major performance troupes are based in Beijing and Tianjin in the north, and Shanghai in the south. Peking Opera features four main types of performers: *Sheng* (the main male roles), *Dan* (the female roles), *Jing* (the painted face male roles) and *Chou* (the male clown roles). Each type has subtypes. Take *Dan* as an example. *Dan* roles are divided into several subtypes, including *laodan*, *wudan*, *daomadan*, *qingyi* and *huadan*.

69 开博 | Blogging

Wǒ kāi bókè le.
我开博客了。
I have registered to start a blog.

句型与替换
Substitution

wēibó
微博
Microblog (twitter or weibo)

liǎnshū
脸书
facebook

扩展/Extension

Nǐ dǎsuàn zài bókè xiě shénme?
1. 你打算在博客写什么？ What do you plan to write on your blog?

Shénmeyàng de rén huì dú nǐ de bókè ne?
2. 什么样的人会读你的博客呢？ Who will read your blog?

Wǎngluò bù ānquán, nǐ de xìnxī huì bàolù chuqu.
3. 网络不安全，你的信息会暴露出去。 The Internet is not secure and your information may be exposed.

Wǒ huì jīngcháng qù kàn nǐ bókè.
4. 我会经常去看你博客。 I will visit your blog often.

甲: Wǒ zuótiān zhùcè kāi bókè le.
我昨天注册开博客了。
I registered to start a blog yesterday.

乙: Shì ma? Nǐ dǎsuàn xiě xiē shénme ne?
是吗? 你打算写些什么 呢?
Really? What do you plan to write?

甲: Xiě xiē wǒ zài Zhōngguó de jīnglì, xué Zhōngwén de tǐhuì.
写些我在中国的经历, 学中文的体会。
Write something about my experience in China and
Chinese learning.

乙: Wǎngluò bìng bù ānquán, nǐ de xìnxī huì bàolù chuqu.
网络 并不安全, 你的信息会暴露出去。
The Internet is not secure and your information may be
exposed.

甲: Wǒ huì xiǎoxīn de.
我会小心的。
I will be very careful.

乙: Xiě bókè yě tǐng huā shíjiān de.
写博客也挺花时间的。
It is time consuming to keep the blog updated.

甲: Méi cuò. Dàn wǒ xǐhuan xiě dōngxi.
没错。但我喜欢写东西。
You are right. But I like writing.

乙: Nà wǒ yǐhòu huì jīngcháng qù kàn nǐ de bókè de.
那我以后会经常去看你的博客的。
I will visit your blog often.

1	zhùcè 注册	to register	6	wǎngluò 网络	the Internet
2	bókè 博客	blog	7	ānquán 安全	secure
3	kāi bó 开博	to start a blog	8	xìnxī 信息	information
4	jīnglì 经历	experience	9	bàolù 暴露	to expose
5	tǐhuì 体会	to experience	10	xiǎoxīn 小心	careful

文化导航
Cultural Navigation

中国是世界上人口最多的国家，也拥有人数众多的互联网用户。这些用户大都集中在城市里，多数在家就可以上网。中国城市的大街小巷里遍布着很多网吧，可以让人们上网浏览，打网络游戏。网吧的价钱不贵，平均每小时三元钱。为了吸引消费者，网吧还出售饮料、食物，因此成了城市年轻人休闲的重要场所。

As the most populous country in the world, China has a large number of Internet users. Though many urban residents have Internet access at home, many young people prefer to go to the Internet café, a kind of commercial facility, to surf the Internet and play online games at about ¥3 per hour. Snacks and beverages can also be bought there. Such a café can be easily found in commercial areas and residential areas and has become a popular place for young people to spend their leisure time.

70 在线聊天 | Online Chatting

核心句
Key Sentence

Hǎojiǔ bú zài wǎngshang lòumiàn le.
好久不在网上露面了。
I haven't seen you online recently.

句型与替换
Substitution

xiànshang
线上
online; on the Internet

lùntán
论坛
forum

liáotiānshì
聊天室
chatting room

扩 展/Extension

Zuìjìn fā tiězǐ le ma?
1. 最近发帖子了吗？

Did you post anything new on the forum recently?

Gēntiě duō bù duō?
2. 跟帖多不多？

Are there a lot of follow-up posts?

Shàng dǎodú le ma?
3. 上导读了吗？

Was it selected into the recommendation section?

Qù wǎngbā shàngwǎng.
4. 去网吧上网。

Go to the Internet café to surf the net.

对话实例/Dialogue

甲：
Nǐ hǎo! Hǎojiǔ bú zài wǎngshang lòumiàn le, qù nǎ le?
你好！好久不在 网 上 露面了，去哪了？
Hello! I haven't seen you online for a while. Where were you?

乙：
Chūchāi le. Nǐ zěnmeyàng? Zài yīnyuè lùntán shang fā xīn tiězi le ma?
出差了。你怎么样？在音乐论坛 上 发新帖子了吗？
I went on a business trip. How are you? Did you post anything new on the Music Forum?

甲：
Qián jǐ tiān fāle yí gè.
前几天发了一个。
I posted one a few days ago.

乙：
Nǎ fāngmiàn de?
哪方面 的？
About what?

甲：
Mínyuè.
民乐。
Folk music.

乙：
Gēntiě duō bù duō?
跟帖 多不多？
Are there a lot of follow-up posts?

甲：
Èrshí jǐ gè ba, hái yǒu jǐ gè dàniú.
二十几个吧，还有几个大牛。
About twenty posts including a few well-known IDs.

乙：
Wǒ yíhuìr qù kànkan.
我一会儿去看看。
I will go and take a look.

1	yīnyuè lùntán 音乐论坛	music forum	6	xiàxiàn 下线	to log off; to go offline
2	shàng tiězi 上 帖子	to post	7	dēnglù 登录	to log in; to sign in
3	gēntiě 跟帖	follow-up post	8	tuìchū 退出	to log out; to sign out
4	dǎodú 导读	recommendation section	9	liáotiān 聊天	to chat
5	shàngwǎng 上 网	to go online; to surf the Internet	10	guānjī 关机	to turn off / shut down a machine

文化导航
Cultural Navigation

　　上班时间使用公司的电脑在网上聊天、玩网络游戏甚至购物，似乎是很多人或多或少会做的事。由于公司性质、企业文化和管理制度的不同，每个公司对此的政策和规定也会不一样。了解并遵守相关规定是很必要的。这不但可以避免误解和不愉快的情形，也是你对企业文化和管理的尊重。

　　It seems to have become a daily routine for many employees to use company computers to chat online, play video games, or even do online shopping while at work. Due to the difference in company nature, corporate culture and management systems, each company has different policies and regulations about these kinds of online activities. It is necessary to get to know and observe these related rules. It may not only save you from misunderstandings and unpleasant situations, but also show your respect for the corporate culture and management.

[出行]
Traveling

核心句 Key Sentence

Jiàqī wǒ xiǎng qù pάshān.
假期我想去爬山。
I want to climb the mountains during the vacation.

句型与替换 Substitution

hǎibiān shài tàiyáng
海边晒太阳
bathe in the sun on the beach

cǎoyuán qímǎ
草原骑马
ride a horse on the grassland

sīchóu zhī lù tànxiǎn
丝绸之路探险
explore along the Silk Road

扩展 / Extension

Jiàqī nǐ dǎsuàn qù nǎr?
1. 假期你打算去哪儿?

Where do you plan to go during the vacation?

Nǐ zìjǐ qù háishi gēn lǚyóu-tuán qù?
2. 你自己去还是跟旅游团去?

Do you plan to go yourself or go with the tour group?

Wǒ zài wǎngshang dìng de lǚguǎn.
3. 我在网上订的旅馆。

I booked the hotel online.

Gēn lǚyóutuán qù tài bú zìyóu.
4. 跟旅游团去太不自由。

There are a lot of restrictions with
the tour group.

对话实例/Dialogue

Jiàqī   nǐ dǎsuàn qù nǎr?
甲：假期你打算去哪儿？

Where do you plan to go during the vacation?

Wǒ xiǎng qù hǎibiān wán jǐ tiān,   yóuyóuyǒng, shàishai tàiyáng.
乙：我想去海边玩几天，游游泳，晒晒太阳。

I plan to go to the beach, swimming and bathing in the sun.

Zìjǐ   qù háishi gēn lǚyóutuán qù?
甲：自己去还是跟旅游团去？

Do you go alone or with a tour group?

Hé péngyou yìqǐ   qù.
乙：和朋友一起去。

I will go with my friends.

Dìng lǚguǎn le ma?
甲：订旅馆了吗？

Did you book the hotel?

Wǎngshang dìng de.   Nǐ yǒu shénme dǎsuàn?
乙：网上订的。你有什么打算？

I did online. What plan do you have?

Wǒ xiǎng zìjǐ   qù páshān.
甲：我想自己去爬山。

I want to climb the mountains myself.

Zhēn de?
乙：真的？

Really?

1	yóuyǒng 游泳	to swim	4	dìng lǚguǎn 订旅馆	to book the hotel
2	shài tàiyáng 晒太阳	to bathe in the sun	5	páshān 爬山	to climb the mountains
3	lǚyóutuán 旅游团	tour group			

文化导航
Cultural Navigation

　　中国国土面积仅次于俄国和加拿大，其九百六十万平方公里的国土占世界总面积的十五分之一。随着人们生活水平的提高，越来越多的中国人有钱出去旅游度假了，因此旅游业已成为中国发展最快的产业之一。中国最佳旅游季节是三月到十一月之间，这段时间气候温和，适合出游。很多企业也会组织职工出去度假旅游。

　　China is the third largest country in the world in size following Russia and Canada, with an area of 9.6 million square kilometers. It is one-fifteenth of the world's land mass. With a rise in living standard, more and more Chinese can afford to have a vacation out of town and thus tourism has become one of the fast developing industries in China. The best travel season in China is between March and November when the weather is mild. Many companies organize tours for employees in appreciation of their hard work.

核心句
Key Sentence

Huānyíng cānjiā Guìlín wǔ rì yóu.
欢迎参加桂林五日游。
Welcome to join the 5-day tour group to Guilin.

句型与替换
Substitution

shuāngfēi tuán
双飞团
double-flight tour

shuāngwò tuán
双卧团
double sleeper-train tour

bànyuè yóu
半月游
a half-month tour group

扩展/Extension

Qù Guìlín de tuán féng zhōuwǔ chūfā.
1. 去桂林的团逢周五出发。

The tour group to Guilin departs every Friday.

Sìqiān wǔbǎi kuài yí wèi.
2. 四千五百块一位。

¥4,500 for each tourist.

Chúle lǚguǎn hái bāo shénme?
3. 除了旅馆还包什么?

What else should be covered besides lodging?

Hái bāo měi rì zǎocān, ménpiào,
dǎoyóu fèiyong.
4. 还包每日早餐、门票、导游费用。

It covers breakfast, entrance, and tour guide.

甲： Dàtóng lǚxíngshè, nín yǒu qù Guìlín de tuán ma?
大同旅行社，您有去桂林的团吗？

Hello, Datong Travel Agency, do you have a tour group to Guilin?

乙： Yǒu, féng zhōuwǔ chūfā.
有，逢周五出发。

Yes, we do. We depart every Friday.

甲： Duōshao tiān?
多少天？

How many days for a trip?

乙： Kàn nín cānjiā nǎ zhǒng tuán le? Wǒmen yǒu wǔ rì yóu, shuāngfēituán
看您参加哪种团了？我们有五日游、双飞团
hé shuāngwòtuán.
和双卧团。

It depends on which package you will choose. We have a 5-day tour, double-flight and double-sleeper groups.

甲： Wǔ rì yóu duōshao qián?
五日游多少钱？

How much is it for a 5-day tour package?

乙： Sìqiān wǔbǎi kuài yí wèi, sān xīngjí lǚguǎn. Sì xīngjí zài jiā
四千五百块一位，三星级旅馆。四星级再加
wǔbǎi.
五百。

¥4,500 each person with 3-star hotel. If you want to stay in a 4-star hotel, it is ¥500 extra.

甲： Chúle lǚguǎn hái bāo shénme?
除了旅馆还包什么？

What else should it cover besides lodging?

乙： Hái bāo měi rì zǎocān, ménpiào, dǎoyóu fèiyong.
还包每日早餐、门票、导游费用。

It covers breakfast, entrance and tour guide.

1	féng 逢	to come upon	6	bāo 包	to include
2	chūfā 出发	to depart	7	ménpiào 门票	entrance ticket
3	sān xīngjí 三星级	3-star	8	dǎoyóu 导游	tour guide
4	zǎocān 早餐	breakfast	9	fèiyong 费用	expense; cost
5	jiā 加	to add; in addition to			

文化导航
Cultural Navigation

中国旅游热点城市有北京、西安、上海等。在北京，可以爬长城、参观紫禁城；到西安可以参观世界八大奇迹之一的兵马俑；而上海是中国经济最发达的城市。其他受欢迎的旅游路线还有丝绸之路、桂林、长江等。各旅行社为了适应不同层次旅游者的需要，还推出不同的旅游套餐项目，如豪华游、简约游、汽车团、飞机团、一日游等。

The top choices for tourists in China include Beijing, the capital of the country where you can climb the Great Wall and walk in the Forbidden City; Xi'an where you can see the Terracotta Warriors and Horses, one of the eight world wonders; and Shanghai, the largest and most developed city in China. In addition, you can participate in the Silk Road Adventure, package tours to Guilin and cruise tours along the Yangtze River. To accommodate customers on different budgets, travel agencies promote different tour packages including luxury tours, budget tours, bus tours, airplane tours and daily tours, etc.

核心句
Key Sentence

Wǒ dìng yì zhāng fēi Shēnzhèn de tóuděngcāng jīpiào.

我订一张飞深圳的头等舱机票。

I want to book a first-class airplane ticket to Shenzhen.

句型与替换
Substitution

gōngwùcāng
公务舱
business class

jīngjìcāng
经济舱
economy class

zhékòupiào
折扣票
discount ticket

értóngpiào
儿童票
children's ticket

扩 展/Extension

Nín yào fēi nǎr?
1. 您要飞哪儿？
Where do you plan to go by plane?

Dānchéng háishi wǎngfǎn?
2. 单程还是往返？
One way or round trip?

Wǒ gěi nín miǎnfèi shēngjí dào yī-
3. 我给您免费升级到一
děngcāng.
等舱。
I will upgrade you to the first-class for free.

Kěyǐ miǎnfèi tuōyùn jǐ jiàn
4. 可以免费托运几件
xíngli?
行李？
How many pieces of luggage can be consigned for free?

甲: Wǒ xiǎng dìng yì zhāng míngtiān fēi Shēnzhèn de gōngwùcāng jīpiào.
我 想 订一 张 明天 飞 深 圳 的 公务舱 机票。

I want to book a business-class airplane ticket to Shenzhen tomorrow.

乙: Dānchéng háishi wǎngfǎn?
单 程 还是 往返?

One way or round trip?

甲: Dàngtiān wǎngfǎn.
当 天 往返。

Same day round trip.

乙: Zǎochen gōngwùcāng màiméi le, jīngjìcāng xíng ma?
早 晨 公务舱 卖没 了, 经济舱 行 吗?

But business-class tomorrow morning is sold out. How about the economy?

甲: Jīngjìcāng jiù jīngjìcāng ba.
经济舱 就 经济舱 吧。

That is fine.

乙: Nín shì wǒmen de lǎohuìyuán le, huíchéng de jīpiào wǒ gěi nín miǎnfèi
您是 我们 的 老会员 了, 回程 的 机票 我给 您 免费
shēngjí dào yīděngcāng.
升级 到 一等舱。

You are our veteran member. I will upgrade you to first-class for free on your return plane.

甲: Xièxie. Kěyǐ miǎnfèi tuōyùn jǐ jiàn xíngli?
谢谢。 可以 免费 托运 几 件 行李?

Thank you. How many pieces of luggage can I consign for free?

乙: Yí jiàn. Qǐng gěi wǒ nín de xìngmíng hé shēnfènzhèng hàomǎ, wǒ
一件。 请 给我 您 的 姓名 和 身份证 号码, 我
xiànzài jiù dìngpiào.
现在 就 订票。

One piece. Please give me your name and identification card number and I will book it for you.

相关词语/Related Words

1	dìngpiào 订票	to book a ticket	7	jīpiào 机票	airplane ticket
2	dānchéng 单程	one way	8	miǎnfèi 免费	free of charge
3	wǎngfǎn 往返	round trip	9	shēngjí 升级	to upgrade
4	dàngtiān 当天	same day	10	tuōyùn 托运	to consign
5	huìyuán 会员	member	11	xíngli 行李	luggage
6	huíchéng 回程	return trip	12	shēnfènzhèng 身份证	identification card

文化导航
Cultural Navigation

　　在中国买飞机票、火车票还是很方便的。一般来说，三星级以上的旅馆都有火车票、飞机票代售点，你也可以到航空公司或火车站的售票处以及代售处买票。很多代售处还可以免费送票，拿到票后再用现金或信用卡付钱。

　　It is rather convenient to purchase tickets in China. In general, you can find a ticket office or counter that sells train and airplane tickets at hotels with a three-star rating or above. You can also buy tickets at travel agencies or the ticket offices of airlines and train stations. Most travel agencies can deliver your ticket to your home at no extra charge and collect the payment then, in cash or by credit card.

Wǒ yào kàochuāng de wèizi.
我要靠窗的位子。
I want a window seat.

句型
与替换
Substitution

kào guòdào de wèizi
靠过道的位子
aisle seat

liǎng zhāng liánzuò
两张连座
two seats together

扩 展/Extension

Xiànzài fēi Shànghǎi de jīpiào yǒu
1. 现在飞上海的机票有
yōuhuì.
优惠。

Airplane tickets to Shanghai are on sale.

Zhékòupiào bù kěyǐ tuìpiào.
2. 折扣票不可以退票。

Discounted tickets cannot be returned.

Máfan gěi wǒ zhǎo yí gè kào
3. 麻烦给我找一个靠
guòdào de wèizi.
过道的位子。

Please help me find an aisle seat.

Jīpiào jiàqián hán shuì.
4. 机票价钱含税。

The price includes tax.

甲：
Xiànzài fēi Shànghǎi de jīpiào yǒu yōuhuì, duì ma?
现在飞上海的机票有优惠，对吗？

You have promotion for tickets to Shanghai, am I right?

乙：
Duì, wǔ zhé. Búguò tíxǐng nín yíxià, zhékòupiào bù kěyǐ
对，五折。不过提醒您一下，折扣票不可以
tuìpiào.
退票。

Yes, we have a 50% discount. But I have to let you know

that discounted tickets cannot be returned.

甲：
Wǒ zhīdào. Qǐng gěi wǒ dìng yì zhāng 9 yuè 10 rì shàngwǔ 10 diǎn
我知道。请给我订一张9月10日上午10点
zuǒyòu de.
左右的。

I know. Please book a ticket at about 10 o'clock on the

morning of September 10th for me.

乙：
Wǒ gěi nín chácha. Hǎo, hái yǒu wèizi.
我给您查查。好，还有位子。

Let me check for you. Good, there are still seats.

甲：
Yǒu kàochuāng de wèizi ma?
有靠窗的位子吗？

Is there a window seat?

乙：
Duìbuqǐ, méiyǒu le.
对不起，没有了。

Sorry, no window seats left.

甲：
Nà jiù máfan gěi wǒ zhǎo yí gè kào guòdào de wèizi.
那就麻烦给我找一个靠过道的位子。

Then please find me an aisle seat.

乙：
Hǎo, zhǎodào yì zhāng. Jiàqián 800 kuài, hán shuì.
好，找到一张。价钱800块，含税。

Good, there is one. The price is ¥800 including tax.

1	wǔ zhé 五折	50% off	5	wèizi 位子	seat	
2	tíxǐng 提醒	to alert	6	máfan 麻烦	trouble	
3	tuìpiào 退票	to return a ticket	7	hán 含	to include	
4	chá 查	to check	8	shuì 税	tax	

文化导航
Cultural Navigation

　　中国跟其他国家一样，飞机上的舱位也分为头等舱、公务舱和经济舱。登机时要出示护照或身份证。现在中国人出行的主要交通工具还是火车，但随着人们生活水平的提高，中国人坐飞机出游的也越来越多。

　　Airplanes in China, as in many other countries in the world, have first class, business class and economy class seats. Passport, or the identification card is required at boarding. Though the railroad is still the major means of domestic travel for most Chinese, more and more people can afford to take airplanes for vacations as the result of the rise of living standards.

75 飞机延时起飞 | The Plane Is Delayed

核心句
Key
Sentence

Yóuyú tiānqì yuányīn, fēijī jiāng yánshí qǐfēi.

由于天气原因,飞机将延时起飞。

Because of the weather, the take-off will be delayed.

句型
与替换
Substitution

jīxiè gùzhàng
机械故障
mechanical problem

duìfāng jīchǎng yuányīn
对方机场原因
problems of the destined airport

jǐnjí qíngkuàng
紧急情况
emergency

扩展/Extension

Fēi wǎng Shànghǎi de gèwèi lǚkè
1. 飞往上海的各位旅客
qǐng zhùyì.
请注意。

Passengers to Shanghai, may I have your attention please?

Hángbān bù néng ànshí qǐfēi.
2. 航班不能按时起飞。

The plane cannot take off on time.

Hángbān bèi qǔxiāo le.
3. 航班被取消了。

The plane has been canceled.

Hángkōng gōngsī yīnggāi fùzé.
4. 航空公司应该负责。

The airline company should be responsible for that.

甲： Gāngcái guǎngbō shuō, wǒmen zhège hángbān bù néng ànshí qǐfēi le.
刚才 广播 说，我们 这个 航班 不能 按时 起飞 了。

The broadcast announced just now that our plane cannot depart on time.

乙： Wèi shénme?
为 什么？

Why?

甲： Shuō shì nàbiān xià bàoyǔ le.
说 是 那边 下 暴雨 了。

It's said there is a thunderstorm on the other side.

乙： Wǒmen zěnmebàn?
我们 怎么办？

What should we do then?

甲： Nàixīn děngzhe ba.
耐心 等 着 吧。

We have to wait patiently.

（广播：各位旅客请注意，本次航班将被取消。

Broadcast：Passengers to Shanghai, attention please, the plane is canceled.)

甲： Hángbān qǔxiāo le, wǒmen děi zhǎo lǚguǎn guòyè.
航班 取消 了，我们 得 找 旅馆 过夜。

Our plane is canceled. We have to find a hotel for tonight.

乙： Hángkōng gōngsī yīnggāi fùzé.
航空 公司 应该 负责。

The airline company should be responsible for that.

甲： Nà wǒmen qù wènwen.
那 我们 去 问问。

Let's go and ask.

1	yánshí 延时	to delay in time	6	hángbān 航班	plane; flight
2	qǐfēi 起飞	to take off; (plane) to depart	7	qǔxiāo 取消	to cancel
3	guǎngbō 广播	broadcast; to broadcast	8	guòyè 过夜	to stay for the night
4	lǚkè 旅客	passenger	9	fùzé 负责	responsible
5	zhùyì 注意	attention			

文化导航
Cultural Navigation

　　中国虽然面积很大，但只有一个时间，即北京时间。北京时间是整个国家的标准时间。北京属东八时区，比格林尼治时间早八个小时。在中国生活要注意时间问题，因为在上海和北京早上8点人们已经开始工作，可在新疆人们还在熟睡。所以打电话时要注意这一点。

　　Though vast in size, China only has one time, Beijing time, as the standard time throughout the country. Beijing is located at E8 time zone, 8 hours earlier than the Greenwich Mean Time (GMT). So be careful if you want to call somebody in Xinjiang at 8:00 in the morning. They may be still in sleep while people in Beijing and Shanghai have already started to work.

Jiùyào gōngyìng wǎncān le, qǐng zuòhǎo.

就要供应晚餐了，请坐好。

Dinner will be served. Please return to
your seat.

句型
与替换
Substitution

dēngjī
登机
aboard

qǐfēi
起飞
take off

jiàngluò
降落
land

qǐng zhǔnbèihǎo dēngjīpái
请准备好登机牌
have your boarding pass ready

qǐng jìhǎo ānquándài
请系好安全带
fasten your seat belt

wèishēngjiān bù néng yòng le
卫生间不能用了
The lavatory will be closed.

扩 展/Extension

1. Jiùyào gōngyìng wǎncān le, qǐng
就要 供应 晚餐 了，请
fàngxia cānzhuō.
放下 餐桌。

Dinner will be served. Please
pull down the seat table.

2. Qǐngwèn, nín yào hē diǎn shénme?
请问，您 要 喝 点 什么？

Excuse me, what do you want
for a drink?

3. 啤酒另付费，一听2块钱。
   Píjiǔ lìng fù fèi, yì tīng 2 kuài qián.
   You need pay extra for beer, two yuan for a can.

4. 您要鸡肉饭还是牛肉面？
   Nín yào jīròufàn háishi niúròumiàn?
   Do you want chicken rice or beef noodles?

对话实例/Dialogue

空中小姐：就要供应晚餐了，请坐好，放下餐桌。
Jiùyào gōngyìng wǎncān le, qǐng zuòhǎo, fàngxia cānzhuō.
Dinner will be served. Please sit properly and pull down the seat table.

空中小姐：请问，您要喝点什么？
Qǐngwèn, nín yào hē diǎn shénme?
What do you want for a drink?

甲：给我一杯橘汁。
Gěi wǒ yì bēi júzhī.
Please give me a cup of orange juice.

空中小姐：您呢？
Nín ne?
How about you?

乙：有啤酒吗？
Yǒu píjiǔ ma?
Do you have beer?

空中小姐：有，但要另付费，5块钱。
Yǒu, dàn yào lìng fù fèi, 5 kuài qián.
Yes. But you need to pay 5 yuan for a can.

……

空中小姐：请问，您要鸡肉饭还是牛肉面？
Qǐngwèn, nín yào jīròufàn háishi niúròumiàn?
Excuse me, do you want chicken rice or beef noodles?

乙：我们两个都要牛肉面。
Wǒmen liǎng gè dōu yào niúròumiàn.
Both of us want beef noodles.

1	gōngyìng 供 应	to supply; to serve		4	cānzhuō 餐桌	table
2	wǎncān 晚餐	dinner		5	jīròufàn 鸡肉饭	chicken rice
3	lāxia 拉下	to pull down		6	niúròumiàn 牛肉面	beef noodles

文化导航
Cultural Navigation

　　春节是中国人最重要的节日。不管多远，人们都要回家与家人团圆。春节一般在一月末或二月初来临，国家为此放春节长假，大学生们开始放寒假，上百万农民工在外工作了一年，也要回家和家人团聚。由于铁路交通是大部分中国人出行的首选，所以，春节前后是中国铁路运输最繁忙的季节。春运期间各火车站排队买票的、在火车站候车的人非常之多，真可谓人山人海。

The Spring Festival is the most important holiday for Chinese people which brings along the busiest travel season in China. The Spring Festival falls either in late January or early February when the winter break starts for college students and when millions of migrant workers go home for family reunions during the holiday season. Since the railroad is the major means of transportation for most people, all the train stations across the country are overcrowded with travelers buying tickets in long lines, or waiting for check-in.

核心句
Key Sentence

Mǎi yì zhāng dào Xī'ān de ruǎnwò.
买一张到西安的软卧。
Please give me a soft sleeper ticket to Xi'an.

句型与替换
Substitution

yìngzuò
硬座
hard seat

yìngwò
硬卧
hard sleeper

xuéshēngpiào
学生票
student ticket

értóngpiào
儿童票
children's ticket

扩展/Extension

Nín yào tèkuài háishi pǔkuài?
1. 您要特快还是普快?

Do you want a ticket of the special express train or the express train?

Pǔkuài zhǐ yǒu yìngzuò hé yìngwò le.
2. 普快只有硬座和硬卧了。

The express train only has hard seats and hard sleepers.

Ruǎnwò shàngpù 600 kuài, xiàpù 750 kuài.
3. 软卧上铺600块,下铺750块。

The soft upper berth is ¥600, and the lower berth ¥750.

Kāichē 30 fēnzhōng zhīqián jiǎnpiào.
4. 开车30分钟之前检票。

Boarding starts 30 minutes before the departure.

甲: Wǒ mǎi yì zhāng jīntiān wǎnshang dào Xī'ān de ruǎnwò.
我买一张今天晚上到西安的软卧。
I want to buy a soft sleeper ticket to Xi'an tonight.

乙: Tèkuài háishi pǔtōng kuàichē?
特快还是普通快车?
The special express train or the express train?

甲: Pǔkuài.
普快。
The express train.

乙: Pǔkuài zhǐ yǒu yìngzuò hé yìngwò le.
普快只有硬座和硬卧了。
The express train only has hard seats and hard sleepers.

甲: Nà jiù tèkuài ba.
那就特快吧。
Then give me a special express train ticket.

乙: Ruǎnwò shàngpù 600 kuài, xiàpù 750 kuài, yào nǎ zhǒng?
软卧上铺600块，下铺750块，要哪种?
The soft upper berth is ¥600 and the lower berth ¥750.

Which one do you want?

甲: Ruǎnwò shàngpù.
软卧上铺。
The soft upper berth.

乙: Hǎo, zhè shì nín de piào. Kāichē 30 fēnzhōng zhīqián jiǎnpiào.
好，这是您的票。开车30分钟之前检票。
Here is your ticket. Boarding starts 30 minutes before the departure.

甲: Xièxie.
谢谢。
Thank you.

	tèkuài 特快	special express train	6	jiǎnpiào 检票	ticket check-in
1					
2	pǔkuài 普快	express train	7	yī děng chēxiāng 一等车厢	first-class coach
3	mànchē 慢车	slow train	8	kèchē 客车	passenger train
4	shàngpù 上铺	upper berth	9	zhàntái 站台	platform
5	xiàpù 下铺	lower berth			

文化导航
Cultural Navigation

中国的火车按速度和舒适程度分几类，票价因此有所不同。不同类型的火车，其代号字母也不同。最舒适快捷的是近几年出现的以C、D、G打头的火车，称为高铁（G train）、动车（D train）、城际列车（C train），时速可达每小时200到300公里。另外有以Z打头的传统直达特快列车，以T打头的特快列车，以K打头的快速列车和以四位数字编号的普通列车。

There are different categories of trains in China according to the speed and comfort. Trains can be distinguished by the letter they start with. Those starting with the letters of C, D & G are top-quality high-speed trains with ultra-modern air-conditioned coaches and some are 200-300km/h daytime electric trains. Trains with Z as the starting letter are the previous top-quality sleeper train. They are now the second best, but still with very modern air-conditioned coaches. T trains are the third best category which is followed by K trains in line. Trains without any letter to start with but have four digit numbers are the regular trains. Higher fares are charged for better categories.

78 在火车上 | On the Train

核心句
Key Sentence

Cānchē zài jǐ hào chēxiāng?
餐车在几号车厢？
Where is the dining car?

句型与替换
Substitution

lièchēzhǎng shì
列车长室
office for the head of the train crew

bǔpiàoshì
补票室
ticket office on the train

ruǎnwò chēxiāng
软卧车厢
soft sleeper coach

扩 展／Extension

Lièchēzhǎng shì zài 6 hào chēxiāng.
1. 列车长室在6号车厢。

The office for the head of the train crew is in Coach No. 6.

Méi láidejí zài chēzhàn mǎipiào
2. 没来得及在车站买票
de kěyǐ zài chēshang bǔpiào.
的可以在车上补票。

Those who did not buy tickets at the station can buy tickets on the train.

Xiànzài bú shì cānchē gōngcān shíjiān.
3. 现在不是餐车供餐时间。

The dining car hasn't opened for business yet.

Chēshang yǒu tuīchē sòng héfàn fúwù.
4. 车 上 有 推车 送 盒饭 服务。There are mobile handcarts selling lunch boxes on the train.

对话实例/Dialogue

Qǐngwèn, cānchē zài jǐ hào chēxiāng?
甲: 请问，餐车在几号车厢？

Excuse me, do you know where the dining car is?

Zài 6 hào chēxiāng. Kě xiànzài bú shì gōngcān shíjiān.
乙: 在6号车厢。可现在不是供餐时间。

It is in Coach No. 6. But it hasn't opened for business yet.

Nà jǐ diǎn yíngyè ne?
甲: 那几点营业呢？

When does it open?

Zài guò yí gè xiǎoshí. Yíhuìr yǒu tuīchē sòng héfàn de.
乙: 再过一个小时。一会儿有推车送盒饭的。

In an hour. Oh, by the way, there is a mobile handcart selling lunch boxes in a moment.

(送盒饭车来了。Handcart that sells lunch boxes comes.)

Nín gěi wǒ yí gè 20 kuài qián de héfàn hé yì píng kuàngquánshuǐ.
甲: 您给我一个20块钱的盒饭和一瓶矿泉水。

Please give me a lunch box of ¥20 and a bottle of water.

Yígòng 22 kuài.
丙: 一共22块。

¥22 altogether.

1	chēxiāng 车厢	coach of the train	5	kuàngquánshuǐ 矿泉水	mineral water
2	gōngcān 供餐	to serve meals	6	lièchē shíkèbiǎo 列车时刻表	train schedule
3	yíngyè 营业	operation	7	lièchēyuán 列车员	train crew
4	héfàn 盒饭	lunch box			

文化导航
Cultural Navigation

中国的火车票分为四个等级，但并不是每辆火车都同时具有四个等级的位子。这四个等级是硬座、硬卧、软座、软卧。硬座最便宜，软卧最贵。硬卧车厢分为三层，不是包厢，车票也分为上、中、下铺。软卧车厢四人一个包厢，分为上下两层，下层较贵。

Chinese trains generally have four classes of seats at different prices, although you won't find every class on every train. They are hard-seat, hard-sleeper, soft-seat, and soft-sleeper tickets with the hard-seat the least expensive and soft-sleeper the most expensive. The hard-sleeper cars have three tiers of bunks with mattresses and do not have compartments. The soft-sleeper cars have four-person compartments. The hard-sleeper tickets are divided into three categories: upper-level berth, mid-level berth, and lower-level berth. The soft-sleeper tickets are upper-level or lower-level. The lower-level berth is more expensive than the upper-level berth.

城市交通
Local Transportation

核心句
Key Sentence

Gōnggòng qìchē zhàn zài nǎr?
公共汽车站在哪儿?
Where is the bus stop?

句型与替换
Substitution

wúguǐ diànchē
无轨电车
trolley bus

qīngguǐ
轻轨
light rail

dìtiě
地铁
subway

扩展/Extension

1. Dào Tiān'ānmén zuò gōngjiāochē
到天安门坐公交车
zěnme zǒu?
怎么走?

How can I take the public transportation to Tian'anmen?

2. Dào Qiánmén, huàn 104 wúguǐ diànchē.
到前门,换104无轨电车。

Change to Trolley Bus 104 at Qianmen.

3. Nín zhīdào dào Kuānjiē yào zuò jǐ
您知道到宽街要坐几
zhàn ma?
站吗?

Do you know how many stops to Kuanjie?

4. Shàngchē wèn shòupiàoyuán jiù
上车问售票员就
zhīdào le.
知道了。

You can ask the conductor on the bus.

甲: Qǐngwèn, rúguǒ wǒ zuò gōngjiāochē qù Běihǎi, zěnme zǒu?
请问，如果我坐公交车去北海，怎么走？
Excuse me, how can I take the public transportation to Beihai?

乙: Nín zuò 104 lù wúguǐ diànchē dào Kuānjiē, huàn 13 lù gōnggòng
您坐104路无轨电车到宽街，换13路公共
qìchē jiù dào Běihǎi le.
汽车就到北海了。
You can take Trolley Bus 104 to Kuanjie, and then change to Bus 13.

甲: 104 lù chēzhàn zài nǎr?
104路车站在哪儿？
Where is the 104 Trolley stop?

乙: Yìzhí wǎng qián zǒu, dào lùkǒu jiù kànjiàn chēzhàn le.
一直往前走，到路口就看见车站了。
Go straight to the intersection, and you can see the bus stop then.

甲: Nín zhīdào yào zuò jǐ zhàn ma?
您知道要坐几站吗？
Do you know how many stops?

乙: Wǒ bù zhīdào, búguò dào zhànpái nàr kěyǐ chá.
我不知道，不过到站牌那儿可以查。
I don't know. But you can find out at the bus stop.

甲: Zài nǎr xiàchē huàn 13 lù?
在哪儿下车换13路？
Where should I get off to change to Bus 13?

乙: Shàngchē wèn shòupiàoyuán jiù zhīdào le.
上车问售票员就知道了。
You can ask the conductor on the bus.

相关词语/Related Words

1	gōnggòng jiāotōng 公共交通	public transportation	3	huàn chē 换（车）	to change
2	zěnme zǒu 怎么走	How to get ...?	4	lùkǒu 路口	crossroads; intersection

5	gōnggòng 公共 qìchē zhàn 汽车站	bus stop	7	shòupiàoyuán 售票员	conductor; ticket seller
6	zhànpái 站牌	route board	8	chéngkè 乘客	rider; passenger

文化导航
Cultural Navigation

　　中国城市的公共汽车有不同种类。最便宜的是普通的公共汽车和无轨电车，但无轨电车行驶起来要慢很多，不过现在的无轨电车越来越少了。稍贵一点的是小公共汽车，多见于开往各旅游景点的公共汽车线路上，速度要快于普通公共汽车。最贵的是空调大巴，价钱按所坐路程计算。除此之外，还有旅游大巴和机场专线大巴。

　　There are several kinds of public buses in China. The cheapest ones are regular buses and trolley buses but the latter run slower and are becoming less and less. The next in line is the van, which usually runs parallel to the busy bus lines that go to tourist areas. The fare is a bit higher but it runs faster than the bus. Then comes the air-conditioned bus whose fare is higher than a regular bus depending on the distance you travel. There are also tourist buses and airport shuttles that run along special routes to tourist attractions or to airports.

核心句 / Key Sentence

Wǒ yào dào Běi Dà qù, zuò dìtiě jǐ hào xiàn?

我要到北大去，坐地铁几号线?

I am going to Peking University. Which subway line should I take?

句型与替换 / Substitution

Wǒ gāi wǎng nǎge fāngxiàng zǒu?

我该往哪个方向走?

Which direction should I go?

Yòng huàn chē ma?

用换车吗?

Should I change to another line?

Yǒu zhídá chē ma?

有直达车吗?

Is there a direct train?

扩展 / Extension

Dào Běi Dà qù, zuò dìtiě yī hào xiàn, èr hào xiàn dōu kěyǐ, rán hòu huànchéng sì hào xiàn.

1. 到北大去，坐地铁一号线、二号线都可以，然后换乘四号线。

To go to Peking University, you can take either Line 1 or Line 2, and then change to Line 4.

2. <ruby>一<rt>Yī</rt></ruby> <ruby>号<rt>hào</rt></ruby> <ruby>线<rt>xiàn</rt></ruby> <ruby>往<rt>wǎng</rt></ruby> <ruby>西单<rt>Xīdān</rt></ruby> <ruby>方向<rt>fāngxiàng</rt></ruby>。

Take Line 1 that goes to Xidan direction.

3. <ruby>这儿<rt>Zhèr</rt></ruby> <ruby>有<rt>yǒu</rt></ruby> <ruby>没<rt>méi</rt></ruby> <ruby>有<rt>yǒu</rt></ruby> <ruby>直达<rt>zhídá</rt></ruby> <ruby>北<rt>Běi</rt></ruby> <ruby>大<rt>Dà</rt></ruby> <ruby>的<rt>de</rt></ruby> <ruby>地铁<rt>dìtiě</rt></ruby>?

Is there a direct line to Peking University from here?

4. <ruby>一<rt>Yī</rt></ruby> <ruby>号<rt>hào</rt></ruby> <ruby>线<rt>xiàn</rt></ruby>、<ruby>二<rt>èr</rt></ruby> <ruby>号<rt>hào</rt></ruby> <ruby>线<rt>xiàn</rt></ruby> <ruby>哪个<rt>nǎge</rt></ruby> <ruby>更<rt>gèng</rt></ruby> <ruby>快<rt>kuài</rt></ruby>?

Which line is faster: Line 1 or Line 2?

对话实例/Dialogue

甲: <ruby>售票员<rt>Shòupiàoyuán</rt></ruby>，<ruby>我<rt>wǒ</rt></ruby> <ruby>要<rt>yào</rt></ruby> <ruby>到<rt>dào</rt></ruby> <ruby>北<rt>Běi</rt></ruby> <ruby>大<rt>Dà</rt></ruby> <ruby>去<rt>qù</rt></ruby>，<ruby>坐<rt>zuò</rt></ruby> <ruby>地铁<rt>dìtiě</rt></ruby> <ruby>几<rt>jǐ</rt></ruby> <ruby>号<rt>hào</rt></ruby> <ruby>线<rt>xiàn</rt></ruby>?
Sir, I want to go to Peking University. Which subway line should I take?

乙: <ruby>一<rt>Yī</rt></ruby> <ruby>号<rt>hào</rt></ruby> <ruby>线<rt>xiàn</rt></ruby>、<ruby>二<rt>èr</rt></ruby> <ruby>号<rt>hào</rt></ruby> <ruby>线<rt>xiàn</rt></ruby> <ruby>都<rt>dōu</rt></ruby> <ruby>行<rt>xíng</rt></ruby>。
Either Line 1 or Line 2.

甲: <ruby>那<rt>Nà</rt></ruby> <ruby>一<rt>yī</rt></ruby> <ruby>号<rt>hào</rt></ruby> <ruby>线<rt>xiàn</rt></ruby> <ruby>怎么<rt>zěnme</rt></ruby> <ruby>走<rt>zǒu</rt></ruby>?
How should I go if I take Line 1?

乙: <ruby>一<rt>Yī</rt></ruby> <ruby>号<rt>hào</rt></ruby> <ruby>线<rt>xiàn</rt></ruby> <ruby>往<rt>wǎng</rt></ruby> <ruby>西单<rt>Xīdān</rt></ruby> <ruby>方向<rt>fāngxiàng</rt></ruby>，<ruby>在<rt>zài</rt></ruby> <ruby>西单<rt>Xīdān</rt></ruby> <ruby>换<rt>huàn</rt></ruby> <ruby>四<rt>sì</rt></ruby> <ruby>号<rt>hào</rt></ruby> <ruby>线<rt>xiàn</rt></ruby>。
If you take Line 1, go towards Xidan direction and change to Line 4 at the Xidan Station.

甲: <ruby>那么<rt>Nàme</rt></ruby> <ruby>麻烦<rt>máfan</rt></ruby>? <ruby>那<rt>Nà</rt></ruby> <ruby>二<rt>èr</rt></ruby> <ruby>号<rt>hào</rt></ruby> <ruby>线<rt>xiàn</rt></ruby> <ruby>呢<rt>ne</rt></ruby>?
It is pretty complicated. How about taking Line 2?

乙: <ruby>二<rt>Èr</rt></ruby> <ruby>号<rt>hào</rt></ruby> <ruby>线<rt>xiàn</rt></ruby> <ruby>也<rt>yě</rt></ruby> <ruby>得<rt>děi</rt></ruby> <ruby>倒车<rt>dǎochē</rt></ruby>，<ruby>这儿<rt>zhèr</rt></ruby> <ruby>没有<rt>méiyǒu</rt></ruby> <ruby>直达<rt>zhídá</rt></ruby> <ruby>北<rt>Běi</rt></ruby> <ruby>大<rt>Dà</rt></ruby> <ruby>的<rt>de</rt></ruby> <ruby>车<rt>chē</rt></ruby>。
You also have to change. There is no direct train to Peking University.

甲: <ruby>一<rt>Yī</rt></ruby> <ruby>号<rt>hào</rt></ruby> <ruby>线<rt>xiàn</rt></ruby>、<ruby>二<rt>èr</rt></ruby> <ruby>号<rt>hào</rt></ruby> <ruby>线<rt>xiàn</rt></ruby> <ruby>哪个<rt>nǎge</rt></ruby> <ruby>更<rt>gèng</rt></ruby> <ruby>快<rt>kuài</rt></ruby>?
Which is faster: Line 1 or Line 2?

乙: <ruby>都<rt>Dōu</rt></ruby> <ruby>差不多<rt>chàbuduō</rt></ruby>。
About the same.

1	wǎng 往	towards (a certain direction)	3	zhídá 直达	non-stop; direct (train)
2	fāngxiàng 方向	direction	4	chàbuduō 差不多	similar

文化导航
Cultural Navigation

　　对北京人来说，最方便快捷的公共交通工具是地铁。2014年年底起，北京地铁调整了价格：三元起，按里程收费，最高可达九元。目前，北京有18条地铁线路，是世界上地铁线路最长的城市。北京地铁线路还在不断增加，以更好地满足城市交通的需要。

The most popular means of public transportation for Beijing local commuters is subway. It is fast and conveninent. Since the end of 2014, the price of subway in Beijing has been adjusted. The charge is based on the distance with the minimum charge of 3 yuan and the maximum charge of 9 yuan. Beijing now has 18 subway lines serving the urban and suburban districts of Beijing municipality. Among the world's metro systems, the Beijing Subway ranks first in track length at present. The subway network of the city is still expanding to meet the city transit needs.

核心句
Key Sentence

Qiánmiàn xiūlù le.
前面修路了。
There is a construction in the front.

句型与替换
Substitution

chū jiāotōng shìgù
出交通事故
car accident

chū chēhuò
出车祸
car accident

sāichē
塞车
traffic jam

扩展/Extension

Zěnme yòu dǔchē le?
1. 怎么又堵车了？
How come there is a traffic jam again?

Wǒmen dǎkāi shōuyīnjī tīngtīng
2. 我们打开收音机听听
lùkuàng ba.
路况吧。
Let's listen to the radio for traffic situations.

Wǒmen ràodào zǒu ba.
3. 我们绕道走吧。
We have to detour.

Wǒmen yīnggāi cóng qiánbiān
4. 我们应该从前边
lùkǒu wǎng yòu zǒu.
路口往右走。
We should turn right from the next intersection.

甲：
Zěnme yòu dǔ le?
怎么 又 堵了？
How come there is a traffic jam again?

乙：
Hǎoxiàng qiánmiàn xiūlù ne.
好像 前面 修路呢。
It looks as if there is a construction in the front.

甲：
Wǒmen ràodào zǒu ba, bù zhī yào dǔ duō jiǔ ne.
我们 绕道 走吧，不知 要 堵多久呢。
How about getting off the road? We don't know how long
we have to wait.

乙：
Hǎo, wǒmen kěyǐ cóng qiánbiān lùkǒu wǎng yòu zǒu.
好，我们 可以 从 前边 路口 往 右走。
OK, we should turn right from the next intersection.

甲：
Wǒ jìde nà tiáo lù shì zuǒxíng dānxíngxiàn.
我记得那条路是左行单行线。
I remember it is one-way drive to the left.

乙：
Nà jiù zài kāi yí gè lùkǒu yòuguǎi.
那就再开一个路口右拐。
Then pass one more traffic light before turning right.

甲：
Nà jiù shì Píng'ān Dàdào le.
那就是平安大道了。
That is Ping'an Street.

乙：
Duì, Píng'ān Dàdào hé zhè tiáo lù shì píngxíng de.
对，平安大道和这条路是平行的。
Good. Ping'an Street is parallel to this street.

相关词语/Related Words

1	dǔchē 堵车	traffic jam	3	dānxíngxiàn 单行线	one-way road
2	ràodào 绕道	to make a detour	4	lùkǒu 路口	intersection

5	yòuguǎi 右拐	to turn right		8	lùkuàng 路况	road condition
6	hóng-lǜdēng 红绿灯	traffic lights		9	jiāotōngtái 交通台	traffic radio station
7	píngxíng 平行	parallel				

文化导航
Cultural Navigation

中国大城市开车的人越来越多，交通堵塞成为人们出行的大问题。为了缓解这个问题，政府采取了很多措施，其中一条是在交通灯上加上电子显示装置，提示人们红绿灯之间转换的等待时间，这样可以让司机和行人更好地掌握时间，安全通过路口。

As more and more people drive cars in large cities in China, traffic jams are a big headache for drivers and commuters. To alleviate the situation, the government takes a lot of measures and one of them is to equip an electronic display in the array of traffic lights. Such an electronic display tells the remaining time before the light turns from green to red or from red to green. This allows drivers and pedestrians to better manage their time in getting through the intersections.

核心句 Key Sentence

Zǒu gāosù háishi zǒu chéngli?
走高速还是走城里？

Shall we go on the highway or through the city?

句型与替换 Substitution

huándào
环道
ring

chéngli
城里
in the city

chéngwài
城外
outside the city

wàihuán
外环
outer ring

nèihuán
内环
inner ring

扩展/Extension

Nín shuō wǒmen zěnme zǒu?
1. 您说我们怎么走？

You decide how we should go.

Zǒu gāosù lù yuǎn dànshì kuài.
2. 走高速路远但是快。

It is faster if we go via the highway though the distance is long.

Chéngli jìn dàoshì jìn, jiùshì
3. 城里近倒是近，就是

If we drive through the city, it is

chē tài duō, jīngcháng dǔ.
车太多，经常 堵。

shorter in distance but there is too much traffic on the way.

Wǒ gěi nín dǎbiǎo.
4. 我给您打表。

I will run the meter for you.

对话实例/Dialogue

甲: Chūzūchē, chūzūchē…… Běi Dà Nánmén.
出租车，出租车……北大 南门 。

Taxi, taxi… I am going to the South Gate of Peking University.

乙: Zěnme zǒu? Zǒu gāosù háishi zǒu chéngli?
怎么 走？走 高速 还是 走 城里？

Tell me how we should go: on the highway or through the city?

甲: Nǎge jìn zǒu nǎge.
哪个 近 走 哪个。

Whichever is shorter in distance.

乙: Gāosù lù yuǎn dànshì kuài
高速 路 远 但是 快。

Highway is longer in distance but much faster.

甲: Chéngli ne?
城里 呢？

How about through the city?

乙: Jìn dàoshì jìn, jiùshì chē tài duō, jīngcháng dǔ.
近 倒是 近，就是 车 太 多，经常 堵。

Though it is shorter in distance, there is too much traffic and too many traffic jams.

甲: Nà jiù zǒu gāosù ba. Dàyuē duōshao qián?
那就 走 高速 吧。大约 多少 钱？

Then let's go on the highway. How much is it approximately?

乙: 100 duō kuài qián ba. Wǒ gěi nín dǎbiǎo. Yǒu shōujù.
100 多 块 钱 吧。我给您打表。有 收据。

A little over ¥100. I will run the meter and give you the receipt.

1	chūzūchē 出租车	taxi	4	dǎbiǎo 打表	to run the meter
2	gāosù 高速	highway	5	shōujù 收据	receipt
3	huánlù 环路	ring road			

文化导航
Cultural Navigation

　　北京大约有70,000辆出租车，除此之外，还有一些没注册的"黑车"。随着物价的上涨，北京出租车的价格也在不断上调。根据政府的规定，除了燃油附加费外，行程中因堵车造成的等待时间也要付钱。夜里出租车的价钱要贵一些。上车后你应要求司机打表，到目的地应要发票，以避免一些不愉快。为了以防万一，最好把司机的号码记下来，如果丢东西，还可以找回来。

There are approximately 70,000 taxis going around in Beijing, plus some illegal ones called "black cars". With the rising commodity price, the price for taking a taxi has been continuously rising. According to the local government, the extra money will be charged to compensate for the high oil price, and waiting time in a traffic jam will also be charged. Mid-night driving is a bit more expensive. Ask the driver to run the meter and request for a receipt to avoid a possible dispute. It is also a good idea to write down the driver's ID number in case you lose anything in the car.

旅馆
At the Hotel

83 旅店设施 | Hotel Facilities

Wǒmen jiǔdiàn yǒu jiànshēnfáng.
我们酒店有健身房。
Our hotel has a gymnasium.

句型
与替换
Substitution

yóuyǒngchí
游泳池
swimming pool

huìyìshì
会议室
conference room

shāngwù zhōngxīn
商务中心
business center

xīcāntīng
西餐厅
Western restaurant

jiǔbā
酒吧
wine bar

扩 展/Extension

Zhè jiā jiǔdiàn dìdiǎn hǎo.
1. 这家酒店地点好。
This hotel has a great location.

Zhè shì yì jiā wǔ xīngjí jiǔdiàn.
2. 这是一家五星级酒店。
This is a 5-star hotel.

Jiǔdiàn yǒu Rìběn liàolǐ hé
3. 酒店有日本料理和
Yìdàlì cāntīng.
意大利餐厅。
The hotel has Japanese and Italian restaurants.

Biāozhǔnjiān duōshao qián yì tiān?
4. 标准间多少钱一天?
How much is a standard room per night?

5. Xiànzài shì yōuhuìjià.
现在是优惠价。   Now it is a promotion price.

对话实例/Dialogue

甲：Xiǎo Wáng, wǒmen děi wèi Měiguó dàibiǎotuán ānpái lǚguǎn le.
小王，我们得为 美国 代表团安排旅馆了。

Xiao Wang, we need to find a hotel for the American delegation.

乙：Nà jiù qù Qiánmén gāng kāi de nà jiā wǔ xīngjí jiǔdiàn ba, shèshī
那就去前门 刚 开的那家五星级酒店吧，设施
hěn qíquán.
很齐全。

That newly opened 5-star hotel on Qianmen Street is great. It has excellent facilities.

甲：Yǒu shāngwù zhōngxīn ma?
有 商务 中心 吗?

Is there a business center?

乙：Dāngrán yǒu, hái yǒu jiànshēnfáng, yóuyǒngchí, jiǔbā, huìyìshì.
当然有，还有健身房、游泳池、酒吧、会议室。

Sure. It has a gym, a swimming pool, a bar as well as conference rooms.

甲：Yǒu shénme fēngwèi de cāntīng?
有 什么 风味 的 餐厅?

What kind of restaurants does it have?

乙：Yǒu Rìběn liàolǐ hé Yìdàlì cāntīng.
有日本料理和意大利餐厅。

It has a Japanese restaurant and an Italian restaurant.

甲：Biāozhǔnjiān duōshao qián yì tiān?
标准间 多少 钱 一天?

How much is it for a standard room per day?

乙: Xiànzài gāng kāizhāng shì yōuhuìjià, cái 1,100 yuán.
现在 刚 开张是优惠价， 才1,100元。

Since it is newly opened, they offer a promotion price at ¥1,100 per night.

甲: Tīngzhe búcuò, jiù nàr ba.
听着不错，就那儿吧。

It sounds good. Let's choose there.

相关词语/Related Words

1	lǚguǎn 旅馆	hotel	7	fēngwèi 风味	cuisine; flavor
2	zhùsù 住宿	to stay in (a hotel)	8	cāntīng 餐厅	restaurant
3	wǔ xīngjí 五星级	5-star (hotel)	9	biāozhǔnjiān 标准间	standard room
4	jiǔdiàn 酒店	(luxurious) hotel	10	kāizhāng 开张	to start business
5	shèshī 设施	facilities	11	yōuhuìjià 优惠价	promotion price
6	qíquán 齐全	all complete			

文化导航
Cultural Navigation

　　在汉语中，对不同等级的旅馆有不同的叫法。以"宾馆"、"饭店"和"酒店"冠名的一般来说是比较高级的，那里的工作人员一般可以用英文跟你交流。如果是以"旅馆"或"旅店"为名的，一般在三星级以下，工作人员很可能不懂英文。过去，招待所是国有企业或政府机构自己的旅馆，但现在也对公众开放。近几年，中国还出现了很多连锁经营的经济型旅馆，各方面都比较实惠。

The terminology for hotels in Chinese generally indicates the level of a hotel. "宾馆", "饭店", and "酒店" are usually luxury hotels, in which English can be a communication language in most cases. "旅馆" and "旅店" are usually three-star hotels or lower and English is often not spoken there. "招待所"（guesthouse or hostel）used to belong to a state-owned company or a government agency and now open to public. In recent years, chains of motels have appeared on the market and received a great deal of popularity.

核心句 Key Sentence

Wǒ dìng yí gè shuāngrén jiān.

我订一个双人间。

I want to book a double room.

句型与替换 Substitution

biāozhǔnjiān
标准间
standard room

dānrénjiān
单人间
single room

tàofáng
套房
suite

xīyānfáng
吸烟房
smoke room

扩 展/Extension

1. Qǐngwèn nín shénme shíjiān rùzhù?
请问您什么时间入住？

May I ask when you are arriving?

2. Qǐngwèn nín zhù jǐ tiān?
请问您住几天？

How long will you stay?

3. 469 yuán yì tiān, bāokuò zǎocān
469元一天，包括早餐
hé shàngwǎng fèi.
和上网费。

It is ¥469 a day including breakfast and the Internet.

4. Huìyuán yǒu 20% de zhékòu.
会员有20%的折扣。

There is a 20% discount for the hotel members.

5. Rùzhù shíjiān shì xiàwǔ 3:00,
入住时间是下午3:00，
jiézhàng shíjiān shì zhōngwǔ 12:00.
结账时间是中午12:00。

The check-in time is 3 pm and check-out time 12 pm.

甲： Nín hǎo! Báiyún Lǚguǎn ma? Wǒ xiǎng yùdìng yí gè shuāngrénjiān.
您好！白云旅馆吗？我想预订一个双人间。

Hello, is it Baiyun Hotel? I want to reserve a double-bed room.

乙： Kěyǐ, qǐngwèn nín shénme shíjiān rùzhù?
可以，请问您什么时间入住？

Sure. May I know your date of arrival?

甲： 10 yuè 5 rì rùzhù, 9 rì líkāi.
10月5日入住，9日离开。

I arrive on Oct. 5th and leave on the 9th.

乙： Wǒ chácha hái yǒu fángjiān ma Èng, hái yǒu fángjiān. 469 yuán,
我查查还有房间吗……嗯，还有房间。469元，
bāokuò zǎocān hé shàngwǎngfèi.
包括早餐和上网费。

Let me check if there is a room available… Yes, there is one. ¥469 per night including breakfast and the Internet.

甲： Yǒu zhékòu ma?
有折扣吗？

Is there any discount?

乙： Huìyuán yǒu 20% de zhékòu.
会员有20%的折扣。

There is a 20% discount for our members.

甲： Wǒ shì huìyuán. Dìng ba.
我是会员。订吧。

Yes, I am your member. Please book it for me.

乙： Hǎo. Wǒmen xiàwǔ 3:00 rùzhù, dì-èr tiān zhōngwǔ líkāi.
好。我们下午3:00入住，第二天中午离开。

OK. Our check-in time is 3 pm and check-out time 12 pm.

1	yùdìng 预订	to book; to reserve	4	fèi 费	expense; cost
2	rùzhù 入住	check-in	5	zhékòu 折扣	discount
3	zǎocān 早餐	breakfast	6	jiézhàng 结账	check-out

文化导航
Cultural Navigation

就时间而言，中国媒体和官方文件都使用24小时制，如火车时刻表、飞机时刻表、办公时间等。在日常生活中，人们通常使用12小时制，但会在前面加上上午、下午、晚上等时间段以示区分。

The 24-hour time system is used in media and all official schedules such as train and airplane schedules and office hours in China. In the daily conversation people usually use the 12-hour system together with the expressions such as morning, afternoon and evening to distinguish.

核心句 Key Sentence

Zhè shì nín de fángkǎ.
这是您的房卡。
This is your room key.

句型与替换 Substitution

fángjiān yàoshi   zǎocānquàn
房间钥匙   早餐券
room key   breakfast coupon

shàngwǎng mìmǎ
上网密码
Internet password

扩展/Extension

Wǒ xiǎng yào yì jiān lóucéng gāo yìdiǎnr de fángjiān.
1. 我想要一间楼层高一点儿的房间。
I want a room on a higher floor.

Zhè shì nín de fángkǎ, zǎocānquàn hé shàngwǎng mìmǎ.
2. 这是您的房卡，早餐券和上网密码。
This is the key to your room, your breakfast coupon and the password for the Internet.

Xūyào bāng nín yùn xíngli ma?
3. 需要帮您运行李吗？
Do you need help with your luggage?

Rúguǒ xūyào shénme fúwù, qǐng gēn qiántái liánxì.
4. 如果需要什么服务，请跟前台联系。
If you need any service, please contact the front desk.

Zhù nín rùzhù yúkuài!
5. 祝您入住愉快！
Wish you a happy stay!

甲: Nín hǎo! Wǒ yùdìngle yí gè shuāngrénjiān.
您好！我预订了一个双人间。

Hello, I have reserved a double room.

乙: Nín hǎo! Qǐng gěi wǒ nín de shēnfènzhèng.
您好！请给我您的身份证。

May I take a look at your ID?

甲: Gěi. Wǒ kěyǐ yào yì jiān lóucéng gāo yìdiǎnr de fángjiān ma?
给。我可以要一间楼层高一点儿的房间吗？

Here it is. Can I have a room on a higher floor?

乙: Méi wèntí. Nín de fángjiān shì 10 lóu 1008 hào, zhè shì nín de
没问题。您的房间是10楼1008号，这是您的
fángkǎ, zǎocānquàn hé shàngwǎng mìmǎ.
房卡、早餐券和上网密码。

No problem. Your room is 1008 on the 10th floor. Here is your room key, your breakfast coupon and the password for the Internet.

甲: Xièxie. Zǎocān jǐ diǎn?
谢谢。早餐几点？

Thank you. When is the time for breakfast?

乙: 6 diǎn dào 9 diǎn, cāntīng zài èr lóu. Xūyào bāng nín ná xíngli ma?
6点到9点，餐厅在二楼。需要帮您拿行李吗？

From 6 am to 9 am on the second floor. Do you need help with your luggage?

甲: Búyòng.
不用。

No, thank you.

乙: Rúguǒ nín xūyào shénme fúwù, qǐng gēn qiántái liánxì. Zhù nín rùzhù
如果您需要什么服务，请跟前台联系。祝您入住
yúkuài.
愉快。

If you need any service, please contact the front desk. Wish you a happy stay!

相关词语／Related Words

1	lóucéng 楼层	storey	4	qiántái 前台	front desk
2	fángkǎ 房卡	key; room card	5	liánxì 联系	to contact
3	fúwù 服务	service	6	rùzhù 入住	to check in

文化导航
Cultural Navigation

汉语里，如果房间号、公共汽车号、楼房号、电话号码等有三位或三位以上的数字，就按顺序一个数字一个数字地念出来。比如说，"一零零三号房间"（Room 1003）、"电话号码二二二三四五六一"（22-234-561）。但如果数字小于三位数，就直接读出整个数字，比如"二十二号房间"（Room 22），"五十六号楼"（Building 56）等。

In Chinese, if a number for room, bus, building, or telephone contains three or more figures, you should read the figures one by one in order. For example, Room 1003 is read as "一零零三号房间", and the telephone number 22-234-561 is read as "二二二三四五六一". However, if such a number has less than three figures, you can just simply read it out. For example, Room 22 is read as "二十二号房间", and Building 56 is read as "五十六号楼".

核心句 / Key Sentence

Wǒ xūyào fángjiān sòngcān fúwù.
我需要房间送餐服务。

句型与替换 / Substitution

jiàozǎo
叫早
morning call

fángjiān qīngsǎo
房间清扫
room cleaning

jiào chūzūchē
叫出租车
taxi calling

扩展/Extension

1. Wǒ gěi nín zhuǎndào cāntīng fúwù bù.
   我给您转到餐厅服务部。

   I will switch you to the cafeteria service department.

2. Nín jǐ hào fángjiān?
   您几号房间?

   Which room are you in?

3. Gěi wǒ sòng yì píng Fǎguó hóngjiǔ, yí gè shuǐguǒpán, liǎng fèn mógutāng.
   给我送一瓶法国红酒,一个水果盘,两份蘑菇汤。

   Please send me a bottle of French red wine, a fruit platter and two portions of mushroom soup.

Nín diǎn de cān 15 fēnzhōng yǐhòu
4. 您 点 的餐15分 钟以后
sòngdào.
送到。

We will have your meal
delivered in 15 minutes.

对话实例/Dialogue

甲： Cāntīng fúwù bù,　wǒ xūyào fángjiān sòngcān fúwù.
餐厅服务部，我需要房间 送餐服务。

Hello, is it restaurant service department? I need meal
delivery service.

乙： Hǎo,　nín jǐ hào fángjiān?
好，您几号房间？

Yes. Which room are you in?

甲： 1023 hào.
1023号。

Room 1023.

乙： Nín xūyào shénme?
您需要什么？

What do you order?

甲： Gěi wǒ sòng yì píng Fǎguó hóngjiǔ,　yí gè shuǐguǒpán,　liǎng fèn
给我送一瓶 法国红酒，一个水果盘，两份
mógūtāng.
蘑菇汤。

Please give me a bottle of French red wine, a fruit platter
and two portions of mushroom soup.

乙： Méi wèntí.　Nín jǐ diǎn yào?
没问题。您几点要？

No problem. When do you want it served?

甲： Yuè kuài yuè hǎo.
越 快 越 好。

The sooner the better.

乙： 15 fēnzhōng hòu sòngdào.
15分 钟后送到。

It will be there in 15 minutes.

1	qiántái 前台	front desk	3	shuǐguǒpán 水果盘	fruit platter
2	fúwùbù 服务部	service department	4	qǐng wù dǎrǎo 请勿打扰	Don't disturb.

文化导航
Cultural Navigation

　　在中国，旅馆退房跟在欧美不一样，你必须到前台亲自退房卡、结账。此时，前台会通知服务员到你住过的房间检查，以确保房间的所有东西都完好无缺，这个过程结束后你才可以结账。这是中国旅馆的正常程序，你不必有不舒服的感觉。

There are some differences in hotel check-out procedure in China. You have to come to the front desk to return the room key and check out. During the procedure, you will be asked to wait for a while when a hotel staff member checks your room to verify if everything is OK. This is a routine part of checking out and you don't have to feel uncomfortable about it.

核心句 Key Sentence

Měiyuán duì Rénmínbì de huìlǜ shì duōshao?
美元对人民币的汇率是多少？

What is the exchange rate between US dollar and RMB?

句型与替换 Substitution

Ōuyuán
欧元
Euro

Rìyuán
日元
Japanese Yen

Gǎngbì
港币
Hong Kong dollar

Jiānádàyuán
加拿大元
Canadian dollar

扩 展/Extension

1. Jīntiān Měiyuán duì Rénmínbì de huìlǜ shì 1 bǐ 6.45.
   今天 美元对人民币的汇率是1比6.45。

   The exchange rate between USD and RMB today is 1:6.45.

2. Wàibì yèwù dào yī hào chuāngkǒu bànlǐ.
   外币业务到一号 窗 口办理。

   Foreign currency service is at the first window.

3. Huàn wàibì, xūyào hùzhào.
   换 外币，需要护照。

   If you want to convert foreign currency into RMB, we need your passport.

4. Líkāi qián qǐng nín diǎn yíxià.
   离开前 请您点一下。

   Please count before you leave.

Qǐngwèn, jīntiān Měiyuán duì Rénmínbì de huìlǜ shì duōshao?
甲：请问，今天美元对人民币的汇率是多少？

Excuse me. What is the exchange rate between USD and RMB today?

1 bǐ 6.45.
乙：1比 6 .45。

1:6.45.

Wǒ huàn 200 Měiyuán.
甲：我 换 200美元。

I want to convert $200.

Nín dài hùzhào le ma?
乙：您带护照了吗？

Do you have your passport with you?

Dài le.
甲：带了。

Yes.

Nín bǎ hùzhào gěi wǒ, zài tián yíxià zhège dānzi.
乙：您把护照给我，再填一下这个单子。

Please give me your passport and fill out this form.

Hǎo.
甲：好。

OK.

Zhè shì nín de Rénmínbì, líkāi qián qǐng nín diǎn yíxià.
乙：这是您的人民币，离开前请您点一下。

This is your RMB. Please count before you leave.

相关词语/Related Words

1	huàn qián 换（钱）	to exchange	3	diǎn qián 点（钱）	to count (the money)
2	hùzhào 护照	passport	4	dānzi 单子	form

5	wàibì 外币	foreign currency	7	chuāngkǒu 窗口	window
6	yèwù 业务	business			

文化导航
Cultural Navigation

　　中国的货币是人民币，符号是"￥"。人民币的单位是元、角、分。一元等于十角，一角等于十分。在人们日常对话中，这三个单位分别是块、毛、分。人民币中常见的纸币共有八种，分别是100元、50元、20元、10元、5元、1元、5角、1角。另外，还有三种常用的硬币，分别是1元、5角、1角。

The Chinese currency is *Renminbi* (RMB) with the symbol of ￥. The units of RMB are yuan, jiao and fen. 1 yuan equals 10 jiao and 1 jiao equals 10 fen. In colloquial Chinese these three units are kuai, mao and fen respectively. There are 8 paper bills which are often used. They are 100 yuan, 50 yuan, 20 yuan, 10 yuan, 5 yuan, 1 yuan, 5 jiao and 1 jiao. And there are 3 frequently-used coins, which are 1 yuan, 5 jiao and 1 jiao.

核心句
Key Sentence

Wǒ xiǎng kāi yí ge chǔxù zhànghù.
我 想 开 一 个 储蓄 账户。
I want to open a saving account.

句型 与替换
Substitution

zhīpiào zhànghù
支票 账户
checking account

xìnyòngkǎ
信用卡
credit card

jièjìkǎ
借记卡
debit card

yínhángkǎ
银行卡
bank card

✚ 扩 展／Extension

1. Wàiguórén kěyǐ kāi chǔxù zhànghù ma?
外国人 可以 开储蓄 账户 吗? Can foreigners open a saving account?

2. Kāi zhànghù xūyào nín de hùzhào.
开 账户 需要 您的 护照。 To open an account here, we need your passport.

3. Nǐ jīntiān cúnqián ma?
你 今天 存钱 吗? Do you want to deposit money today?

4. Nín yǐhòu píng cúnzhé cúnqián, qǔqián.
您 以后 凭 存折 存钱、取钱。 You will use the bankbook to deposit or withdraw money.

甲: Wǒ shì yí gè wàiguórén, xiǎng kāi gè chǔxù zhànghù, kěyǐ ma?
我是一个外国人，想开个储蓄账户，可以吗？

I am a foreigner and want to open a saving account, can I?

乙: Kěyǐ. Dàn xūyào nín de hùzhào hé línshí jūzhù dēngjìbiǎo.
可以。但需要您的护照和临时居住登记表。

Sure, you can. But I need your passport and temporary residency registration form.

甲: Wǒ dōu dài le.
我都带了。

I have them with me.

乙: Hǎo, wǒ xiànzài jiù gěi nín bàn. Nín tián yíxià zhè fèn biǎo.
好，我现在就给您办。您填一下这份表。

Good. Let me do it for you. Please fill out this form.

甲: Hǎo.
好。

Yes.

乙: Nín jīntiān cúnqián ma?
您今天存钱吗？

Do you want to deposit money today?

甲: Cún 500 Měiyuán.
存500美元。

Yes, $500.

乙: Hǎo, gěi nín cún qilai le. Zhè shì nín de cúnzhé, yǐhòu píng
好，给您存起来了。这是您的存折，以后凭
tā cúnqián, qǔqián.
它存钱、取钱。

OK. It's done. This is your bankbook. You will need it when you deposit or withdraw money.

1	chǔxù 储蓄	saving	5	cúnzhé 存折	bankbook
2	zhànghù 账户	account	6	cúnqián 存钱	to deposit
3	línshí 临时	temporary	7	qǔqián 取钱	to withdraw (money)
4	dēngjìbiǎo 登记表	registration form			

文化导航
Cultural Navigation

　　外币可以在当地银行兑换，也可以在国际机场、高档酒店及一些大型商店兑换。兑换时要出示护照或其他身份证件。兑换率在不同的地方可能略有不同。比较划算的是使用旅行支票。国外信用卡也可以在ATM机上兑换人民币，但要收一定数量的手续费。

　　Foreign currency can be exchanged at almost all local banks, international airports, large hotels, and some large department stores. You need to show your passport or ID card. The exchange rate varies a little from place to place. A slightly more favorable rate is given for traveler's checks. Foreign credit cards can also be used to obtain RMB from Chinese ATM machines. Some service fees will be charged for such transactions.

核心句 Key Sentence

Wǒ xiǎng bǎ zhè zhāng zhīpiào cún qǐlai.
我 想 把 这 张 支票 存 起来。
I want to deposit this check.

句型与替换 Substitution

zhè bǐ xiànjīn
这 笔 现金
this amount of cash

zhè zhāng shāngyè huìpiào
这 张 商业汇票
this commercial draft

zhè zhāng lǚxíng zhīpiào
这 张 旅行支票
this traveler's check

扩展/Extension

Nín zài wǒmen háng yǒu zhànghù ma?
1. 您在我们 行 有 账户 吗? Do you have an account with our bank?

Nín shì àn Měiyuán cún háishi huàn
2. 您是按美元 存还是 换 Do you want to deposit it in USD or in RMB?
chéng Rénmínbì cún?
成 人民币存?

wǒ shénme shíhou kěyǐ yòng zhè
3. 我什么 时候可以 用 这 When can I use the money?
bǐ qián?
笔钱?

4. Wǒ xiǎng yòng zhè zhāng zhīpiào duì
   我 想 用 这 张 支票 兑   I want to cash this check.
   xiànjīn.
   现金。

对话实例/Dialogue

甲: Wǒ xiǎng bǎ zhè zhāng zhīpiào cún qilai.
我 想 把 这 张 支票 存 起来。

I want to deposit this check.

乙: Nín zài wǒmen háng yǒu zhànghù ma?
您 在 我们 行 有 账户 吗?

Do you have an account with our bank?

甲: Yǒu, zhè shì wǒ de cúnzhé hé hùzhào.
有, 这 是 我 的 存折 和 护照。

Yes, I do. This is my bankbook and passport.

乙: Nà nín shì àn Měiyuán cún háishi huànchéng Rénmínbì cún?
那 您 是 按 美元 存 还是 换 成 人民币 存?

Do you want to deposit it in USD or RMB?

甲: Àn Rénmínbì cún.
按 人民币 存。

I will go with RMB.

乙: Nín zài zhèr qiān gè míng.
您 在 这儿 签 个 名。

Please sign your name here.

甲: Wǒ shénme shíhou kěyǐ yòng zhè bǐ qián?
我 什么 时候 可以 用 这 笔 钱?

When can I use the money?

乙: Yí gè yuè yǐhòu.
一个 月 以后。

In a month.

1	zhīpiào 支票	check	3	qiānmíng 签名	signature; to sign
2	àn 按	based on	4	duì xiànjīn 兑现金	to cash

文化导航
Cultural Navigation

　　银行的营业时间一般是星期一到星期五的早上8:30 到下午5:30，节假日办公时间会缩短。政府部门的办公时间跟银行的办公时间差不多一样（有些政府部门节假日不办公），但商店、饭馆一周七天都开门，公共假期也营业。

Business hours for a bank are generally 8:30 am-5:30 pm from Monday to Friday. They are open on weekends and public holidays, with less working hours. Government agencies have the similar working hours while some have days off on weekends and public holidays. However, stores and restaurants are open seven days a week including public holidays.

核心句
Key Sentence

Nǐ děi mǎshàng dǎ diànhuà kǒutóu guàshī.
你得马上打电话口头挂失。

You have to call and orally report the loss immediately.

句型与替换
Substitution

zhèngshì guàshī
正式挂失
report the loss officially

dòngjié zhànghù
冻结账户
freeze the account

bàn bǔkǎ shǒuxù
办补卡手续
have a new card issued

扩 展/Extension

1. Guàshī hòu, nín de zhànghù jiù huì bèi dòngjié.
挂失后，您的账户就会被冻结。

After your report for loss, your account will be frozen.

2. Zànshí dòngjié zhànghù yǒuxiàoqī 5 tiān.
暂时冻结账户有效期5天。

Temporary account freeze will expire in five days.

3. Wǔ tiān nèi bìxū dào yínháng bàn zhèngshì guàshī hé bǔkǎ shǒuxù.
五天内必须到银行办正式挂失和补卡手续。

You have to go to the bank to officially report the loss and have a new card issued within five days.

Shǒuxù bìxū běnrén bàn.
4. 手续必须本人办。

Yí gè xīngqī yǐhòu zhànghù cái néng shǐyòng.
5. 一个星期以后账户才能使用。

You must go through the procedures in person.
The account cannot be used until a week later.

对话实例/Dialogue

Wǒ bǎ yínhángkǎ diū le, zěnme bàn?
甲: 我把银行卡丢了，怎么办？

I have lost my bank card. What should I do?

Nǐ xiān dǎ diànhuà kǒutóu guàshī, dòngjié zhànghù.
乙: 你先打电话口头挂失，冻结账户。

You have to call to report the loss orally to freeze the account.

Ránhòu ne?
甲: 然后呢？

And then?

Wǔ tiān nèi nǐ běnrén dào yínháng bàn zhèngshì guàshī hé bǔkǎ shǒuxù.
乙: 五天内你本人到银行办正式挂失和补卡手续。

Within five days, you have to go to the bank to report the loss officially and have a new card issued.

Yào shénme zhèngjiàn?
甲: 要什么证件？

What kind of documents do they need?

Hùzhào yuánjiàn hé fùyìnjiàn.
乙: 护照原件和复印件。

Your passport and its copy.

Yào děng jǐ tiān zhànghù cái néng jiědòng?
甲: 要等几天账户才能解冻？

How many days will I wait before it is unfrozen?

Yí gè xīngqī.
乙: 一个星期。

One week.

1	yínhángkǎ 银行卡	bank card	6	bǔkǎ 补卡	to issue a replaced card
2	kǒutóu 口头	oral; orally	7	zhèngjiàn 证件	document
3	guàshī 挂失	to report the loss	8	yuánjiàn 原件	original document
4	dòngjié 冻结	to freeze	9	fùyìnjiàn 复印件	copied document
5	zhèngshì 正式	officially	10	jiědòng 解冻	to unfreeze

文化导航
Cultural Navigation

　　中国大部分银行都有自动取款机，例如中国银行和中国工商银行，但有的银行取款机不接受外国卡取款。中国的自动取款机屏幕显示中、英文两种语言。有时机器显示不能取钱，往往是因为这台机器当时没有与国际联网。此时你可以试试其他机器，或第二天再来。用取款机取款每笔有最高限额，有的是2,500元，有的是1,500元。如果需要，你可以多取几次，直到当日限额为止。

　　In China, there are many banks with ATMs including the Bank of China and the Industrial and Commercial Bank of China, but some machines don't accept foreign cards. These ATMs in China work in both Chinese and English. If you are told by a machine that your transaction has been declined, contact your bank and do not panic. This often just means that the international network is unavailable. You should try other machines or return the next day. The maximum you will be able to withdraw in one request is about ¥2,500, sometimes as little as ¥1,500. You can press the "continue" button and try to get more cash out up to the ATMs' daily limit.

核心句
Key Sentence

Zhànghù mìmǎ bú duì.
账户 密码不对。
The code of the account is incorrect.

句型与替换
Substitution

jùjué jiāoyì
拒绝交易
refuse to transact

chūxiàn ānquán wèntí
出现安全问题
have security issue

rì jiāoyì cìshù guò duō
日交易次数过多
have too many daily transactions

扩展/Extension

1. Wǒ zuótiān zài ATM jī shang
我 昨天在ATM机 上
qǔqián, kě qǔ bù chūlái.
取钱，可取不出来。

I tried to withdraw money from an ATM machine yesterday but failed.

2. Píngmù tíshì shì jùjué jiāoyì.
屏幕提示是 "拒绝交易"。

The message on the screen is "transaction denied".

3. Nǐ shū de mìmǎ kěnéng bú duì.
你输的密码可能不对。

The code you entered may be wrong.

4. Dàngtiān de jiāoyì cìshù guò duō.
当天的交易次数过多。

There are too many transactions for the day.

甲: Wǒ zuótiān wǎnshang qù ATM jī qǔqián, kě qǔ bù chūlái.
我 昨天 晚上 去ATM机取钱，可取不出来。

Last night, I tried to withdraw money from the ATM
machine but failed.

乙: Píngmù tíshì shì shénme?
屏幕 提示 是 什么？

What is the message on the screen?

甲: Jùjué jiāoyì.
"拒绝 交易"。

"Transaction denied".

乙: Nǐ dào wǎngshang chá nǐ de zhànghù le ma?
你到 网 上 查你的账户 了吗？

Did you check your account online?

甲: Chá le, yíqiè zhèngcháng.
查了，一切 正常。

I did and everything looks good.

乙: Nà kěnéng nǐ shū de mìmǎ bú duì, yě kěnéng shì dàngtiān de jiāoyì
那可能你输的密码不对，也可能是 当天 的 交易

cìshù guò duō, yě kěnéng jīqì tài lǎo le.
次数过多，也可能机器太老了。

You might have entered the wrong code or made more transactions than allowed for a day or the machine is too old.

甲: Nà zěnme bàn?
那怎么 办？

What should I do then?

乙: Wèile nǐ zhànghù de ānquán, gǎnkuài dào yínháng qù chácha.
为了 你账户 的 安全，赶快到 银行 去查查。

For the safety of your account, go to the bank to have a
check.

相关词语／Related Words

1	píngmù 屏幕	screen	5	zhèngcháng 正常	normal
2	tíshì 提示	indication	6	yìcháng 异常	abnormal
3	jùjué 拒绝	to refuse	7	ānquán 安全	safety
4	jiāoyì 交易	transaction			

文化导航
Cultural Navigation

　　在中国，当你用自动取款机提取人民币时，钱其实取自你的海外账户，其间的兑换率一般来说都很合理，至于手续费多少则取决于你的卡所属银行的规定。如果你用ATM卡或借记卡，手续费比较低，跟你在本国取钱的手续费差不多。但如果用信用卡，手续费就会较贵，因为这等于你在借钱花。

　　When you use an ATM to withdraw money in China, the money obviously is taken from your foreign bank account usually at a quite reasonable rate. The commission and transaction charges are dependent upon your own bank's policies. If you are using an ATM / debit card, usually the charges are comparable to drawing money in your own country. If you are using a credit card, it can be relatively expensive since it is "cash advance".

健康保健
Health

核心句
Key Sentence

Zhèr de jiànshēnfáng tài shǎo le.
这儿的健身房太少了。
There are very few gyms here.

句型与替换
Substitution

wǎngqiúchǎng
网球场
tennis court

yóuyǒngchí
游泳池
swimming pool

tǐyùchǎng
体育场
sportsground

扩 展／Extension

Zhèr nǎ yǒu jiànshēnfáng?
1. 这儿哪有 健身房？

Where can I find a gym here?

Jiànshēnfáng de qìcái
2. 健身房的器材
zěnmeyàng?
怎么样？

How about the facilities of the gym?

Jiànshēnfáng yuèfèi duōshao?
3. 健身房月费多少？

How much is the monthly fee for the gym?

Jiànshēnfáng jǐ diǎn kāimén?
4. 健身房几点开门？
Jǐ diǎn guānmén?
几点 关门？

What is the business hour of the gym?

甲：
Zhèr de jiànshēnfáng tài shǎo le.
这儿的健身房太少了。
There are very few gyms here.

乙：
Tīngshuō dōngqū yǒu yì jiā.
听说东区有一家。
I've heard there is one in the East District.

甲：
Wǒ qùguo yí cì, tài yuǎn le, yào dǎo liǎng cì chē.
我去过一次，太远了，要倒两次车。
I've been there once, but it is too far. I have to change two buses to get there.

乙：
Jiànshēn qìcái zěnmeyàng?
健身器材怎么样？
How about its facilities?

甲：
Hái xíng, búguò rén tǐng duō de.
还行，不过人挺多的。
Fine but there are too many people.

乙：
Fèiyong ne?
费用呢？
How about the fees?

甲：
Tāmen yǐ jìdù wéi dānwèi shōufèi, kě wǒ zhǐ zài zhèr dāi liǎng gè yuè.
他们以季度为单位收费，可我只在这儿呆两个月。
They collect fees on the quarterly basis, but I only stay here for two months.

乙：
Nà nǐ zěnme bàn?
那你怎么办？
What do you do then?

甲：
Méi bànfǎ, jiù zài fùjìn pǎopaobù.
没办法，就在附近跑跑步。
I can't do anything. I am jogging in the vicinity.

1	jiànshēn qìcái 健身器材	fitness facilities	4	hùwài 户外	outdoor
2	dānwèi 单位	unit (to collect fees)	5	pǎobù 跑步	running; jogging
3	shōufèi 收费	to collect fees			

文化导航
Cultural Navigation

　　上世纪七十年代以前中国食物匮乏，人们见面之后说对方"你胖了"被视为恭维话，说明对方有钱能吃饱。改革开放后，人们生活水平提高，吃饱饭已不是问题，人们的胖与瘦不再是评判是否有钱的标准，"你胖了"也不再是恭维话了。事实上，现在人们摄入的热量较以前大大增加，肥胖，尤其是儿童肥胖已成为一种疾病，减肥产品的研制生产已成为一种新兴产业。

Before the 1970s, the comment "you have put on weight" was considered as a compliment implying that the person who received the compliment was the one who had money to eat to his full. As living standards have improved in recent years, this comment has changed its implication and people are careful with this expression. In fact, the intake of calories from rich food has been on the rise. Obesity has become a problem especially among children. Weight-loss products and medicines have become a new industry.

Wǒ   kāishǐ   liàn   yújiā   le.
我开始练瑜伽了。
I have begun practicing yoga.

liàn   wǔshù
练武术
practice martial arts

xué chàng   jīngjù
学唱京剧
learn to sing Peking Opera

tiào Zhōngguó   wǔdǎo
跳中国舞蹈
practice traditional Chinese dance

xué Zhōngguóhuà
学中国画
learn to paint Chinese paintings

扩 展/Extension

Yújiā nàn xué ma?
1. 瑜伽难学吗?

Is it difficult to learn yoga?

Wǒ měi tiān liàn liǎng gè xiǎoshí de
2. 我每天练两个小时的
yújiā.
瑜伽。

I practice yoga two hours every day.

Wǒ duì yújiā yuè lái yuè zháomí.
3. 我对瑜伽越来越着迷。

I have become more and more enchanted in yoga.

4. Yújiābān de lǎoshī hěn yǒu
   瑜伽班的老师很有
   nàixīn.
   耐心。

The yoga teacher is very patient.

对话实例/Dialogue

甲：Měi tiān xiàkè dōu kàn bú jiàn nǐ, gàn shénme qù le?
每天下课都看不见你，干什么去了？

I didn't see you recently after school. Where were you?

乙：Wǒ qù shàng yújiābān le.
我去上瑜伽班了。

I went to the yoga class.

甲：Shénme shíhou yòu liàn qǐ yújiā le?
什么时候又练起瑜伽了？

When did you start yoga?

乙：Nà tiān wǒ shìle yí cì yújiābān, jiù liàn qilai le.
那天我试了一次瑜伽班，就练起来了。

The other day I tried the yoga class and began to practice it.

甲：Gǎnjué zěnmeyàng?
感觉怎么样？

How do you like it?

乙：Yuè liàn yuè zháomí.
越练越着迷。

The more I practice, the more I like it.

甲：Nà wǒ yě qù shìshi.
那我也去试试。

I will try then.

乙：Hǎo a, wǒmen yìqǐ qù.
好啊，我们一起去。

Why not? Let's go together.

1	liàn 练	to practice	4	gǎnjué 感觉	to feel
2	yújiā 瑜伽	yoga	5	yuè 越⋯⋯	the more...
				yuè 越⋯⋯	the more
3	shì 试	to try	6	zháomí 着迷	enchanted

文化导航
Cultural Navigation

　　在中国，健康养生已成为人们之间的热门话题。市场上有不少以此为题目的书籍，电视台和电台这类节目也很受欢迎。这股潮流的另一个表现是中国城市里的公园每天清晨都会聚集很多人练太极，这些人大都是老人和退休人员。

How to live a healthy and long life is a hot topic among Chinese people. There have been numerous books published on the topic, and TV stations and radios feature a lot on the topic. As another sign of the trend, one of the most spectacular scenes in Chinese cities is that crowds of people gather in the park in early mornings to practice tai chi. Most of them are old people and retirees.

核心句
Key Sentence

Wǒ guà yí gè nèikēhào.
我挂一个内科号。
Please register with the internal medicine department for me.

句型与替换
Substitution

wàikē
外科
surgical department

zhuānjiā ménzhěn
专家门诊
specialist

xīnzàng zhuānkē
心脏专科
cardiologist

zhōngyīkē
中医科
Chinese medicine department

扩 展/Extension

Wǒ juéde tóu tèbié tòng,
1. 我觉得头特别痛，
yīnggāi guà nǎ kē?
应该挂哪科？

I have a severe headache. Which department should I register with?

Nǐ kànkan zhōngyī ba.
2. 你看看中医吧。

You may need to see a Chinese medicine practitioner.

Nǐ zuò yí gè xiōngtòu ba.
3. 你做一个胸透吧。

I will prescribe you a chest X-ray.

Nǐ duō xiūxi jiù hǎo le.
4. 你多休息就好了。　　You should take more rest.

对话实例/Dialogue

Dàifu,　　wǒ tóutòng,　tóuyūn,　húnshēn fālěng.
甲: 大夫，我头痛、头晕、浑身 发冷。

Doctor, I have a headache and feel dizzy and chilly all over.

Xiān shìshi biǎo...　　nǐ fāshāo le.　　Wǒ lái jiǎnchá yíxià　fèibù.
乙: 先试试表……你发烧了。我来检查一下肺部。

Check the temperature first…You have a fever. Let me check your lungs.

Dàifu,　yánzhòng ma?
甲: 大夫，严重 吗?

Doctor, is it serious?

Nǐ dé liúgǎn le.　　dàn bú tài yánzhòng. Wǒ xiān gěi nǐ kāi liǎng zhǒng yào.
乙: 你得流感了，但不太严重。我先给你开两 种 药。

You've got the flu but not serious. I will prescribe you two medicines.

Zěnme chī?
甲: 怎么 吃?

How to take them?

Měi rì sān cì,　　měi cì liǎng piàn.
乙: 每日三次，每次两 片。

Take them three times a day and two pills a time.

Hǎo.
甲: 好。

OK.

Hái yào duō hēshuǐ,　　zhùyì bǎonuǎn,　duō xiūxi.　Shāo bú tuì,
乙: 还要多 喝水，注意 保暖，多 休息。烧 不退，
zài huílái kàn.
再回来 看。

Drink a lot of water, keep warm and have more rest. If the fever continues, come to see me again.

1	tóutòng 头痛	headache	7	fèibù 肺部	chest
2	tóuyūn 头晕	dizzy	8	yánzhòng 严重	serious
3	húnshēn 浑身	all over the body	9	liúgǎn 流感	flu
4	shìbiǎo 试表	to check the temperature	10	kāi yào 开药	to prescribe
5	fāshāo 发烧	to have a fever	11	bǎonuǎn 保暖	to keep warm
6	jiǎnchá 检查	to examine	12	xiūxi 休息	to rest

文化导航
Cultural Navigation

　　在中国医院看病，病人首先要自己选定要看哪一科，然后到挂号处挂号，挂号费一般是五元。但如果你要看专家门诊，挂号费会高很多。在大医院里，病人先由护士接待，然后在门诊室外面等候看医生。

　　At a Chinese hospital, an outpatient has to decide which department he/she will go to and pay registration fees at the registration window before seeing a doctor. The fee is about ¥5. But if you choose to see a better-known specialist, the fee will be much higher. In a big hospital, the patient will see a nurse first and wait in line with other patients outside the doctor's examination room.

叫救护车 | Calling an Ambulance

核心句 Key Sentence

Wǒmen děi mǎshàng sòng tā qù yīyuàn.
我们得马上送他去医院。
We have to send him to hospital right away.

句型 与替换 Substitution

jiào jiùhùchē
叫救护车
call an ambulance

jiào yīshēng chūzhěn
叫医生出诊
ask the doctor for a home visit

dào yīyuàn jiùzhěn
到医院就诊
go to hospital

扩 展/Extension

Wǒ péngyou tóutòng de lìhai.
1. 我朋友头痛得厉害。

My friend suffers a severe headache.

Tā gāoyā 180, dīyā 120.
2. 他高压180，低压120。

His systolic pressure is 180 and diastolic pressure 120.

Tā xiōngbù téngtòng, hūxī yǒu
3. 他胸部疼痛，呼吸有
kùnnan.
困难。

He has a severe chest pain and can hardly breathe.

Ràng tā píngtǎngzhe. Wǒmen mǎ-
4. 让 他 平躺着。我们 马
shàng pàichē.
上 派车。

Let him lie down and we
will dispatch an ambulance
immediately.

对话实例/Dialogue

甲:
120, wǒ péngyou tóutòng de lìhai. děi mǎshàng qù yīyuàn.
120，我朋友 头痛得厉害，得马上去医院。

120, my friend has a severe headache and needs to go to the
hospital right away.

乙:
Tā xuèyā zěnmeyàng?
他血压怎么样？

How about his blood pressure?

甲:
Gāoyā 180, dīyā 120.
高压180，低压120。

His systolic pressure is 180 and diastolic pressure 120.

乙:
Hái yǒu shénme bù hǎo?
还有什么 不好？

What else?

甲:
Tā xiōngbù téngtòng, hūxī yǒu kùnnan.
他胸部 疼痛，呼吸有 困难。

He has a severe chest pain and can hardly breathe.

乙:
Ràng tā píngtǎngzhe. Wǒmen mǎshàng pàichē. Gàosu wǒ nǐ de dìzhǐ.
让 他 平躺着。我们 马上 派车。告诉我你的地址。

Let him lie down and we will dispatch an ambulance
immediately. Your address please?

甲:
Chéngnán Qū Tàiyuán Jiē 125 hào. Jiùhùchē shénme shíhou dào?
城 南区 太原街125号。救护车什么 时候到？

125 Taiyuan Street, Chengnan District. When can the
ambulance be here?

乙:
Dàyuē 15 fēnzhōng.
大约15分钟。

In about 15 minutes.

1	yīyuàn 医院	hospital	7	kùnnan 困难	difficulty
2	xuèyā 血压	blood pressure	8	píngtǎng 平躺	to lie down
3	gāoyā 高压	systolic pressure	9	pài chē 派车	to dispatch a vehicle
4	dīyā 低压	diastolic pressure	10	jiùhùchē 救护车	ambulance
5	téngtòng 疼痛	pain	11	dìzhǐ 地址	address
6	hūxī 呼吸	to breathe			

文化导航
Cultural Navigation

在中国医院，病人看病、接受治疗以前都要先到收费处付费，项目包括检查、试验、打针、输液、照X光、CT等。医院有自己的药房，病人到收费处交完费用后，再到药房取药。当然也可以到外面的药店买药。

At a Chinese hospital, an outpatient has to pay all the prescribed treatments up front including examinations, tests, injections, intravenous infusion, X-rays, CT, etc. at the payment window. The hospitals have their own pharmacies. After you pay for the prescriptions and get a receipt, you will go to the pharmacist window to fulfill your prescription. You can also get the medicine from an independent pharmacy.

其他服务
Other Services

wǒ yào jì yí gè kuàidì.
我要寄一个快递。
I want to send this by express mail.

句型
与替换
Substitution

yì fēng píngxìn
一封平信
a regular letter

yì fēng guàhàoxìn
一封挂号信
a registered letter

yì zhāng míngxìnpiàn
一张明信片
a postcard

yí gè bāoguǒ
一个包裹
a package/parcel

扩展/Extension

Dào Shànghǎi de kuàidì yào duōshao qián?
1. 到上海的快递要多少钱？ How much is it for express delivery service to Shanghai?

Qǐng tiánhǎo kuàijiànbāo.
2. 请填好快件包。 Please complete the express mail envelope.

Jì de dōngxi děi zài kuàijiànbāo shang
3. 寄的东西得在快件包 上
zhùmíng.
注明。 The contents should be listed on the envelope.

Yòng shōujù hàomǎ kěyǐ shàngwǎng
4. 用收据号码可以上网
gēnzōng cháxún.
跟踪查询。 The package can be tracked online with the receipt number.

甲: Wǒ yào jì yí gè kuàidì. Zhè shì tiánhǎo de kuàijiànbāo.
我要寄一个快递。这是填好的快件包。

I want to send a package by express mail. This is the completed express mail envelope.

乙: Lǐmiàn jì de shì shénme?
里面寄的是什么?

What is inside?

甲: Shì rùxué shēnqǐng cáiliào hé shēnqǐng zhīpiào.
是入学申请材料和申请支票。

My university application package and a check for application.

乙: Nà nǐ děi zài kuàijiànbāo shang zhùmíng.
那你得在快件包上注明。

You need to list them on the envelope.

甲: Hǎo. Dàyuē jǐ tiān néng dào?
好。大约几天能到?

OK. How many days will it take to arrive there?

乙: Liǎng tiān dào sì tiān.
两天到四天。

Two to four days.

甲: Duōshao qián?
多少钱?

How much is it?

乙: Rúguǒ bù chāozhòng, kuàijiànbāo 1 kuài, yóufèi 20 kuài.
如果不超重,快件包1块,邮费20块。

If it is not overweight, one yuan for the envelope and 20 yuan for the postage.

1	tián 填	to complete (forms)	6	yóufèi 邮费	postage
2	kuàijiànbāo 快件包	express delivery package	7	shōujù 收据	receipt
3	jì 寄	to mail	8	gēnzōng 跟踪	to track
4	zhùmíng 注明	to indicate	9	cháxún 查询	to check
5	chāozhòng 超重	overweight			

文化导航
Cultural Navigation

中国邮局是传统的邮递渠道，提供国内、国际间的信件、包裹、汇款、电报、传真等邮政服务。但近年来，中国城市出现很多快递公司，业务范围以国内城市为主，提供文件、票据、样品等的传递。因为这类公司服务灵活、方便、便宜，很受客户的欢迎。

Chinese post offices function as a traditional mailing channel through which letters, parcels, remittances, telegrams and faxes are delivered domestically and internationally. In addition, there are many local express delivery companies that deliver files, vouchers, and sample products nationwide. Since these companies are more flexible and cheaper, they gain more and more popularity.

核心句
Key Sentence

Bàogào jiāotōng shìgù, bō 122.
报告 交通 事故，拨122。
To report a car accident, call 122.

句型与替换
Substitution

bàogào qiǎngjié
报告 抢劫
report a robbery

cháxún diànhuà hàomǎ
查询 电话 号码
check a telephone number

jíjiù zhōngxīn
急救 中心
emergency medical center

扩 展/Extension

1. 122, zhèr fāshēngle yì qǐ
   122, 这儿 发生了 一起
   jiāotōng shìgù.
   交通 事故。

   122, there is a traffic accident here.

2. 110, wǒ yào bàogào yì qǐ
   110, 我 要 报告 一起
   qiǎngjié'àn.
   抢 劫案。

   110, I want to report a robbery here.

3. 114, qǐngwèn Shānxī Lù xiǎoxué
   114, 请问 山西路 小学
   de diànhuà hàomǎ shì duōshao?
   的 电话 号码 是 多少？

   114, can you check for me the number of Shanxilu Elementary School?

甲: Zāogāo, qiánmiàn zhuàngchē le.
糟糕，前面 撞 车 了。

It is too bad that there is a car accident.

乙: Bàogào jiāotōng shìgù, dǎ 122.
报告 交通 事故，打122。

Call 122 to report the accident.

......

甲: Wèi, 122 ma? Zhèr fāshēngle yì qǐ jiāotōng shìgù.
喂，122吗？ 这儿发生了一起 交通 事故。

Hello, 122? There is a car accident here.

丙: Yǒu shāngwáng ma?
有 伤 亡 吗？

Is there any injury and death?

甲: Bú tài qīngchu, liǎng liàng chē zhuàngdào yìqǐ le.
不太清楚，两 辆 车 撞 到一起 了。

I don't know but two cars hit each other.

丙: Zài nǎlǐ?
在哪里？

Where is it?

甲: Nánkāi Dàxué dōngmén fùjìn.
南开大学 东门 附近。

Close to the east gate of Nankai University.

丙: Wǒmen mǎshàng jiù dào.
我们 马上就到。

We will be right there.

1	zāogāo 糟糕	too bad		6	dǎ diànhuà 打电话	to make a call
2	zhuàngchē 撞车	car collision		7	fāshēng 发生	to take place
3	bàogào 报告	to report		8	shāngwáng 伤亡	casualty
4	jiāotōng 交通	traffic		9	qīngchu 清楚	clear
5	shìgù 事故	accident		10	fùjìn 附近	close to

文化导航
Cultural Navigation

中国的座机号码和手机号码是两个不同的系统。座机有地区号，用来区分不同地区的电话，如北京是"010"，天津是"022"。大城市的座机号码一般是八位数，其他地区是七位数。手机号码一般是11位数字，没有地区号。

The Chinese Telephone Code Plan is the way to group telephone numbers. Landlines and mobile phones follow different systems: landlines use area codes, for example, "010" for Beijing and "022" for Tianjin, while mobile phones do not. Domestic landline numbers in large cities have 8 digits, and in other areas have 7 digits. Mobile phone numbers have 11 digits without area codes.

打长途电话 | Making a Long-distance Call

核心句 Key Sentence

Gěi Měiguó dǎ diànhuà, xiān bō 001.
给美国打电话，先拨001。

If you call the United States, please dial 001 first.

句型与替换 Substitution

dǎ guójì diànhuà
打国际电话
make an international call

dǎ chángtú diànhuà
打长途电话
make a long-distance call

bō 00 jiā guójiāhào
拨00加国家号
dial 00 plus the country code

bō qūhào
拨区号
dial the area code

扩展/Extension

1. Dǎ guójì chángtú diànhuà jǐ kuài qián yì fēnzhōng?
   打国际长途电话几块钱一分钟？

   How much is it per minute to make an international phone call?

2. Mǎi yí gè chángtú diànhuàkǎ, dǎ guójì diànhuà liǎng-sān máo qián yì fēnzhōng.
   买一个长途电话卡，打国际电话两三毛钱一分钟。

   If you buy a long-distance phone card, it only costs 20 to 30 fen a minute to make an international call.

3. Qǐng gěi wǒ jiē duìfāng fùfèi diànhuà.
请 给我接对方付费 电话。

I would like to make a collect call.

4. Kěyǐ yòng Skype dǎ guójì chángtú.
可以用Skype打国际 长途。

You can use Skype to make an international call.

💬 **对话实例/Dialogue**

甲: Wǒ láile jǐ tiān le, xiǎng gěi jiālǐ dǎ gè diànhuà.
我来了几天了，想给家里打个电话。
I have been here for a few days and want to call my home.

乙: Gěi Měiguó dǎ diànhuà, xiān bō 001, zài bō nǐ jiā de diànhuà hàomǎ.
给美国打电话，先拨001，再拨你家的电话
号码。
If you call the US, dial 001 first and then dial your home number.

甲: 001 shì shénme hào?
001是什么号？
What is 001?

乙: 00 shì guójì diànhuà dàimǎ, 1 shì Měiguó guójiāhào.
00是国际电话代码，1是美国国家号。
00 is the international code and 1 is the country code of the US.

甲: Zài lǚguǎn dǎ diànhuà guì bú guì?
在旅馆打电话贵不贵？
Is it expensive if I use the hotel phone?

乙: Guì, jǐ kuài qián yì fēnzhōng, yǒu de diànhuà hái bù néng dǎ.
贵，几块钱一分钟，有的电话还不能打。
Yes, it is. About a few yuan a minute and some phones have the long-distance call blocked.

甲: Zěnme dǎ bǐjiào piányi?
怎么打比较便宜？
What is a cheaper way?

乙: Mǎi yí gè chángtú diànhuàkǎ, liǎng-sān máo qián yì fēnzhōng.
买一个长途电话卡，两三毛钱一分钟。
You can buy a long-distance phone card and it is only 20 or 30 fen a minute.

1	dàimǎ 代码	code	5	chángtú 长途	long-distance
2	guójiāhào 国家号	country code	6	diànhuàkǎ 电话卡	phone card
3	bō 拨	to dial	7	shēngyīn 声音	voice
4	guójì 国际	international	8	qīngchu 清楚	clear

文化导航
Cultural Navigation

对中国人来说，有的数字会给人带来好运，被视为幸运数字，有的数字就不那么幸运。比方说，数字"9"是所有数字中最大的，因此被视为数字中最幸运的——比如故宫有9999间房。数字"8"听起来像发财的"发"，也是个幸运数字，2008年奥运会的开始时间是2008年的8月8号8点。数字"6"的发音在方言里像顺溜的"溜"，也是幸运数字。但是数字"4"听起来像死亡的"死"，所以人们尽量避免在自己的电话号码和家庭住址里出现这个数字。

For Chinese, some numbers are luckier than others. For example, the number 9 is the biggest number and thus regarded as the luckiest number among all. For example, in the Forbidden City there are 9999 rooms. Number 8 sounds like "fā" which means "fortune". The 2008 Olympic Games started at 8 o'clock, August 8th, 2008. Number 6 sounds like "liu" in "shūnliu" which means "smooth". However, the number 4 sounds like "sǐ" which means "death", thus people try to avoid it in phone numbers or home addresses.

99 买手机 | Purchasing a Cell Phone

Zhè kuǎn shǒujī yǒu wúxiàn shàngwǎng gōngnéng.

这款手机有无线上网功能。

This kind of cell phone has wireless Internet function.

句型与替换
Substitution

lùyīn
录音
audio-tape

lùxiàng
录像
video-tape

tīng yīnyuè
听音乐
listen to music

tīng guǎngbō
听广播
listen to the radio

kàn diànshì
看电视
watch TV

扩展/Extension

Zhè kuǎn shǒujī yǒu shénme gōngnéng?
1. 这款手机有什么功能？

What features does this kind of cell phone have?

Zhè kuǎn shǒujī gōngnéng qíquán.
2. 这款手机功能齐全。

It has a lot of extra features.

Zhè shì jīnnián de xīnkuǎn.
3. 这是今年的新款。

This is the newly released style this year.

Zhè kuǎn shǒujī nèicún dà.
4. 这 款 手机内存大。　　　This cell phone has a large storage space.

对话实例/Dialogue

Láojià, wǒ xiǎng kànkan zuì xīn kuǎn shǒujī.
甲: 劳驾，我 想 看看iPhone最新 款 手机。

Excuse me, can I take a look at the latest version of iPhone?

Zhè jiù shì, nín kàn yàngshì duō shíshàng.
乙: 这就是，您看样式多时尚。

Here it is. It looks so fashionable.

Chúle zhàoxiàng, hái yǒu shénme gōngnéng?
甲: 除了 照相，还有什么 功能？

Other than taking photos, what functions does it have?

Zhè kuǎn shǒujī kěyǐ wúxiàn shàngwǎng, hái kěyǐ lùyīn,
乙: 这 款 手机可以无线 上网，还可以录音、

lùxiàng, tīng yīnyuè ne, nín shìshi.
录像、听音乐呢，您试试。

It has the wireless Internet function. It also can record, shoot videos and has an MP3 player. Try it.

Zhēn búcuò.
甲: 真 不错。

It is really great.

Nín kěyǐ yòng tā chá tiānqì, zhǎolù, tīng guǎngbō, kàn diànshì.
乙: 您可以用它查天气、找路、听广播、看电视。

You can also use it to check the weather, locate a place, listen to the radio and watch TV.

Nèicún duōshao?
甲: 内存多少？

What's the storage space?

Nèicún 32 GB, zúgòu yìbān rén yòng de.
乙: 内存32GB，足够一般人用 的。

It is 32 GB, quite enough for everyday use.

1	kuǎn 款	style		4	gōngnéng 功能	feature
2	yàngshì 样式	looks; type		5	nèicún 内存	storage space
3	shíshàng 时尚	fashionable		6	zúgòu 足够	enough

文化导航
Cultural Navigation

　　中国手机出售和手机服务是分开的。你可以买电话卡充值或到银行为手机付费。如果你的电话丢了或被人偷走了，你得马上到电话公司取消你的电话芯片，并同时要求保留电话号码和话费余额。中国年轻人很喜欢用手机发短信，因为短信收费比电话通话要便宜得多。

　　There is a clear distinction between cell phone purchase and cell phone service in China. Cell phone service payment can be made by buying a card and calling the cell phone company, or through commercial banks. When a cell phone is stolen, the owner must visit the cell phone service company to cancel the previous card, at the same time retaining the previous phone number and pre-payment. Texting is cheaper than calling so it is more popular among young people.

Shīfu, wǒ xiǎng lǐfà.
师傅，我想理发。
Sir, I want to have a haircut.

tàngfà
烫发
perm the hair

rǎnfà
染发
dye the hair

chuī xià tóufà
吹下头发
dry the hair with a blower

xǐtóu
洗头
wash the hair

扩展/Extension

Nǐ xiān xǐtóu zài lǐfà.
1. 你先洗头再理发。

You wash your hair first before the haircut.

Nín xiǎng zěnme lǐ?
2. 您想怎么理?

How do you want your haircut?

Liǎng biān gěi wǒ jiǎnduǎn yìdiǎn.
3. 两边给我剪短一点。

Cut a bit short on the sides.

Tóudǐng dǎbáo diǎnr.
4. 头顶打薄点儿。

Trim the top a bit.

甲： Shīfu, wǒ xiǎng lǐfà.
师傅，我想理发。

Hello, Master, I want to have a haircut.

乙： Hǎo, xiān xǐtóu.
好，先洗头。

OK. Wash your hair first.

......

乙： Nín xiǎng zěnme lǐ?
您想怎么理？

How do you want your haircut?

甲： Liǎng biān gěi wǒ jiǎnduǎn yìdiǎn.
两边给我剪短一点。

Cut short on the sides.

乙： Shàngbiān ne?
上边呢？

How about the top?

甲： Dǎbáo diǎnr.
打薄点儿。

Trim just a bit.

......

乙： Nín kàn zhèyàng xíng ma?
您看这样行吗？

How do you like it?

甲： Hěn hǎo, xièxie.
很好，谢谢。

Pretty good. Thank you.

1	lǐfà 理发	haircut	5	lǐfàdiàn 理发店	barber's shop
2	xǐtóu 洗头	to wash the hair	6	lǐfàshī 理发师	barber; hairdresser
3	jiǎnduǎn 剪短	to cut short	7	fàxíng 发型	hair style
4	dǎbáo 打薄	to trim			

文化导航
Cultural Navigation

你可能会发现中国人使用"谢谢你"这三个字的频率远远低于西方人。"谢谢"一般不用在家庭成员和朋友之间，因为中国人认为感谢是让对方感觉出来的，而不是说出来的。你会对向你提供服务的人道谢，但服务行业的人很少会因为你给他们带来了生意机会，对你说谢谢。不过，近几年，中国人说"谢谢"的次数越来越多了。

You may find that Chinese people say "thank you" much less than Westerners. They seldom say it within families and with friends in the belief that appreciation is something to be felt rather than spoken out. If you receive a kind of service, you may say "thank you" to the people who serve you. But people in the service industry seldom say "thank you" to show their appreciation for the business opportunity you as a consumer provide to them. But in recent years, people say "thank you" much more frequently than before.

Wǒ yào zhào yì zhāng hùzhào zhàopiàn.
我要照一张护照照片。
I want to take a passport photo.

qiānzhèng	xuéshēngzhèng
签证	学生证
visa	student ID
dìnghūn	hūnlǐ
订婚	婚礼
engagement	wedding

扩 展／Extension

Hùzhào zhàopiàn mǎshàng kě qǔ.
1. 护照 照片 马上 可取。

You can get your passport photos in minutes.

Nín yào zhào jǐ cùn de zhàopiàn?
2. 您要 照几寸的照片？

What size of the photo do you want?

Gěi wǒ xǐ yì zhāng bā cùn cǎisè
3. 给我洗一 张 八寸彩色
zhàopiàn.
照片。

I want to develop an 8-inch color photo.

Bǎ nǐ yào xǐ de zhàopiàn chuándào
4. 把你要洗的照片 传到
wǒ de diànzǐ yóuxiāng.
我的电子邮箱。

Email me the pictures you want to develop.

对话实例/Dialogue

甲: Xiānsheng, wǒ yào zhào yì zhāng hùzhào zhàopiàn.
先生，我要照一张护照照片。

Sir, I want to take a passport photo.

乙: Hǎo, nín bǎ màozi zhāi xialai.
好，您把帽子摘下来。

Sure. Please take your hat off.

甲: Kěyǐ dài yǎnjìng ma?
可以戴眼镜吗?

Can I wear my glasses?

乙: Kěyǐ. Hǎo, nín wǎng hòu zhàn yìdiǎn, kàn qiánmiàn
可以。好，您往后站一点，看前面……
fàngsōng, zhùyì, zhào le!
放松，注意，照了!

Yes, you can. OK, please step back a bit, look front, relaxed, attention, shoot!

甲: Xièxie nín. Wǒ hái xiǎng xǐ yì zhāng bā cùn cǎisè zhàopiàn.
谢谢您。我还想洗一张八寸彩色照片。

Thank you. I also want to develop an 8-inch color photo.

乙: Gěi wǒ U pán, wǒ bǎ zhàopiàn xiàzǎi dào jìsuànjī shang.
给我U盘，我把照片下载到计算机上。

Please give me your flash drive and I will download the picture to my computer.

甲: Zài zhèr, jiù xǐ zhè zhāng.
在这儿，就洗这张。

Here is the flash drive. Here is the picture I want to develop.

乙: Hǎo le. Qǐng dào shōuyíntái jiāo qián, liǎng tiān hòu qǔ zhàopiàn.
好了。请到收银台交钱，两天后取照片。

It is done. Please pay at the cashier. Your pictures will be ready in two days.

1	洗（照片） xǐ zhàopiàn	to develop (a picture)	5	相机 xiàngjī	camera
2	八寸 bā cùn	8 inches	6	下载 xiàzǎi	to download
3	彩色 cǎisè	color	7	取 qǔ	to pick up
4	黑白 hēibái	black and white			

文化导航
Cultural Navigation

　　自改革开放以来，中国的服务业发展迅猛，主要表现在两方面：一是规模扩大，二是成为吸引就业的主要渠道。中国的服务业包括餐饮业、旅游业、零售业、金融、保险、信息产业、交通、广告、法律、会计、房地产等。据中国发展规划，到2020年服务业的增加值将占国内生产总值的百分之五十，而2004年只占百分之三十三，2008年占百分之四十。

　　Since the reform and opening up at the end of the 1970s, China's service industry has developed rapidly. It is reflected in two aspects. First, the scale of service industry is expanding. Second, it has become a main channel to attract social employment. China's service industry includes business on food and drinks, tourism, retail sales, finance, insurance, information, transportation, advertisement, law, accounting and real estate management, etc. According to China's development plan, by 2020, service industry will account for more than 50% of GDP compared to 33% in 2004 and 40% in 2008.

附 录

一、紧急情况用句

1. 卫生间在哪?	Where is the rest room?
2. 我现在遇到大麻烦了。	I'm in big trouble now.
3. 我该怎么办呢?	What should I do?
4. 小心!	Watch out!
5. 你要干什么?	What do you want?
6. 好的,别伤害我。	Okay. Don't hurt me.
7. 你是谁?	Who are you?
8. 别碰我!	Don't touch me!
9. 离我远点儿!	Leave me alone!
10. 我叫警察啦!	I'll call the police!
11. 救命呀!	Help!
12. 来人呀!	Somebody!
13. 警察!	Police!
14. 你能帮我叫警察吗?	Can you call the police for me?
15. 抓住他!	Get him!
16. 着火啦!	Fire!
17. 开门!	Open the door!
18. 站住! 小偷!	Stop! Thief!
19. 我的护照丢了。	I lost my passport.
20. 您能马上注销我的信用卡吗?	Will you cancel my credit card immediately?
21. 我的行李找不到了。	I can't find my baggage.
22. 警察局在哪儿?	Where is the police station?
23. 我遇到交通事故了。	I am in a car accident.
24. 请叫救护车!	Please call an ambulance!
25. 我什么也不知道。	I don't know anything about it.
26. 我是受害者。	I'm the victim.
27. 这是哪儿呀?	Where am I?
28. 我迷路了。	I'm lost.
29. 我找不到我的朋友了。	I can't find my friend.
30. 我的汽车坏了。	My car broke down.
31. 请叫医生来。	Please call a doctor.

二、度量衡换算表

1. 重量

克 g (gram)	千克 kg (kilogram)	盎司 oz (ounce)	磅 lb (pound)
1,000	1	35.27	2.205
28.3	0.0283	1	0.062
454	0.454	16.00	1

1盎司 ≈ 28克

1磅 ≈ 454克

2. 长度

厘米 cm (centimeter)	米 m (meter)	千米 km (kilometer)	英寸 inch	英尺 feet	码 yard	英里 mile
1	0.01	—	0.394	—	—	—
100	1	0.001	39.37	3.28	1.09	—
100,000	1,000	1	39,370	3,280	1,094	0.62
2.54	—	—	1	0.083	0.028	—
30.48	0.305	—	12.00	1	0.333	—
91.44	0.914	—	36.00	3	1	—
—	1,609	1.61	—	—	1,760	1

1英寸 ≈ 2.54厘米

1码 ≈ 0.91米

1英尺 ≈ 0.31米

1英里 ≈ 1.61千米

3. 容量

升 l (liter)	加仑 gal (gallon)	夸脱 qt (quart)	品脱 pt (pint)
1	0.264	1.057	2.114
3.785	1	4	8
0.946	0.25	1	2
0.473	—	0.5	1

1品脱 ≈ 0.47升

1夸脱 ≈ 0.94升

1加仑 ≈ 3.79升

4. 面积

平方米 m² (square meter)	平方千米 km² (square kilometer)	平方英尺 ft² (square feet)	平方码 yd² (square yard)	公顷 ha (hectare)	英亩 acre
1	—	10.764	1.1960	—	—
1,000,000	1	—	—	100.00	247.11
0.0929	—	1	0.1111	—	—
0.8361	—	9.00	1	—	—
—	0.010	—	—	1	2.4711
—	0.004	—	—	0.4047	1

1平方英尺 ≈ 0.09平方米

1平方码 ≈ 0.84平方米

1英亩 ≈ 0.405公顷

三、温度比较

1. 温度计

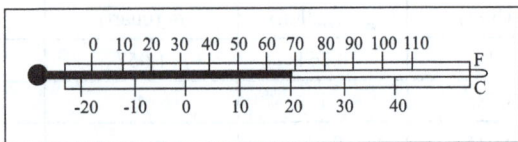

2. 体温计

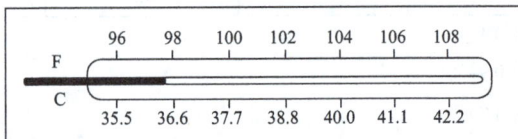

F=华氏温度　　　　C=摄氏温度

四、服装、鞋号码对照表

1. 男码

1) 衬衫

日本	36	37	38	39	40	41	42
英美	14	14.5	15	15.5	16	16.5	17
澳大利亚	36	37	38	39	40	41	42

2) 西服/大衣

日本	S		M		L		LL
英美	34	36	38	40	42	44	46
澳大利亚	S		M		L		LL

3) 鞋

日本	24	24.5	25	25.5	26	26.5	27
美国	6	6.5	7	8	8.5	9	9.5
英国	5.5	6	6.5	7	7.5		8
澳大利亚	7	7.5	8	8.5	9	9.5	10

2. 女码

1) 女装

日本	7	9	11	13	15	17	19
美国	8	10	12	14	16	18	20
英国	32	34	36	38	40	42	44
澳大利亚	6	8	10	12	14	16	18

2) 罩衫

日本	7	9	11	13	15		
英国	32	34	36	38	40	42	44

3) 鞋

日本	22	22.5	23	23.5	24	24.5	25
美国	4.5	5	5.5	6	6.5	7	7.5
英国			4	4.5	5	5.5	6
澳大利亚	5	5.5	6	6.5	7	7.5	8

Note